BOOK 3 – FINANCIAL STATEMENT ANALYSIS

Readings and Learning Outcome Statements   3

Study Session 7 – Financial Statement Analysis: Basic Concepts, Cash Flow Analysis and IASB GAAP   9

Study Session 8 – Financial Statement Analysis: Financial Ratios and Earnings Per Share   77

Study Session 9 – Financial Statement Analysis: Inventories, Long-Term Assets and Economic Reality   123

Study Session 10 – Financial Statement Analysis: Deferred Taxes, On- and Off-Balance-Sheet Debt and Economic Reality   185

Formulas   243

Index   247

READINGS AND
LEARNING OUTCOME STATEMENTS

READINGS

The following material is a review of the Financial Statement Analysis principles designed to address the learning outcome statements set forth by CFA Institute.

STUDY SESSION 7

Reading Assignments

33. "Framework for Financial Statement Analysis," Ch. 1, *The Analysis and Use of Financial Statements*, 3rd edition, Gerald I. White, Ashwinpaul C. Sondhi, and Dov Fried (Wiley, 2003)   page 9

34. "Accounting Income and Assets: The Accrual Concept," Ch. 2, including Box 2-5 *The Analysis and Use of Financial Statements*, 3rd edition, Gerald I. White, Ashwinpaul C. Sondhi, and Dov Fried (Wiley, 2003)   page 17

35. "The Statement of Cash Flows," Ch. 14, *Financial Accounting*, Belverd E. Needles, Jr., and Marian Powers, 8th edition, (Houghton Mifflin, 2004)   page 42

36. "Analysis of Cash Flows," Ch. 3, pp. 74–82, 84 (Box 3-1), and 87–99, including Box 3-1, *The Analysis and Use of Financial Statements*, 3rd edition, Gerald I. White, Ashwinpaul C. Sondhi, and Dov Fried (Wiley, 2003)   page 51

37. "Worldwide Accounting Diversity and International Accounting Standards," Ch. 11, *Advanced Accounting*, 7th edition, Joe B. Hoyle, Thomas F. Schaefer, and Timothy S. Doupnik (McGraw-Hill, 2004)   page 71

STUDY SESSION 8

Reading Assignments

38. "Analysis of Financial Statements," Ch. 10, pp. 319–358 and Exhibits 10.1, 10.2, and 10.3, *Investment Analysis and Portfolio Management*, 7th edition, Frank K. Reilly and Keith C. Brown (Dryden, 2003)   page 77

39. "Dilutive Securities and Earnings per Share," Ch. 16, pp. 788–801 and Appendix 16B, pp. 809–814, *Intermediate Accounting*, 11th edition, Donald E. Kieso, Jerry J. Weygandt, and Terry D. Warfield (Wiley, 2004)   page 106

STUDY SESSION 9

Reading Assignments

40. "Analysis of Inventories," Ch. 6, pp. 192–215 and pp. 219–220, *The Analysis and Use of Financial Statements*, 3rd edition, Gerald I. White, Ashwinpaul C. Sondhi, and Dov Fried (Wiley, 2003)   page 123

41. "Long-Term Assets," Ch. 10, *Financial Accounting*, Belverd E. Needles, Jr., and Marian Powers, 8th edition, (Houghton Mifflin, 2004)   page 145

42. "Analysis of Long-Lived Assets: Part I - The Capitalization Decision," Ch. 7, pp. 227–240, including Box 7-1, and pp. 242–244, *The Analysis and Use of Financial Statements*, 3rd edition, Gerald I. White, Ashwinpaul C. Sondhi, and Dov Fried (Wiley, 2003)   page 154

43. "Analysis of Long-Lived Assets: Part II - Analysis of Depreciation and Impairment," Ch. 8, pp. 257–278 and pp. 280–282, *The Analysis and Use of Financial Statements*, 3rd edition, Gerald I. White, Ashwinpaul C. Sondhi, and Dov Fried (Wiley, 2003)   page 167

STUDY SESSION 10

Reading Assignments

44. "Analysis of Income Taxes," Ch. 9, pp. 290–314, including Boxes 9-1 and 9-2, *The Analysis and Use of Financial Statements*, 3rd edition, Gerald I. White, Ashwinpaul C. Sondhi, and Dov Fried (Wiley, 2003)   page 185
45. "Analysis of Financing Liabilities," Ch. 10, pp. 322–332 and 337–343, *The Analysis and Use of Financial Statements*, 3rd edition, Gerald I. White, Ashwinpaul C. Sondhi, and Dov Fried (Wiley, 2003)   page 206
46. "Leases and Off-Balance-Sheet Debt," Ch. 11, pp. 363–383, including Box 11-1 and pp. 386–393, *The Analysis and Use of Financial Statements*, 3rd edition, Gerald I. White, Ashwinpaul C. Sondhi, and Dov Fried (Wiley, 2003)   page 222

LEARNING OUTCOME STATEMENTS (LOS)

STUDY SESSION 7

The topical coverage corresponds with the following CFA Institute assigned reading:

33. **Framework for Financial Statement Analysis**

The candidate should be able to:

a. discuss the general principles of the financial reporting system and explain the objectives of financial reporting according to the Financial Accounting Standards Board (FASB) conceptual framework. (page 9)

b. identify the two primary qualities of accounting information (i.e., relevance and reliability), the ingredients of relevance (i.e., predictive value, feedback value and timeliness), the ingredients of reliability (i.e., verifiability, neutrality and representational faithfulness), the two secondary qualities of accounting information (i.e., comparability and consistency), and discuss how these qualities provide useful information to an analyst. (page 11)

c. describe and explain the purposes of the five principal financial statements (i.e., Balance Sheet, Income Statement, Statement of Comprehensive Income, Statement of Cash Flows and Statement of Stockholders' Equity) and discuss the additional sources of information accompanying the financial statements, including the financial footnotes, supplementary schedules, Management Discussion and Analysis (MD&A) and proxy statements. (page 11)

d. discuss the role of the auditor and the meaning of the audit opinion. (page 13)

The topical coverage corresponds with the following CFA Institute assigned reading:

34. **Accounting Income and Assets: The Accrual Concept**

The candidate should be able to:

a. describe the format of the income statement and discuss the components of net income. (page 18)

b. describe the criteria for revenue and expense recognition and discuss major issues in revenue and expense recognition including the affect on reported earnings and their implications for financial analysis. (page 19)

c. compare the percentage-of-completion method with the completed contract method and contrast the effects of the two methods on the income statement, balance sheet, statement of cash flows and selected financial ratios. (page 21)

    d.   describe the types and analysis of unusual or infrequent items, extraordinary items, discontinued operations, accounting changes, and prior period adjustments. (page 24)

    e.   discuss managerial discretion in areas such as classification of good news/bad news, income smoothing, big bath behavior and accounting changes, and explain how this discretion can affect the financial statements. (page 26)

    f.   describe the format and the components of the balance sheet and the format, classification, and use of each component of the statement of stockholders' equity. (page 27)

The topical coverage corresponds with the following CFA Institute assigned reading:

35.   The Statement of Cash Flows

The candidate should be able to:

    a.   identify the principal purposes and uses of the statement of cash flows. (page 42)

    b.   compare and contrast the three major classifications (i.e., cash provided or used by operating activities, investing activities, and financing activities) in a statement of cash flows, and describe how noncash investing and financing transactions are reported. (page 43)

    c.   calculate and analyze, using the indirect method, the net cash flow provided or used by operating activities, investing activities and financing activities. (page 44)

The topical coverage corresponds with the following CFA Institute assigned reading:

36.   Analysis of Cash Flows

The candidate should be able to:

    a.   classify a particular transaction or item as cash flow from 1) operations, 2) investing, or 3) financing. (page 51)

    b.   compute and interpret a statement of cash flows, using the direct method and the indirect method. (page 53)

    c.   convert an indirect statement of cash flows to a direct basis. (page 59)

    d.   explain the two primary factors (i.e., acquisitions/divestitures and translation of foreign subsidiaries) that may cause discrepancies between balances of operating assets and liabilities reported on the balance sheet and those reported in the cash flow statement. (page 60)

    e.   describe and compute free cash flow. (page 60)

    f.   distinguish between U.S. GAAP and IAS GAAP classifications of dividends paid or received and interest paid or received for statement of cash flow purposes. (page 60)

The topical coverage corresponds with the following CFA Institute assigned reading:

37.   Worldwide Accounting Diversity and International Standards

The candidate should be able to:

    a.   discuss the factors influencing and leading to diversity in accounting and reporting practices throughout the world and explain why worldwide accounting diversity causes problems for capital market participants. (page 71)

    b.   discuss the importance of the hierarchical model of accounting diversity. (page 73)

    c.   discuss the arguments for and against harmonization and discuss the role of the International Accounting Standards Board (IASB). (page 73)

STUDY SESSION 8

The topical coverage corresponds with the following CFA Institute assigned reading:

38.   Analysis of Financial Statements

The candidate should be able to:

    a.   interpret common-size balance sheets and common-size income statements, and discuss the circumstances under which the use of common-size financial statements is appropriate. (page 77)

b. discuss the purposes and limitations of financial ratios and why it is important to examine a company's performance relative to the economy and its industry. (page 79)

c. calculate, interpret and discuss the uses of measures of a company's internal liquidity, operating performance (i.e., operating efficiency and operating profitability), risk analysis, and growth potential. (page 80)

d. calculate and interpret the various components of the company's return on equity using the original and extended DuPont systems and a company's financial ratios relative to its industry, to the aggregate economy, and to the company's own performance over time. (page 88)

The topical coverage corresponds with the following CFA Institute assigned reading:

39. **Dilutive Securities and Earnings per Share**
The candidate should be able to:

a. differentiate between simple and complex capital structures for purposes of calculating earnings per share (EPS), describe the components of EPS, and calculate a company's EPS in a simple capital structure. (page 106)

b. calculate a company's weighted average number of shares outstanding. (page 107)

c. determine the effect of stock dividends and stock splits on a company's weighted average number of shares outstanding. (page 108)

d. distinguish between dilutive and antidilutive securities and calculate a company's basic and diluted EPS in a complex capital structure, and describe and determine the effects of convertible securities, options and warrants on a company's EPS. (page 109)

e. compare and contrast the requirements for EPS reporting in simple versus complex capital structures. (page 114)

STUDY SESSION 9

The topical coverage corresponds with the following CFA Institute assigned reading:

40. **Analysis of Inventories**
The candidate should be able to:

a. compute ending inventory balances and cost of goods sold using the LIFO, FIFO, and average cost methods to account for product inventory and explain the relationship among and the usefulness of inventory and cost of goods sold data provided by the LIFO, FIFO, and average cost methods when prices are 1) stable or 2) changing. (page 124)

b. analyze the financial statements of companies using different inventory accounting methods to compare and describe the effect of the different methods on cost of goods sold and inventory balances, discuss how a company's choice of inventory accounting method affects other financial items such as income, cash flow, and working capital, and compute and describe the effects of the choice of inventory method on profitability, liquidity, activity, and solvency ratios. (page 128)

c. discuss the reasons that a LIFO reserve might decline during a given period and discuss the implications of such a decline for financial analysis. (page 135)

d. discuss how inventories are reported in the financial statements and how the lower of cost or market principle is used and applied. (page 135)

The topical coverage corresponds with the following CFA Institute assigned reading:

41. **Long-Term Assets**
The candidate should be able to:

a. describe the factors that distinguish long-term assets from other assets and identify the common types of long-term assets and how carrying value is determined on the balance sheet. (page 145)

b. determine the costs that are capitalized to property, plant and equipment and determine which costs are expensed as incurred. (page 146)

    c. explain depreciation accounting (including the reasons for depreciation), calculate depreciation using the straight-line, production (also known as units-of-production), and declining-balance methods, and calculate depreciation after revising the estimated useful life of an asset. (page 146)

    d. describe how to account for the sale, exchange, or disposal of depreciable assets, and determine whether a gain or loss is recorded. (page 148)

    e. identify assets that should be classified as natural resources, determine their carrying values on the balance sheet and calculate depletion. (page 149)

    f. identify the types of intangible assets and describe how the accounting treatment for goodwill under U.S. GAAP differs from the accounting treatment for other intangible assets. (page 149)

The topical coverage corresponds with the following CFA Institute assigned reading:

42. **Analysis of Long-Lived Assets: Part I — The Capitalization Decision**

The candidate should be able to:

    a. compute and describe the effects of capitalizing versus expensing on net income, shareholders' equity, cash flow from operations, and financial ratios including the effect on the interest coverage ratio (times interest earned) of capitalizing interest costs. (page 154)

    b. explain the circumstances in which intangible assets, including software development costs and research and development costs are capitalized. (page 160)

    c. calculate and describe both the initial and long-term effects of asset revaluations on financial ratios. (page 161)

The topical coverage corresponds with the following CFA Institute assigned reading:

43. **Analysis of Long-Lived Assets: Part II — Analysis of Depreciation and Impairment**

The candidate should be able to:

    a. identify the different depreciation methods and discuss how the choice of depreciation method affects a company's financial statements, ratios, and taxes. (page 167)

    b. explain the role of depreciable lives and salvage values in the computation of depreciation expenses, and compute and describe how changing depreciation methods or changing the estimated useful life or salvage value of an asset affects financial statements and ratios. (page 172)

    c. discuss the use of fixed asset disclosures to compare companies' average age of depreciable assets, and calculate, using such disclosures, the average age and average depreciable life of fixed assets. (page 173)

    d. define impairment of long-lived assets and explain what effect such impairment has on a company's financial statements and ratios. (page 175)

    e. discuss the liability for closure, removal, and environmental effects of long-lived operating assets, and discuss the financial statement impact and ratio effects of that liability. (page 177)

STUDY SESSION 10

The topical coverage corresponds with the following CFA Institute assigned reading:

44. **Analysis of Income Taxes**

The candidate should be able to:

    a. discuss the key terms (e.g., deferred tax asset, valuation allowance, deferred tax liability, taxes payable, income tax expense, temporary difference, permanent difference, etc.) used in income tax accounting, explain why and how deferred tax liabilities and assets are created, and describe the liability method of accounting for deferred taxes. (page 185)

    b. discuss the implications of a valuation allowance for deferred tax assets (i.e., when it is required, what impact it has on the financial statements, and how it might affect an analyst's view of a company). (page 188)

    c. explain the factors that determine whether a company's deferred tax liabilities should be treated as a liability or as equity for purposes of financial analysis. (page 188)

    d.   distinguish between temporary and permanent items in pretax financial income and taxable income. (page 189)

    e.   determine income tax expense, income taxes payable, deferred tax assets, and deferred tax liabilities, and calculate and interpret the adjustment to the financial statements related to a change in the tax rate. (page 191)

    f.   analyze disclosures relating to deferred tax items and the effective tax rate reconciliation and discuss how information included in these disclosures affects a company's financial statements and financial ratios. (page 194)

    g.   compare and contrast a company's deferred tax items and effective tax rate reconciliation between reporting periods and/or to other companies. (page 194)

The topical coverage corresponds with the following CFA Institute assigned reading:

45.   **Analysis of Financing Liabilities**

The candidate should be able to:

    a.   compute the effects of debt issuance and amortization of bond discounts and premiums on the financial statements and ratios, and discuss the effect on the financial statements from issuing zero-coupon debt. (page 207)

    b.   determine the appropriate classification for debt with equity features and calculate the effect of issuance of such instruments on the debt to total capital ratio. (page 213)

    c.   describe the disclosures relating to financing liabilities, and discuss the advantages/disadvantages to the company of selecting a given instrument and the effect of the selection on a company's financial statements and ratios. (page 213)

    d.   determine the effects of changing interest rates on the market value of debt and on financial statements and ratios. (page 215)

    e.   explain the role of debt covenants in protecting creditors by limiting a company's freedom to invest, pay dividends, or make other operating and strategic decisions. (page 216)

The topical coverage corresponds with the following CFA Institute assigned reading:

46.   **Leases and Off-Balance-Sheet Debt**

The candidate should be able to:

    a.   discuss the motivations for leasing assets instead of purchasing them and the incentives for reporting the leases as operating leases rather than capital leases. (page 222)

    b.   determine the effects of capital and operating leases on the financial statements and ratios of the lessees and lessors. (page 223)

    c.   describe the types and economic consequences of off-balance-sheet financing and determine how take-or-pay contracts, throughput arrangements, and the sale of receivables affect selected financial ratios. (page 227)

    d.   distinguish between a sales-type lease and a direct financing lease and determine the effects on the financial statements and ratios of the lessors. (page 228)

          ©2007 Schweser

FRAMEWORK FOR FINANCIAL STATEMENT ANALYSIS

EXAM FOCUS

The understanding of financial statements and their analysis is the key to making sound investment decisions. The Financial Accounting Standards Board sets accounting standards used in the creation of financial statements for U.S.-based companies. Along with the Financial Accounting Standards Board, the standards of the International Accounting Standards Board are used either explicitly or as the basis for most accounting standards prescribed by individual countries around the world. The Financial Accounting Standards Board's standards are codified into a set of Generally Accepted Accounting Principles, which are intended to result in financial statements that are useful, reliable, and comparable across companies. From this topic review, you should recognize how all financial statements—the balance sheet, income statement, statement of cash flows, statement of comprehensive income, and statement of stockholder's equity—are each linked to one another. You should also know that the footnotes and Management Discussion and Analysis help to add detail and explain information summarized in the financial statements.

LOS 33.a: Discuss the general principles of the finandcial reporting system and explain the objectives of financial reporting according to the Financial Accounting Standards Board (FASB) conceptual framework.

One purpose of financial statements is to help investors and creditors make more informed economic decisions. Under **Generally Accepted Accounting Principles** (GAAP), financial statements are based on selective reporting of events and choices of accounting methods, and are only an approximation of economic reality.

Because economic events and accounting recognition of these events diverge across the dimensions of timing, recognition, and measurement, financial statement analysis (interpretation) is required.

Timing. Economic events and the accounting entries for those events may take place at different times. For example, under U.S. GAAP, if a real estate investment is sold for a gain, the appreciation of the investment is recognized only after the sale. No accounting gain is recognized during the holding period, even though the economic value of the asset is increasing through time. Thus, the economic value of the asset is not recognized in an accounting sense until the asset is actually sold.

Accounting for impaired fixed assets presents a similar problem. An asset becomes "impaired" when managers recognize that the economic value of the asset is materially less than the book value and that the value is unlikely to recover to previous levels. Impairment is recognized, and fixed assets are written down during the period of management's choice, not during the period when impairment occurred.

Recognition. Many economic events do not receive accounting recognition. For example, many financial commitments enforced by signed contracts are not recognized on the financial statements. Fortunately, supplementary footnote information helps the financial analyst interpret and adjust the financial statements (including financial ratios) in order to make them comparable, consistent, and more reflective of economic reality. The analytical treatment of "off-balance-sheet" financing (obligations which are not on the balance sheet) is an example of this process.

Measurement. Accounting rules permit economic events to be reported in different ways by different financial statement preparers. For example, one firm may use the first in, first out (FIFO) method of inventory accounting for computing inventory and cost of goods sold, while a virtually identical firm may choose to use the last in, first out (LIFO) method. The different accounting choices would likely result in materially different cost of goods sold and inventory carrying values. Moreover, all performance measures and any ratios that include those accounts would also be affected. A casual user of financial statements would probably conclude that the two firms are different when they are actually economical equivalents.

Analysts also need to learn how to use supplementary information contained in the financial reports as well as information from outside the financial reporting process to make the financial data more useful.

Objectives of Financial Reporting

Statement of Financial Accounting Concepts (SFAC) 1 states that financial statements should provide useful information to investors and creditors for evaluating the amount, timing, and uncertainty of future cash flows. Said differently, the objective of financial analysis is the comparative measurement of risk and return as it relates to investment choices or credit decisions.

- Equity investors are interested in identifying firms with long-term earning power, growth opportunities, and ability to pay dividends.
- Short-term creditors are more concerned with the liquidity of the business.
- Long-term creditors (investors in bonds) focus on the long-term asset position and earning power.

In the U.S., financial statements are prepared according to U.S. GAAP. In developing countries, financial statements are often prepared according to the standards of the International Accounting Standards Board (IASB), U.S. GAAP, or U.K. GAAP. It is noteworthy that these standards boards assume the primary users of financial statements are investors and creditors and generally tailor their standards to satisfy the needs of these groups. However, other outside users depend upon these statements to provide them with useful financial information.

Classes of users. The concepts and techniques of financial statement analysis are aimed at external users, such as:

- Investors: both creditors and equity investors.
- Government: regulators and taxing authorities.
- Others: general public, special interest groups, labor, etc.

Financial information and capital markets. Some academic research is critical of the accounting process and the benefit of financial analysis. However, conclusions critical of market efficiency have proven to be somewhat premature. More recent research demonstrates the market's reliance on fundamental analysis as a form of processing information in order to better understand the relationship between risk and return for individual securities.

The financial reporting system depends on data stemming from accounting events or transactions and selected economic events. The following principles are the foundation of accrual accounting:

- *Recognition principle:* revenue is recognized when goods are delivered or services are performed and the associated expenses are recorded, not necessarily when cash is received for the goods or services.
- *Matching principle:* revenues and associated costs are recognized in the same accounting period.
- *Historical cost principle:* represents a transaction's original value. For example, the historical cost of a fixed asset is its original purchase price plus any installation and shipping fees. One advantage to historical cost is that it is objective and verifiable.

LOS 33.b: Identify the two primary qualities of accounting information (i.e., relevance and reliability), the ingredients of relevance (i.e., Predictive value, fedback value and timliness),the ingredients of reliability (i.e., verfiability, neutrality and representational faithfulness),the two secondary qualities of accounting information (i.e., Comparability and consistency),and discuss how these qualities provide useful information to an analyst.

Statement of Financial Accounting Concepts (SFAC) 2 mandates the qualitative characteristics of accounting information. Financial statement information should facilitate comparisons of firms using alternative reporting methods and be useful for decision-making. For accounting information to be useful for an analyst, it should have the following characteristics:

Relevance means that information could potentially affect a decision. The relevance of accounting information depends to a large extent on the purpose of the analysis. For example, an equity analyst is most concerned with earnings and growth rates. The ingredients of relevance are *timeliness, predictive value*, and *feedback value*.

Timeliness is important because information loses value rapidly in the financial world. Timely data is helpful in making the projections on which market prices are based. For equity and credit analysts, relevance clearly requires that accounting disclosures have *predictive value* as well. Since both equity valuation and analysis of the risk of a firm's debt are based on future results, information about past results is only of value to the extent that it is useful for predicting future results. *Feedback value* refers to the usefulness of accounting data in providing the information necessary to update or correct prior predictions.

Reliability refers to information that can be *verified* (measured accurately) and has *representational faithfulness* (it is what it is reported to be). Without these two characteristics, data cannot be relied upon in making investment decisions. Reliable information should also reflect *neutrality* (does not consider the economic impact of the reported information).

Professor's Note: The qualities of relevance and reliability can often be at odds with one another. For example, market value data is relevant but may not be reliable; on the other hand, historical cost data is highly reliable but may have little relevance.

- *Consistency.* Accounting information should be reported using the same accounting principles over time.
- *Comparability.* Information should allow comparisons among companies. Comparability is often a problem in financial analysis because companies use different accounting methods and estimates.
- *Materiality.* Material data are important enough for inclusion in the financial statements. Many analysts define materiality in quantitative terms (e.g., 5% of assets); however, most analysts agree that an item is material if it affects the value of the firm.

LOS 33.c: Describe and explain the purposes of the five principal financial statements (i.e., Balance Sheet, Income Statement, Statement of Comprehensive Income, Statement of Cash Flows and Statement of Stockholders' Equity) and discussthe additional sources of information accompanying the financial statements, including the financial footnotes, supplementary schedules, Management Discussion and Analysis (MD&A) and proxy statements.

The output of the accounting process is a set of financial statements, footnotes, and supplemental data.

The **balance sheet** reports financial position:

- *Assets* are probable current and future economic benefits obtained or controlled by a particular entity as a result of past transactions or events.
- *Liabilities* are probable future sacrifices of economic benefits. They arise from present obligations of a particular entity to transfer assets or provide services to other entities in the future as a result of past transactions or events.

- *Equity* is the residual interest in the net assets of an entity that remains after deducting its liabilities.

Transactions are measured so that the following fundamental balance sheet equation holds:

assets = liabilities + stockholders' equity, or A = L + E

The **income statement** reports on the performance of the firm and explains some, but not all, of the changes in the assets, liabilities, and equity of the firm between two balance sheet dates. The income statement is governed by accrual concepts and the matching principle. The *elements of the income statement* include:

- *Revenues* that are inflows from delivering or producing goods, rendering services, or other activities that constitute the entity's ongoing major or central operations.
- *Expenses* that are outflows from delivering or producing goods or services that constitute the entity's ongoing major or central operations.
- *Gains and losses* that are increases (decreases) in equity or net assets from peripheral or incidental transactions.

The **statement of comprehensive income** reports the change in equity from transactions and from non-owner sources. It includes all changes in equity during a period except those resulting from investments by owners and distributions to owners. The purpose of the statement of comprehensive income is to help distinguish income from continuing operations from changes in carrying amounts of assets and liabilities.

The results of continuing operations, unusual or infrequent operations, taxes, discontinued operations, extraordinary items, and the effects of accounting changes are reported separately on the typical income statement. In many cases, however, the classification of items is subject to management discretion.

The **statement of cash flows** reports the cash receipts and outflows classified as operating, investing, and financing activities. These cash flows are defined as follows:

- *Investing cash flows* are those resulting from acquisition or sale of property, plant, and equipment, of a subsidiary or segment, and purchase or sale of investments in other firms. Note that these must be reported on a gross basis (e.g., acquisitions separate from sale of property).
- *Financing cash flows* are those resulting from issuance or retirement of debt and equity securities and dividends paid to stockholders.
- *Cash from operations* includes the cash effects of all transactions that are neither investing nor financing as defined above.

The **statement of stockholders' equity** reports the amounts and sources of changes in equity from transactions with owners and may include the following components: preferred shares, common shares at par, additional paid-in-capital, retained earnings, Treasury shares, employee stock ownership plan adjustments, minimum pension liability, valuation allowance for changes in the values of marketable securities, and cumulative foreign currency translation adjustment.

Financial footnotes include disclosures that help explain the information summarized in the financial statements. Footnotes are required by GAAP or the SEC to allow users to improve assessments of the amount, timing, and uncertainty of the estimates reported in the financial statements. Footnotes:

- Provide information about accounting methods and the assumptions and estimates used by management.
- Are audited, whereas other disclosures, such as supplementary schedules, are not audited.
- Provide additional information on such items as fixed assets, inventory, income taxes, pensions, debt, contingencies and commitments, marketable securities, significant customers, sales to related parties, and export sales.
- Often contain disclosures relating to contingent losses. Firms are required to accrue a loss when (1) it is probable that assets have been impaired or a liability has been incurred and (2) when the amount of the loss

can be reasonably estimated. A range of possible losses from a minimum to a maximum range is estimated. If it is only reasonably possible that a loss has been incurred, then footnote disclosure of that loss contingency is required. Examples include litigation, expropriation, and repurchase agreements.

Supplementary schedules contain additional information. Examples of such disclosures are:

- Operating income or sales by region or business segment.
- Reserves for an oil and gas company.
- Information about hedging activities and financial instruments.

The **Management Discussion and Analysis** (MD&A) portion of a financial disclosure provides an assessment of the financial performance and condition of a company from the perspective of the company. The MD&A is required by the SEC.

The MD&A is required to discuss:

- Results from operations, with a discussion of trends in sales and expenses.
- Capital resources and liquidity, with a discussion of trends in cash flows.
- A general business overview based on known trends.

Additional areas include:

- Discussion of significant effects of currently known trends, events, and uncertainties (may voluntarily disclose forward-looking data).
- Liquidity, capital resources, and transactions or events with liquidity implications.
- Discontinued operations, extraordinary items, and other unusual or infrequent events.
- Extensive disclosures in interim financial statements.
- Disclosures of a segment's need for cash flows or contribution to revenues or profit.

Proxy statements are issued to shareholders when there are matters that require a shareholder vote. These statements are a good source of information about the election of (and qualifications of) board members, compensation, management qualifications, and the issuance of stock options.

Other data sources are also available. Remember that corporate reports and other publications are written by management and are often viewed as public relations or sales materials. Not all of the material is independently reviewed by outside auditors. Internet sources of such unaudited information include the company's home page, EDGAR (Electronic Data Gathering Analysis, Retrieval System, www.sec.gov), that contains SEC filings, market data from exchanges, tax, and economic information.

LOS 33.d: Discuss the role of the auditor and the meaning of the audit opinion.

An **audit** is an independent review of an entity's financial statements. Public accountants conduct the audit, and examine the financial reports and supporting records. The auditor provides an opinion on the fairness and reliability of the financial reports. The independent certified public accountant employed by the board of directors is responsible for seeing that the financial statements conform to GAAP. The auditor examines the company's accounting and internal control systems, confirms assets and liabilities, and generally tries to be confident that there are no material errors in the financial statements. Reading the *auditor's report* is important.

The **standard auditor's opinion** contains three parts stating that:

- Whereas the financial statements are prepared by management and are its responsibility, the auditor has performed an independent review.
- Generally accepted auditing standards were followed, thus providing reasonable assurance that the financial statements contain no material errors.

- The auditor is satisfied that the statements were prepared in accordance with GAAP and that the accounting principles chosen and estimates made are reasonable. The auditor's report must also contain an additional explanation when accounting methods have not been used consistently between periods.

An *unqualified opinion* indicates that the auditor believes the statements are free from material omissions and errors. A *qualified opinion* may be issued if the auditor has concerns about omissions and errors.

The auditor's opinion will also contain an explanatory paragraph when a material loss is probable but the amount cannot be reasonably estimated. These "uncertainties" may relate to the going concern assumption, the valuation or realization of assets, or to litigation. This type of disclosure may be a signal of serious problems and call for closer examination by the analyst.

KEY CONCEPTS

1. Financial statements should serve investors and government, as well as other users such as labor unions, and offer information about the amount, timing, and uncertainty of future cash flows.
2. Accounting statements should be relevant to users, contain reliable figures, and be presented in a timely fashion in order to have predictive value for users.
3. The income statement shows the effects of transactions completed over the period; the balance sheet shows assets, liabilities, and owners' equity at a point in time; and the cash flow statement shows the sources and uses of cash over the period.
4. Other sources of information in a company's financials are the Management Discussion and Analysis, supplementary schedules, and the footnotes to the financial statements.
5. The auditor's opinion gives evidence of an independent review of the financial statements that verifies that GAAP were used and that standard auditing procedures were used to establish that the statements contain no material errors.

CONCEPT CHECKERS: FRAMEWORK FOR FINANCIAL STATEMENT ANALYSIS

1. Interpretation of financial statements is required because the accounting treatment of economic events diverges in all of the following dimensions **EXCEPT**:
    A. recognition.
    B. timing.
    C. measurement.
    D. class of users.

2. Information about accounting estimates, assumptions, and methods chosen for reporting is *most likely* found in:
    A. the Management Discussion and Analysis.
    B. the auditor's opinion.
    C. the footnotes to the accounting statements.
    D. supplementary schedules.

3. If an auditor has reservations about errors or misstatements in a company's financial statements, she will issue a:
    A. qualification letter.
    B. dissenting opinion.
    C. cautionary note.
    D. qualified opinion.

ANSWERS – CONCEPT CHECKERS: FRAMEWORK FOR FINANCIAL STATEMENT ANALYSIS

1. **D** In preparing financial statements, choices must be made within the limits of GAAP as to what events to recognize (e.g., off-balance-sheet items), the period that they will be reported in (e.g., revenue recognition), and the amount to be reported (e.g., inventory costing method). Financial statements are written for a variety of users but not specifically for one class or another.

2. **C** Information about accounting methods and estimates is contained in the footnotes to the financial statements.

3. **D** If an auditor has reservations about errors or misstatements in a company's financial statements, she will issue a qualified opinion.

ACCOUNTING INCOME AND ASSETS: THE ACCRUAL CONCEPT

EXAM FOCUS

The key to this topic review is to recognize the difference between cash basis and accrual basis accounting, and to understand why accrual basis accounting is the standard. On a cash basis, income and deductions are recognized when cash is received or paid. Because the timing of a cash flow could be far removed from the process that generated the cash flow, cash basis accounting is not very useful. Accrual basis accounting follows the matching principle—expenses are recognized in the same period in which the associated revenues are generated. Accrual basis statements are also more relevant to projecting the firm's ability to generate future cash flows. For success on the Level 1 exam, you should be prepared for questions identifying the five methods of revenue recognition, the ways management can manipulate earnings, and the four types of non-recurring items reported on the income statement.

EARNINGS, INCOME, AND ACCRUAL ACCOUNTING

There are many definitions of income. These definitions differ in terms of their use, their measurement, and how they are operationalized.

- *Economic earnings* equal net cash flow plus the change in the market value of the firm's assets. In a world of certainty, with a known interest rate, market values equal the present value of cash flows. Hence, there is a direct relationship between economic income, cash flows, and asset values. However, in the real world, where neither future cash flows nor future interest rates are known with certainty, the concepts and relationships are not so simple. Income, however defined, will only be a proxy for economic income, thus we need other definitions.
- *Distributable earnings* equal the amount of earnings that can be paid out as dividends without changing the value of the firm.
- *Sustainable income* equals the level of income that can be sustained in the future given the firm's stock of capital investment.
- *Permanent income* equals the amount of income that can normally be earned each period given the firm's assets:

$$\text{permanent earnings} = \left(\begin{array}{c} \text{market value} \\ \text{of firm's assets} \end{array} \right) \left(\begin{array}{c} \text{required rate} \\ \text{of return} \end{array} \right)$$

The financial reporting concept of income, *accounting income*, is quite different. Accounting income is based on the accrual concept and deals with the firm's ability to generate future cash flows.

Accrual vs. cash accounting. The idea behind cash accounting, simply stated, is that revenue or income is recognized when cash is received, and expenses are recognized when the firm pays out cash. The firm's cash flow is measured as cash in less cash out. This method, while intuitive, typically results in highly volatile, less predictable cash flows and income streams and is not desirable for firms with complex operations and financing strategies. It also increases the difficulty of analyzing balance sheets.

Accrual accounting allows us to allocate revenues and expenses to time periods other than those in which the cash flows occurred. One result of accrual accounting is smoothed earnings streams. For example, depreciation is designed to recognize the cost of an asset over its useful life. Depreciating the asset spreads the cost over many periods and reduces profits over the same periods. The alternative under cash accounting is to recognize the expense when cash is paid for the asset. Under cash accounting, profits in the period of purchase will be extremely low. All the subsequent periods will show profits much higher than under accrual accounting. Accrual accounting also has important implications for the balance sheet that will be discussed shortly.

Empirical results suggest that two benefits arising from accrual accounting are: (1) enhanced predictability of future cash flows and (2) given cash flow from operations, accrual accounting provides incremental information related to a firm's profitability. The tradeoff for these benefits is that accrual accounting can be confusing and the recognition of many important transactions and events is left to managerial discretion. The ramification of this discretion is that managers can time the effects of certain transactions in order to manage earnings. We will discuss some of the methods used to manage earnings later in this review. Before proceeding to that discussion, we will discuss the accounting information and how it is presented on the income statement and balance sheet, and the effects of accrual accounting on each of those financial statements.

LOS 34.a: Describe the format of the income statement and discuss the components of net income.

The **income statement** is prepared using the *accrual method*, in which past, present, and future cash flows are recognized as income or expense only during the period that goods and services are provided (revenue) or used (expense). Cash flows may occur before, during, or after revenue or expense is recognized. The differences between recognized income and cash flow are accrued as assets or liabilities.

U.S. Generally Accepted Accounting Principles (GAAP) do not require any particular format for the presentation of the income statement. International Accounting Standards (IAS) GAAP also allow broad flexibility in the presentation of financial statements as long as all required information is provided in the financial statements or the accompanying footnotes. Although formats can and do vary across firms, the following is a generalized design. The items in italics are classified as **components of net income**:

Income Statement Format

Revenues from the sale of goods and services
− Operating expenses

Operating income from continuing operations
+ Other income and revenues

Recurring income before interest and taxes from continuing operations
− Financing costs

Recurring (pretax) income from continuing operations
+/− Unusual or infrequent items

Pretax earnings from continuing operations
− Income tax expense

Net income from continuing operations
+/− Income from discontinued operations (reported net of tax)
+/− Extraordinary items (reported net of tax)
+/− Cumulative effect of accounting changes (reported net of tax)

Net income

Professor's Note: This topic review will use the terms "above the line" and "below the line." The "line" referred to is the subtotal "net income from continuing operations." Items reported "above the line" do not include a tax impact; items reported "below the line" are net of taxes.

The components of net income can be described in the following ways:

Operating income from continuing operations includes revenues from the continuing businesses of the firm less the costs and expenses associated with those revenues. It is independent of the company's capital structure because it does not yet reflect the charges related to the cost of debt capital; namely, interest expense. At this point, we can characterize this income as belonging to three parties: creditors, the government, and the shareholders. Most income statements divide operating expenses into two parts: cost of goods sold, which is the cost of manufacturing or purchasing products; and the remaining expenses, which include selling, general, administrative, and research expenses. Revenues less the cost of goods sold (COGS) is referred to as gross profit. Firms frequently report COGS and gross profit as separate line items appearing before operating income on the income statement.

Recurring income before interest and taxes from continuing operations includes recurring income resulting from other activities, including investment income from unconsolidated subsidiaries or other investments and gains (or losses) from sales of assets. In the typical income statement, this means segregating the results of normal, recurring operations from the effects of "nonrecurring" or "extraordinary" items in order to improve the forecasting of future earnings and cash flows. The idea here is that *recurring income is persistent.*

Recurring (pre-tax) income from continuing operations is net of financing costs. Note that this income stream is now a function of the capital structure. If a firm is borrowing liberally or if the cost of borrowing is high, then, all else equal, recurring income from continuing operations will be relatively lower and vice versa. Once the interest payments have been accounted for, only the government and the shareholders have claim to the remaining income. Because analysts seek data with predictive characteristics, *recurring income from continuing operations is generally considered to be the best indicator of future earnings.*

Pretax earnings from continuing operations include unusual or infrequent items, which will be discussed in more detail later.

Net income from continuing operations includes the impact of taxes. At this point, the government takes its share of the income and any remaining income belongs to the shareholders.

Net income includes income from discontinued operations, extraordinary items, and the cumulative effect of accounting changes. Note that all of these adjustments to income are made net of tax. Each of these adjustments will be discussed in more detail later.

LOS 34.b: Describe the criteria for revenue and expense recognition and discuss major issues in revenue and expense recognition including the affect on reported earnings and their implications for financial analysis.

Accounting for revenues and expenses is based on the **matching principle**, which states that revenues and expenses incurred to generate those revenues must be accounted for in the same time period. This is important because it makes operating income a better indicator of how much income the firm was able to generate over the period in question.

The Requirements for Revenue Recognition

There are two requirements for **revenue recognition** to occur: (1) completion of the earnings process and (2) reasonable assurance of payment.

Completion of the earnings process. The firm must have provided virtually all of the goods or services for which it is to be paid, and the expected cost of providing the service must be measurable. In most cases, these costs are measurable. In situations where there are contingent costs of completing the sale and those costs are not measurable, recognition of revenue is deferred until the costs become measurable.

For longer-term projects where cost of sales expenditures span accounting periods, the amount of cumulative revenue that can be recognized is calculated by:

$$\left(\frac{\text{cost of goods provided to date}}{\text{total cost of goods to be provided}} \right) \left(\begin{array}{c} \text{total expected} \\ \text{revenue} \end{array} \right)$$

Assurance of payment. The company must be able to estimate the probability of payment. If the seller cannot reasonably estimate the probability of payment (or nonpayment), this second condition is not met because realization is not reasonably assured.

Specific methods of recognizing revenue are discussed later in this topic review.

Appropriate Revenue Recognition Method Based on the Status of the Earning Process and the Assurance of Payment

There are five **revenue recognition methods**:

- The *sales basis method* is the most common, and most businesses generate revenue under these assumptions. The sales basis method is the standard to which we will compare all other methods.
- The *percentage-of-completion method* approximates the sales basis method and is a logical extension of the sales basis method for long-term contracts. It is designed to measure current operating performance.
- The *completed contract method* is more conservative than the percentage-of-completion method—revenues will lag those of the percentage-of-completion method. Also, income will be less stable under the completed contract method than under the percentage-of-completion method. It is impossible to gauge the profitability of long-term contracts using the income statement—an analyst must rely on the statement of cash flows.
- The *installment method* is similar to the percentage-of-completion method in how it accounts for earnings in stages. Nonetheless, it still lags the sales basis method, and an analyst must compare the cash flow statement with the income statement to fully understand the future profitability of the company.
- The *cost recovery method* is similar to the completed contract method (in the same manner that the installment method is similar to the percentage-of-completion method) in that profit is not recognized until all aspects of the sale (revenues and costs) are made. An analyst must rely on the cash flow statement for some measure of sales profitability.

If a *firm recognizes revenue prior to fulfilling the two conditions for revenue recognition*, then its *current assets* will be *overstated* (overstatement of accounts receivable at sales price less the understatement of inventory at cost). Its *retained earnings* will also be *overstated* by the net income that should not have been recorded.

The choice of which recognition method should be used is dependent upon two factors: the status of completion of the earnings process and the assurance of payment.

Implications for Financial Analysis of Different Revenue Recognition Methods

Professor's Note: I list the five methods of revenue recognition here to highlight the roles of completion of the earnings process and assurance of payment in determining how longer-term contracts are reported in the financial statements. More detail on the completed contract and percentage-of-completion methods are covered in the next LOS.

1. Under the **sales basis method**, goods or services are provided when the sale is made, and the sale is for cash or credit to a customer with a high probability of repayment.

    If cash is received before goods or services are provided, the revenue is not recognized until it is earned. Examples of this include:

    - Revenue from the sale of magazines is not recognized until delivery.

©2007 Schweser

- Credit card fees received in advance are not revenue until time passes.
- Money received from equipment leases based on usage is not revenue until the equipment is used.

In each of these cases, revenue is not recognized until it is earned and cash collection is assured. The cost of the goods or services will be recognized as expense only when its corresponding revenue is recorded.

2. The **percentage-of-completion method** is used for long-term projects when there is a contract and there are reliable estimates of the revenues, costs and completion time. It recognizes revenues (and corresponding costs) in proportion to the work completed. There are two methods that can be used to measure the proportion of work completed:

   - An engineering estimate or physical milestone.
   - The ratio of incurred costs to the total estimated cost—even if the total estimated cost has changed.

3. The **completed contract method** is used for long-term projects when there is no contract or estimates of revenues or costs are unreliable. In this method, revenues and expenses are not recognized until the entire project has been completed. The completed contract method must be used for short-term contracts as well.

4. The **installment sales method** is used when there is no way to estimate the likelihood of collecting the sales proceeds, but the costs of the goods and services are known. It recognizes sales and cost of goods sold as proportions of cash collected each period, based on the gross profit margin.

5. The **cost recovery method** is used when the costs to provide goods or services are not known or when there are uncertainties surrounding the collection of the proceeds from the sale. Under this method, sales are recognized when cash is received, but no gross profit is recognized until the seller's cost of goods is fully recovered by buyer's cash payments.

LOS 34.c: Compare the percentage-of-completion method with the completed contract method and contrast the effects of the two methods on the income statement, balance sheet, statement of cash flows and selected financial ratios.

The **percentage-of-completion method** is used when ultimate payment is assured and revenue is earned as costs are incurred. If, however, a reliable estimate of the total costs of the contract does not exist, the amount of profit cannot be determined until the contract is finished. In this situation, the **completed contract method** should be used. The percentage-of-completion method recognizes revenue and income earlier than the completed contract method. Hence, the percentage-of-completion method generally is viewed as a better predictor of trends in earnings power.

The effect of using the different revenue recognition methods for long-term contracts on financial statements is illustrated in the following example. Assume that AAA Construction Corp. has a contract to build a ship for $1,000 while a reliable estimate of the contract's total cost is $800. Assume further that the project produces the year-end billings, collections, and incurred costs shown in Figure 1.

Figure 1: AAA Contract Estimates

	2004	2005	2006	Total
Amounts billed	$600	$200	$200	$1,000
Cash received	$400	$400	$200	$1,000
Cost incurred	$400	$300	$100	$800

In 2004, since one-half of the total contract cost has been incurred ($400/$800), one-half of the total revenue is recognized under the percentage-of-completion method [(1/2)($1,000) = $500]. Under the percentage-of-completion method, expenses are $400, and the resulting net income in 2004 is $100. Under the completed contract method, revenue, expenses, and income are not recognized until the contract is completed and the title is transferred. Let's look more carefully at the balance sheet under both methods, shown in Figures 2 and 3.

Figure 2: AAA Balance Sheet Using Percentage-of-Completion

Balance Sheet (cumulative)	2006	2005	2004
Cash (asset)[1]	$200	100	0
Accounts receivable (asset)[2]	0	0	600 – 400 = 200
Memo: Construction-in-progress year-end balance (not shown explicitly on the balance sheet – netted with advance billings)[3]	0	700 + [(7/8) × 200] = 875	400 + [(4/8) × 200] = 500
Net construction-in-progress (asset)	0	875 – 800 = 75	0
Total assets	$200	175	200
Memo: Advance billings year-end balance (not shown explicitly on the balance sheet – netted with construction-in-progress)[4]	$0	800	600
Net advance billings (liability)	0	0	600 – 500 = 100
Total liabilities	$0	0	100
Retained earnings (equity)[5]	200	[7/8 × 200] = 175	[4/8 × 200] = 100
Total liabilities and equity	$200	175	200

Notes:

1. Cash: In 2004, cash received and costs incurred are equal. Hence, the cash balance is zero. In 2005, cash receipts exceed cash costs by $100, and in 2006, receipts exceed costs once again by $100 for a total cash balance of $200.

2. Accounts receivable: In 2004, amounts billed exceed cash received by $200 for an accounts receivable of $200. In 2005, this reverses as cash received exceeds amounts billed by $200. This results in a zero A/R balance at the end of 2005.

3. Construction-in-progress represents the costs incurred plus the cumulative pro rata share of gross profit. For 2004, this amount is $500 [$400 of costs incurred plus ($400/$800) times the estimated gross profit of the contract ($1,000 – $800)]. The pro rata share is computed as costs incurred to date divided by total estimated costs. For 2005, construction-in-progress is $700 of cumulative cost incurred plus ($700/$800) × $200 = $875.

4. Advance billings are also cumulated over the project's life. A key for the exam is to know that *construction-in-progress and advance billings are netted.* What does this mean? This means that the amount of cumulative construction in progress minus cumulative advance billings is posted to the financial statements. If this number is positive, then an asset called "construction-in-progress" is shown on the assets side of the balance sheet. If this number is negative, then a liability called "advance billings" is shown on the liabilities side. In 2004, construction-in-progress was $500, and advance billings were $600. Since $500 – $600 is a negative number, $100 is posted to the liabilities side of the balance sheet under "advance billings." In 2005, construction-in-progress was $875 while advance billings totaled $800. Since the difference between these values is positive, $75 is posted to the assets side of the balance sheet under "construction-in-progress."

5. Retained earnings represents the cumulative share of total gross profit to date. Calculate this value by taking total costs to date divided by total estimated costs and applying this to the total estimated gross profit.

Professor's Note: As we will soon see, cash and accounts receivable are the same under both methods. As we work through the completed contract method, focus on the differences in how construction-in-progress and retained earnings are calculated.

Figure 3: AAA Balance Sheet Using the Completed Contract Method

Balance Sheet (cumulative)	2006	2005	2004
Cash (asset)[1]	$200	100	0
Accounts receivable (asset)[2]	0	0	600 – 400 = 200
Memo: Construction-in-progress year-end balance (not shown explicitly on the balance sheet – netted with advance billings)[3]	0	700	400
Net construction-in-progress (asset)	0	0	0
Total assets	$200	100	200
Memo: Advance billings year-end balance (not shown explicitly on the balance sheet – netted with construction-in-progress)	$0	800	600
Net advance billings (liability)[4]	0	800 – 700 = 100	600 – 400 = 200
Total liabilities	$0	100	200
Retained earnings (equity)[5]	200	0	0
Total liabilities and equity	$200	100	200

Notes:

1. Cash: In 2004, cash received and costs incurred are equal. Hence, the cash balance is zero. In 2005, cash receipts exceed cash costs by $100, and in 2006, receipts exceed costs once again by $100 for a total cash balance of $200. This is the same as when using the percentage-of-completion method.

2. Accounts receivable: In 2004, amounts billed exceed cash received by $200 for an accounts receivable of $200. In 2005, this reverses as cash received exceeds amounts billed by $200. This results in a zero A/R balance at the end of 2005, same as when using the percentage-of-completion method.

3. Under the completed contract method, construction-in-progress does not include the cumulative effect of gross profit recognition. Or, to think of this another way, the calculation is the same as before, only no gross profit is recognized until the end of the project's life.

4. The *netting of construction-in-progress and advance billings* still occurs under the completed contract method. However, since gross profit is not recognized until the end of the contract's life, liabilities will most likely be greater (or assets less) under the completed contract method compared to the percentage-of-completion method.

5. As before, retained earnings represents the cumulative share of total gross profit to date. Since there is no profit recognition until the end of the contract, the balance of retained earnings is zero until the final year of the contract.

Note that several of the balance sheet items are identical for both revenue recognition methods during the course of the contract. Under both methods, at the end of the contract only cash and retained earnings are listed on the balance sheet.

The example also illustrates that the earnings trend under the completed contract method is more volatile. This is because the completed contract method does not recognize profit until the completion of the contract. This volatility would make the analysis of the cash flow statement (especially cash flow from operations which is unchanged by the revenue recognition method used) very important in assessing the recurring profitability of the firm.

If a firm has several long-term contracts that are completed uniformly over many periods, the time trend of net income under the completed contract method would be much less volatile.

Differences in Cash Flows and Selected Items and Ratios

The table in Figure 4 allows you to compare the financial effects on companies using either of the methods in the periods *before* the construction project is completed:

Figure 4: Financial Component Impacts (during the project)

	Percentage-of-Completion	*Completed Contract*
Cash flows	Same	Same
Net income	Greater—% of profit is recognized	Less—none until final year
Income volatility	Less—some recognized each year	Greater—all at completion
Total assets	Greater—% of profit recognized	Less—no profit until complete
Construction in progress account	Greater—profit included in construction in progress	Less
Amounts billed	Same	Same
Net [construction in progress minus advance billings]	Greater (greater assets or smaller liability)	Less (greater liability or smaller assets)
Shareholder equity	Greater	Less
Ratio of liabilities-to-equity and liabilities-to-assets	Less	Greater

In the percentage-of-completion method, any net construction-in-progress is considered a *current asset*. Thus, this accounting method affects only current assets. Long-term assets are not affected by the selection of the percentage-of-completion or completed contract methods.

LOS 34.d: Describe the types and analysis of unusual or infrequent items, extraordinary items, discontinued operations, accounting changes, and prior period adjustments.

Unusual or infrequent items. The definition of these items is obvious from the title—these events are either unusual or infrequent in occurrence but not both unusual and infrequent. Examples of unusual or infrequent items include:

- Gains or losses from the disposal of a portion of a business segment (e.g., employee separation costs, plant shutdown costs).
- Gains or losses from the sale of assets or investments in subsidiaries.
- Provisions for environmental remediation.

- Impairments, write-offs, write-downs, and restructuring costs.
- Integration expenses associated with businesses that have been recently acquired.

Unusual or infrequent items are reported pre-tax before net income from continuing operations (i.e., above the line).

Analytical implications: Even though unusual or infrequent items do affect net income from continuing operations, an analyst may want to review them to determine whether they should truly be included when forecasting future income. It is important for the analyst to distinguish among recurring items that have no cash flow effect, affect only current period cash flow, and affect future cash flow.

Moreover, management often buries these items in other income or includes them as operating expenses, so an analyst should try to find these items and segment them out to find out the true measure of recurring income. A careful reading of the Management Discussion and Analysis (MD&A) and footnotes will facilitate the identification of these items and help an analyst determine their impact on future performance and profitability.

Extraordinary items. This definition is similar to unusual or infrequent items, except extraordinary items are events that are *both* unusual *and* infrequent in occurrence, and material in nature. Examples of these include:

- Losses from expropriation of assets.
- Gains or losses from early retirement of debt (when it is judged to be both unusual and infrequent).
- Uninsured losses from natural disasters that are both unusual and infrequent.

Extraordinary items are reported net of tax after net income from continuing operations (i.e., below the line).

Analytical implications: Although extraordinary items do not impact net income from continuing operations, an analyst may want to review them to determine whether some portion should be included when forecasting future income. Some companies appear to be accident prone and have extraordinary losses every year.

Discontinued operations. A discontinued operation is one that management has decided to dispose of but either has not yet done so or did so in the current year after it had generated income or losses. To be accounted for as a discontinued operation, the business—in terms of assets, operations, and investing and financing activities—must be physically and operationally distinct from the rest of the firm.

The date when the company develops a formal plan for disposing of an operation is referred to as the *measurement date*, and the time between the measurement period and the disposal date is referred to as the *phaseout period*. The income or loss from discontinued operations is reported separately, and past income statements must be restated, separating the income or loss from the discontinued operations. On the measurement date, the company will accrue any estimated loss during the phaseout period and any estimated loss on the sale of the business. Any expected gain on the disposal cannot be reported until after the sale is completed.

Income and losses from discontinued operations are reported net of tax after net income from continuing operations (i.e., below the line).

Analytical implications: The analysis is straightforward. Discontinued operations do not affect net income from continuing operations. The actual event of discontinuing a segment or selling assets may provide information about the future cash flows of the firm.

Accounting changes. There are two types of accounting changes: (1) a *change in an accounting principle* and (2) a change in *an accounting estimate*.

A *change in accounting principle* refers to the change in one GAAP method to another GAAP method; for example, a change in method of inventory accounting from LIFO to FIFO. When a change in accounting principle is made, the firm is required to restate the financial statements to reflect the change. The impact of the change in method on prior period earnings is typically recorded net of tax after net income from continuing operations (below the line) on the current year's income statement. However, in certain cases it may be reported directly in the current year's retained earnings account.

The cumulative effect on prior period earnings resulting from a change in accounting methods is reported on an after-tax basis below the line. In general, prior years' financial statements do not need to be restated unless the change involves one of the following:

- A change in inventory accounting method from LIFO to another method.
- Change to or from the full-cost method [full cost or successful efforts accounting is typically used in oil and gas exploration and relates to the capitalization (full cost) versus expensing (successful efforts) of well-drilling activities].
- Change to or from the percentage-of-completion revenue recognition method.
- Any change just prior to an initial public offering.

For example, if a firm changes from LIFO to FIFO in 2006, then the 2005 financial statements must be restated using FIFO. The impact of the change in method on prior period earnings is recorded net of tax (below the line).

Generally, a change in *accounting estimate* is the result of a management change in judgment, usually due to gaining new information. For example, management may change the estimated useful life of an asset because new information indicates the asset has a longer life than originally thought. A change in estimate does not require the restatement of prior financial statements.

Analytical implications: Any impact of prior period income resulting from an accounting change does not affect net income from continuing operations. Accounting changes typically do not affect cash flow. An analyst should review any accounting change to determine whether it might have an impact on future operating results.

Prior-period adjustments. A change from an incorrect accounting method to one that is acceptable under GAAP (correction of an accounting error) is reported as a *prior period adjustment*. Adjustments are typically reported in net income, but in some cases are made directly to retained earnings. Disclosure of the error's nature and its effect on net income is required.

Analytical implications: Because they deal with accounting errors, prior period adjustments will typically not affect cash flow. Analysts should review adjustments to determine whether they might have an impact on future operating results.

LOS 34.e: Discuss managerial discretion in areas such as classification of good news/bad news, income smoothing, big bath behavior and accounting changes, and explain how this discretion can affect the financial statements.

A weakness of accrual accounting is that it is subject to management discretion, and a company can use that discretion to manipulate earnings. There are two different types of discretion: the timing of the occurrence and the classification of the item. Earnings manipulation can be classified into four categories.

Classification of good news/bad news. Analysts tend to focus on net income from continuing operations because it tends to be the best indicator of future earnings. Hence, companies prefer to put good news items in categories that will appear above the line of net income from continuing operations and bad news items below the line of net income from continuing operations (i.e., in income from discontinued operations or extraordinary items). Consider the sale of a subsidiary as an example of selective classification. If a subsidiary is sold for a profit, it is likely to appear above the line. If it is sold at a loss, management may seek to define the subsidiary as a discontinued operation and report the loss below the line.

Income smoothing. Firms try to reduce earnings in good years and increase earnings in bad years to make earnings appear to be more stable than they would be otherwise. There are two types of smoothing:

- *Intertemporal smoothing* occurs when a company either alters the timing of expenditures or chooses accounting methods that smooth out earnings. For example, timing expenditures (e.g., repairs or R&D) or choosing between capitalization and expensing can facilitate earnings smoothing.
- *Classification smoothing* occurs when an item is reported in a category above or below the line (that either will or will not impact net income from continuing operations) in order to smooth earnings. As observed earlier, classification of asset sales are an example of this form of earnings smoothing. Some recent studies have focused on income smoothing as a means for companies to meet (or beat by a penny) analysts' earnings expectations. Results indicate that managers tend to manage earnings upward to avoid missing analyst forecasts.

Big bath behavior. When firms are already having a bad year, they try to recognize all potential expenses and losses and report all of their bad news at one time. From management's perspective, this behavior may produce two benefits. First, most of the bad news will be reported below the line. If the investing community is focused on above-the-line performance, big bath behavior will minimize the impact of the bad news. Second, following the reporting of the bad news, the firm will appear to be more profitable going forward and may be rewarded for improved accounting performance even though there may be no improvement in economic performance.

Accounting changes. Firms will use accounting changes to smooth earnings (e.g., changing the inventory cost-flow assumption, the capitalization versus expensing decision, or depreciation methodology). Because these accounting changes can have a material impact on earnings while producing no impact on cash flows, they are seen as a means to manipulate reported earnings and should become the focus of analysis.

LOS 34.f: Describe the format and the components of the balance sheet and the format, classification, and use of each component of the statement of stockholders' equity.

The **balance sheet** reports three main categories of accounts: *assets*, which are the resources of the company; *liabilities*, which are the claims against those assets; and *stockholders' equity*, which is the difference between the value of the assets and the liabilities. With the exception of marketable securities, balance sheet items are reported at historical cost, although in some cases, an impairment (damage) of an asset or a specific rule requiring the lower of cost or market value may require a write-down. Accounts that are denominated in a foreign currency are translated to the local currency using the prevailing exchange rate on the financial statement date.

The value of assets and liabilities must be subject to reasonable measurement to be included on the balance sheet. Examples of assets omitted from the balance sheet include brand names, customer lists, and future benefits from R&D investment, which is expensed rather than capitalized. An example of a hard-to-measure liability that may not be presented on the balance sheet is the potential losses related to legal action against the firm. However, this liability may be disclosed in a footnote. Thorough analysis should include consideration for the effects of assets and liabilities not found on the balance sheet.

Assets are divided into two groups, current and long-term, according to their liquidity.

Current assets are assets that are expected to be converted into cash within one year and are listed first. Within the current assets section, assets are listed in the order of their liquidity. They include:

- *Cash and cash equivalents*. Risk-free securities with original maturities of 90 days or less.
- *Marketable securities*. Includes equity securities (trading securities) which are carried at market value, and fixed-income securities, which are carried at cost or amortized value.
- *Accounts and notes receivable*. Trade accounts receivable, which are part of the sales process, should be analyzed separately from notes receivable. Accounts receivable often have an allowance for bad debt expense as a contra-asset account.

- *Inventories.* Analysts should focus on the accounting method used to value inventory.
- *Prepaid expenses.* Items that will show up on future income statements as expenses.
- *Deferred taxes.* Although these are usually liabilities, deferred taxes occasionally show up as assets.

Long-term assets provide benefits or services over periods exceeding one year. Tangible assets are typically reported before intangible assets. Long-term assets include:

- *Property, plant, and equipment.* Includes a contra-asset account for accumulated depreciation. It also should include capital leases.
- *Investment in affiliates.* The investment in and advances to affiliates.

Liabilities are also divided into two groups, current and long-term, according to liquidity.

Current liabilities are liabilities that are expected to be paid within the next year. Within the current liabilities section, they are listed in order according to when they come due. Current liabilities include:

- *Accounts and notes payable.* Trade accounts payable are part of the operating cycle, while notes payable represent a financing decision.
- *Income taxes payable.* The taxes accrued during the past year but not yet paid.
- *Current portion of long-term debt and capital lease obligations.* The part of these long-term instruments that is due within the next year.

Long-term liabilities are liabilities that are expected to be paid after the next year. They include:

- *Long-term debt* and *capital lease obligations.*
- *Deferred taxes.* Deferred taxes are the cumulative difference between what the income statement has reported as income taxes and what the company has paid in taxes. The difference usually arises because of differences between the accounting methods used for financial reporting and tax filing.

Stockholders' equity includes owners' investment, retained earnings, and various adjustments. Equity components are listed in the order of priority in the event of liquidation. There is a separate statement of stockholders' equity that presents a more detailed breakdown of the accounts than what appears on the balance sheet.

Sample balance sheet. Figure 5 presents a sample balance sheet to provide you with a feel for the format of the balance sheet.

Figure 5: Sample Balance Sheet

Assets		Liabilities and Owners' Equity	
Current assets		**Current liabilities**	
Cash and cash equivalents	$300,000	Accounts & notes payable	$200,000
Marketable securities	200,000	Income taxes payable	100,000
Accounts and notes receivable	300,000	Current portion of long-term debt	100,000
Inventories	100,000	Unearned revenue	50,000
Prepaid expenses	50,000	Miscellaneous other payables	50,000
Deferred taxes	25,000		
Miscellaneous current assets	25,000	**Total current liabilities**	$500,000
Total current assets	$1,000,000	Long-term debt	$2,500,000
		Capital lease obligations	400,000
Plant, property, and equipment	$2,000,000	Deferred taxes	100,000
Investment in affiliates	1,500,000		
Other fixed assets	500,000	**Total other liabilities**	$3,000,000
Total other assets	$4,000,000	**Owners' Equity**	
		Preferred stock	$900,000
Total assets	$5,000,000	Common stock	250,000
		Retained earnings	250,000
		Other equity items	100,000
		Total owners' equity	$1,500,000
		Total liabilities and owners' equity	$5,000,000

The Components of the Statement of Stockholders' Equity

The **components of the statement of stockholders' equity** include:

- *Preferred stock.* Various elements of the preferred stock must be disclosed, including the rights to dividends (whether they are fixed, floating, cumulative, or tied to common stock dividends), and any call or conversion provisions. If preferred stock is redeemable by the holder, then it is to be excluded from the shareholders' equity section and reported immediately after the liabilities section.
- *Common stock.* The company must separate out the different classes of common stock. Common stock is reported at par value. Proceeds from common stock sales above par value are reported as additional paid-in capital. Treasury stock is a contra-account, representing share repurchases that the company has made.
- *Retained earnings.* Both the beginning and ending balance of retained earnings are reported, as well as net income for the year and preferred and common dividends paid.
- *Other items.* These might include a minimum liability for underfunded pension plans, market value changes in noncurrent investments, cumulative effect of exchange rate changes, and unearned shares issued to employee stock ownership plans.

Figure 6 shows the consolidated changes in common shareholders' equity for the Washington Post Company (WPC) for the period December 30, 2001 through December 29, 2002.

Figure 6: WPC Consolidated Changes in Common Shareholders' Equity

	Class A Common Stock	Class B Common Stock	Capital in Excess of Par Value	Retained Earnings	Cumulative Foreign Currency Translation Adjustment	Unrealized Gain on Available-for-Sale Securities	Treasury Stock
Balance, December 30, 2001 (in thousands)	$1,722	$18,278	$142,814	$3,029,595	$(9,678)	$24,281	$(1,523,527)
Net income for the year				204,268			
Dividends paid on common stock: $5.60 per share				(53,223)			
Dividends paid on redeemable preferred stock				(1,033)			
Repurchase of 1,229 shares of Class B common stock							(786)
Issuance of 17,156 shares of Class B common stock, net of restricted stock award forfeitures			4,440				2,507
Change in foreign currency translation adjustment (net of taxes)					2,167		
Change in unrealized gain on available-for-sale securities (net of taxes)						(6,368)	
Stock option expense			45				
Tax benefits arising from employee stock plans			1,791				
Balance, December 29, 2002 (in thousands)	1,722	18,278	149,090	3,179,607	(7,511)	17,913	(1,521,806)

Let's look more closely at the changes from 2001 to 2002. The Washington Post's statement of shareholders' equity lists the transaction affecting equity on the left-hand side of the statement, and then records the amount by the components of the statement of stockholders' equity. For instance, issuance of 17,156 shares of Class B common stock affected the balance of Capital in Excess of Par Value ($4,440) and Treasury Stock ($2,507).

Let's look at the common shareholders' equity section of the Washington Post's balance sheet (shown in Figure 7) to illustrate how the statement of shareholders' equity supports the balance sheet.

Figure 7: Washington Post Company—Partial Balance Sheet

Common Shareholders' Equity	December 29, 2002	December 30, 2001
Common Stock		
Class A common stock, $1 par value; 7,000,000 shares authorized; 1,722,250 shares issued and outstanding	$1,722	$1,722
Class B common stock, $1 par value; 40,000,000 shares authorized; 18,277,750 shares issued and 7,788,543 and 7,772,616 shares outstanding	18,278	18,278
Capital in excess of par value	149,090	142,814
Retained earnings	3,179,607	3,029,595
Accumulated other comprehensive income (loss), net of taxes		
Cumulative foreign currency translation adjustment	(7,511)	(9,678)
Unrealized gain on available-for-sale securities	17,913	24,281
Cost of 10,489,207 and 10,505,134 shares of Class B common stock held in treasury	(1,521,806)	(1,523,527)
	1,837,293	1,683,485

Note how each of the balance sheet components is supported by a calculation of the changes in the statement of shareholders' equity. The statement of owners' (or stockholders') equity is a valuable source of information for the financial analyst providing detail on changes during the year affecting a firm's equity position.

Also notice that while 7,000,000 shares of the Class A common are authorized, only 1,722,250 are issued and outstanding. At one time there were 18,277,750 shares of Class B common stock outstanding. The par value of these shares has remained, and as shares have been repurchased (now held in treasury), only the capital in excess of par value (additional paid-in capital) has changed. Notice the other categories that include items that have not passed through the income statement: adjustment for losses on foreign currency translation and unrealized gains on securities classified as available-for-sale securities.

KEY CONCEPTS

1. The income statement has several components, the most important being recurring income from continuing operations because it gives the best indicator of future earnings.
2. The matching principle states that revenues and the expenses incurred to generate those revenues should be accounted for in the same time period.
3. Revenue is recognized when two conditions are met: (1) the firm has provided virtually all of the goods or services for which it is to be paid, and (2) the company is able to estimate the probability of payment.
4. There are five specific methods by which revenue is recognized:
   * Sales basis method—earnings process complete and revenue assured.
   * Percentage-of-completion method—earnings process incomplete, costs estimable, and revenue assured.
   * Completed contract method—earnings process incomplete, but either costs inestimable or revenue not assured.
   * Installment sales method—earnings process complete and revenue not assured.
   * Cost recovery method—earnings process complete but contingencies of unknown cost exist.
5. Construction-in-progress under percentage-of-completion represents cumulative costs plus cumulative gross income. Under the completed contract method, construction-in-progress is only the cumulative project costs.

6. Prior to completion, a company using the percentage-of-completion method will have greater total assets, greater shareholder equity, and lower liabilities than a company that uses the completed contract method. Cash flows are the same under each method.

7. Advance billings represent the amounts that have been billed to the client on a cumulative basis prior to the completion of the project. Construction-in-progress (CIP) and advance billings (AB) are netted in the computation of the balance sheet asset or liability. If CIP – AB > 0, then a current asset is posted. If CIP – AB < 0, then a liability is posted.

8. There are four nonrecurring items in the income statement:
   - Unusual or infrequent items.
   - Extraordinary items.
   - Income or loss from discontinued operations.
   - Cumulative effect of accounting changes.

   Analysts should be careful when forecasting income to only include items that are likely to recur in the future.

9. There are four ways in which management can manipulate earnings:
   - Classification of good and bad news.
   - Income smoothing.
   - Big bath technique.
   - Accounting changes.

10. The balance sheet reports three main categories of accounts: assets, which are the resources of the company; liabilities, which are the claims against those assets; and stockholders' equity, which is the difference between assets and liabilities.

11. The components of the statement of stockholders' equity include preferred stock, common stock, retained earnings, and treasury stock.

CONCEPT CHECKERS: ACCOUNTING INCOME AND ASSETS: THE ACCRUAL CONCEPT

1. Which of the following statements about accrual accounting is **FALSE**?
    A. Net income before taxes is considered the best indicator of future earnings.
    B. The completed contract method produces more volatile earnings than does the percent-of-completion method.
    C. Revenue should be recognized when the earnings process is complete, costs can be reliably determined, and payment is assured.
    D. Under the accrual concept, revenue is recognized when the earnings process is completed and ultimate realization is assured.

2. Accounting income could be *best described* as being based on the:
    A. firm's economic rate of return adjusted for risk.
    B. cash flows occurring during the accounting period.
    C. firm's current and probable future cash collections and expenses.
    D. matching of expenses with the revenues generated by those expenses.

3. Which of the following is **NOT** necessary to recognize revenue?
    A. Revenue and expenses must be estimable or measurable.
    B. The activity must be substantially complete and ownership must have been transferred.
    C. The transaction must be an arm's length transaction with an independent party.
    D. The transaction must be either for cash or in the company's main line of business.

4. Which principle requires that the cost of goods sold be recognized in the same period in which the sale of the related inventory is recorded?
    A. Accrual.
    B. Certainty.
    C. Matching.
    D. Economic.

5. Revenues that are collected in the same accounting period as the time of sale should be accounted for using the:
    A. sales basis method.
    B. installment sales method.
    C. completed contract method.
    D. percentage-of-completion method.

6. A difference between the percentage-of-completion method and the completed contract method is:
    A. interim equity is lower under the completed contract method.
    B. income is reported earlier under the percentage-of-completion method.
    C. sales and net income are more volatile under the completed contract method.
    D. all of the above.

Use the following data to answer Questions 7 and 8.

AAA has a contract to build a building for $100,000 with an estimated time to completion of three years. A reliable cost estimate for the project would be $60,000. In the first year of the project, AAA incurred costs totaling $24,000.

7. Under the percentage-of-completion method, AAA will report a first-year profit of:
   A. $16,000.
   B. $36,000.
   C. $40,000.
   D. $76,000.

8. Under the completed contract method, AAA will report a first-year profit of:
   A. $0.
   B. $16,000.
   C. $36,000.
   D. $40,000.

9. All of the following items are reported net of taxes below net income from continuing operations on the income statement EXCEPT:
   A. extraordinary items.
   B. unusual or infrequent items.
   C. income from discontinued operations.
   D. the cumulative effect of accounting changes.

10. Which of the following would *least likely* be classified as an extraordinary item?
    A. Uninsured losses from earthquakes.
    B. Expropriations by a foreign government.
    C. Losses from the early retirement of debt.
    D. Losses from the disposal of a business segment.

11. Which of the following statements about nonrecurring items is FALSE?
    A. Cumulative effects resulting from a change in the accounting method for inventory are reported in the cost of goods sold.
    B. Unusual or infrequent items are reported before taxes above net income from continuing operations.
    C. A change in accounting principle is reported in the income statement net of taxes after extraordinary items and before net income.
    D. Gains or losses from extraordinary items and discontinued operations are reported net of taxes at the bottom of the income statement before net income.

12. Which of the following statements about accounting for revenues or costs under the percentage-of-completion method is TRUE?
    A. All current and estimated future costs are charged off as an expense in the first year of the project.
    B. The costs that can be charged against income are calculated by multiplying the total estimated cost by the proportion of revenues paid thus far to the total estimated revenues.
    C. Revenues can be recognized based on engineering estimates of the proportion of work completed.
    D. No costs can be charged off until all revenues are received.

13. Which of the following statements about stockholders' equity is **FALSE**?
    A. The statement of stockholders' equity lists ownership interest in order of payment preference upon liquidation of the firm.
    B. Retained earnings are the total earnings of the company since its inception less all the dividends ever paid out.
    C. Common stock is listed at its sale price with the excess over par listed in a contra account called additional paid-in capital.
    D. Preferred stock receives dividends and any cash during liquidation before common shareholders.

14. In the case of long-term contracts, the method prescribed when there is a contract for the goods and it is possible to reliably estimate revenues and costs is the:
    A. installment method.
    B. percentage-of-completion method.
    C. cost recovery method.
    D. completed contract method.

15. Which of the following would **NOT** be found in the statement of stockholders' equity?
    A. Extraordinary items.
    B. The cumulative effect of exchange rate changes.
    C. The minimum liability for underfunded pension plans.
    D. The changes in the market value of noncurrent investments.

16. Which of the following choices is **NOT** a common method used by management to manipulate earnings?
    A. Make losses appear to be extraordinary so that they will not affect income from continuing operations.
    B. Adjust the timing of costs so that earnings are increased in bad years and decreased in good years, thereby smoothing earnings.
    C. Adjust the timing of costs so that earnings are further decreased in bad years.
    D. Make financing costs appear to be operating expenses, so that they will not affect net income from continuing operations.

17. Under which revenue recognition method is income the *poorest* measure of the future earning power of the company, requiring an analyst to use the cash flow statement to gain an understanding of the operating process?
    A. Sales basis method.
    B. Percentage-of-completion method.
    C. Completed contract method.
    D. Installment sales method.

18. When accounting for long-term projects, which revenue recognition method should be used when the revenues are paid up front, but the costs, which can be estimated, will be incurred over the next three years?
    A. Sales basis method.
    B. Percentage-of-completion method.
    C. Completed contract method.
    D. Installment sales method.

19. When accounting for long-term projects, which revenue recognition method should be used when the revenues are paid up front, but the costs are highly uncertain and will be incurred over the next three years?
    A. Sales basis method.
    B. Percentage-of-completion method.
    C. Completed contract method.
    D. Installment sales method.

20. Which revenue recognition method should be used when the costs are all incurred at the time of sale, but the proceeds will be received over the next year with a high likelihood of collection?
    A. Sales basis method.
    B. Completed contract method.
    C. Installment sales method.
    D. Cost recovery method.

21. Which of the following tactics would *least likely* be used to make earnings appear more stable?
    A. Classification of good news/bad news.
    B. Income smoothing.
    C. Big bath behavior.
    D. Accounting changes.

22. Which of the following statements concerning when a company announces it is discontinuing a business segment is FALSE?
    A. The income or loss from the discontinued operations is reported separately.
    B. Past income statements must be restated, separating the income or loss from the discontinued operations.
    C. Any expected gain on the disposal is reported in the year of the announcement.
    D. Income and losses from discontinued operations are reported net of tax after net income from continuing operations.

23. Assuming a project is in process, which of the following *best describes* a difference between the percentage-of-completion method versus the completed contract method for revenue recognition? The:
    A. completed contract method generates higher cash flows.
    B. percentage-of-completion method results in higher earnings volatility.
    C. completed contract method results in a lower liabilities-to-equity ratio.
    D. percentage-of-completion method generally results in higher total assets.

24. Firms with a continuing flow of profitable projects that use the percentage-of-completion method as opposed to the completed contract method to recognize revenue generally have which of the following?
    A. Higher liabilities.
    B. Lower total assets.
    C. Lower shareholder equity.
    D. Lower ratio of liabilities-to-equity.

25. An analyst gathered the following information for the current fiscal year on a construction company:
    - The company has a 10-year project to build a canal for $5,000,000.
    - Cash received on the contract is $500,000.
    - The firm incurred costs of $400,000 during the fiscal year.
    - An unreliable estimate of the total project cost is $4,000,000.
    In the current fiscal year, the firm would report gross profit for the project of:
    A. $0.
    B. $100,000.
    C. $600,000.
    D. $1,000,000.

26. Construction Project R has both a reliable contract price and an unknown cost estimate. Construction Project S has an unreliable cost estimate. Which revenue recognition method(s) should be used?

	Project R	Project S
A.	Completed contract	Percentage-of-completion
B.	Completed contract	Completed contract
C.	Percentage-of-completion	Completed contract
D.	Percentage-of-completion	Percentage-of-completion

Use the following data to answer Questions 27 and 28.

DDD Inc. has a 5-year construction contract to build a canal for $600,000. The estimate of total costs is $400,000. Year 1 and Year 2 incurred costs are, respectively, $100,000 and $20,000.

27. If ultimate payment is assured and the cost estimate is reliable, DDD would report realized profits of:

	Year 1	Year 2
A.	$0	$0
B.	$10,000	$50,000
C.	$40,000	$40,000
D.	$50,000	$10,000

28. If the estimate of costs is unreliable, DDD would report the following realized profits of:

	Year 1	Year 2
A.	$0	$0
B.	$10,000	$50,000
C.	$40,000	$40,000
D.	$50,000	$10,000

29. Which of the following statements about the percentage-of-completion and completed contract methods during the life of a project is TRUE?
    A. Reported earnings are higher under the completed contract method than the percentage-of-completion method.
    B. The percentage-of-completion method can be used with unreliable cost estimates.
    C. The completed contract method must be used if reliable cost estimates can be obtained.
    D. Periodic profit is not recognized under the completed contract method prior to the project completion.

30. RRR, Inc., has a $500,000 airport construction project contract. The estimated total costs are $400,000. In the first year, incurred costs are $200,000. What is the firm's change in retained earnings at the end of the first fiscal year if it uses the following revenue recognition methods?

	Percentage-of- Completion Method	Completed Contract Method
A.	$0	$0
B.	$50,000	$50,000
C.	$50,000	$0
D.	$100,000	$50,000

COMPREHENSIVE PROBLEM – ACCOUNTING INCOME AND ASSETS: THE ACCRUAL CONCEPT

Acme has entered into a project to build a bridge which it estimates will cost $1.5 million and take three years to complete. Assume the following: total revenues on the project will be $2.3 million; billings will be $800,000 for each of the first two years and $700,000 in the final year; costs will be $500,000 each year; cash flows will be $600,000 in years 1 and 2 and $1.1 million in year 3.

Complete the following entries for the second year of the project under the two methods of revenue recognition:

	Percentage of Completion	Completed Contract
Revenue		
Expense		
Net income		
Cash flow		
Net CIP or AB (identify which and whether asset or liability)		
Accounts receivable		

ANSWERS – CONCEPT CHECKERS: ACCOUNTING INCOME AND ASSETS: THE ACCRUAL CONCEPT

1. **A** Income from continuing operations is considered the best indicator of future earnings.

2. **D** Accounting income is based on the matching principle.

3. **D** There is no requirement for the company to make a sale in its normal line of business.

4. **C** The matching principle facilitates the measurement of periodic income.

5. **A** The sales-basis method recognizes revenue at the time of sale, where title is transferred and the sale is for cash or accounts receivable.

6. **D** All statements are differences between the percentage-of-completion method and the completed contract method.

7. **A** $24,000/$60,000 = 40% of the project completed. 40% of $100,000 = $40,000 revenue. $40,000 – $24,000 = $16,000 profit for the period.

8. **A** The completed contract method does not recognize any revenue until the entire project is complete.

9. **B** Unusual or infrequent items are reported below recurring items from continuing operations, but above net income from continuing operations.

10. **D** Losses from the disposal of a business segment would be reported as part of operating income (or as discontinued operations when appropriate).

11. **A** Effects of accounting changes are reported after net income from continuing operations.

12. **C** Engineering estimates can be used to estimate proportionate revenues.

13. **C** Common stock is recorded at *par value* with the excess over par recorded as additional paid-in capital.

14. **B** Percentage-of-completion method is used for long-term contracts when there is a reliable estimate for revenues and costs.

15. **A** Extraordinary items are found in the income statement.

16. **D** Interest expenses and operating expenses equally affect net income from continuing operations. The other responses are all earnings manipulation techniques: A is income classification, B is income smoothing, and C is big bath behavior.

17. **C** Since revenues are not recognized until the end of the project under the completed contract method, income is a poor measure of economic activity.

18. **B** The percentage-of-completion method is used when there are reliable estimates of revenues and expenses.

19. **C** The completed contract method is used when estimates of costs are unreliable.

20. **A** The sales basis method is used when the goods or services have been provided when the sale was made, and there is a high likelihood of payment.

21. **C** Big bath behavior makes earnings look even worse during a bad year. Classification of good news/bad news may be used to smooth earnings.

22. **C** Any expected gain on the disposal cannot be reported until after the sale is completed.

23. **D** Both methods generate the same cash flows, while the percentage-of-completion method has higher total assets and lower income volatility.

24. **D**   Generally, firms with a continuing flow of profitable projects will have higher total assets, lower liabilities, higher shareholder equity, and a lower ratio of liabilities-to-equity by using the percentage-of-completion method as compared to the completed contract method.

25. **A**   Since the cost estimate is unreliable, the completed contract method for the revenue recognition should be used. This method does not recognize periodic profit prior to the completion of the contract period.

26. **B**   The completed contract method should be used when the selling price or cost estimates are unreliable, while the percentage-of-completion method can be used when payment is assured and cost estimates are reliable. Neither Project R or S meets the requirements for using percentage-of-completion.

27. **D**   Since ultimate payment is assured and the cost estimate is reliable, DDD may use the percentage-of-completion method. Total expected profit is $600,000 – $400,000 = $200,000. In year 1, 25% of the total costs of the project ($100,000/$400,000) are incurred, hence, reported year 1 profit is 25% × $200,000 = $50,000. In year 2, 5% of the total costs of the project ($20,000/$400,000) are incurred. Hence, year 2 profit is 5% × $200,000 = $10,000.

28. **A**   Since the estimate of costs is unreliable, the company must use the completed contract method and defer all profit recognition until the end of the contract.

29. **D**   Generally, firms with a continuing flow of profitable projects will have higher total assets, lower liabilities, higher shareholder equity, and a lower ratio of liabilities-to-equity by using the percentage-of-completion method as compared to the completed contract method. The completed contract method should be used when the selling price or cost estimates are unreliable while the percentage-of-completion method can be used when ultimate payment of the contract is assured and cost estimates are reliable. The completed contract method does not report periodic profit.

30. **C**   The completed contract method does not report periodic profit. Hence, if the firm uses the completed contract method, retained earnings will be $0 in year 1. If the percentage-of-completion method is used, retained earnings will increase by $50,000 = [(200,000/400,000) × (500,000 – 400,000)].

ANSWER – COMPREHENSIVE PROBLEM: ACCOUNTING INCOME AND ASSETS: THE ACCRUAL CONCEPT

Percentage of completion year 2:

$$revenue = \frac{\$500,000}{\$1,500,000} \times \$2,300,000 = \$766,667$$, expense = \$500,000, net income = \$266,667, cash flow = \$600,000, construction in progress = \$1,533,334, advance billings = \$1.6 million

Net balance sheet entry is as follows:

advance billings = \$66,666 (liability), accounts receivable = \$1.6 million – \$1.2 million = \$400,000

Completed contract year 2:

revenue = 0, expense = 0, net income = 0, cash flow = \$600,000, construction in progress = \$1 million, advance billings = \$1.6 million, net difference is advance billings = \$600,000 (liability), accounts receivable = \$1.6 million – \$1.2 million = \$400,000

	Percentage of Completion	Completed Contract
Revenue	\$766,667	0
Expense	\$500,000	0
Net income	\$266,667	0
Cash flow	\$600,000	\$600,000
Net CIP or AB (identify which and whether asset or liability)	\$66,666 Advance billings liability	\$600,000 Advance billings liability
Accounts receivable	\$400,000	\$400,000

THE STATEMENT OF CASH FLOWS

EXAM FOCUS

The statement of cash flows is one of the most important topics in the Level 1 accounting curriculum. It provides information on a firm's operating, investing, and financing activities and is the link between the firm's income statement and the changes in its cash balances. On the Level 1 exam, candidates should be prepared to classify a firm's cash flows into one of the three categories. Candidates should also be prepared to calculate cash flows from operation using the indirect method, starting with net income and adjusting for noncash items and changes in balance sheet accounts to arrive at CFO.

CHANGES IN CASH

Net income based on accrual accounting is not cash earnings. Therefore we need a statement of cash flows to provide information about a company's sources and uses of cash. Remember, 'cash and cash equivalents' includes currency, coins, bank deposits, money market funds, and T-bills and other debt securities with maturities of less than 90 days.

Some understanding of the basics of constructing a statement of cash flows can be gained by looking at our basic accounting relations. Since:

assets = liabilities + equity, it must be that:

Δassets = Δliabilities + Δequity, and we can write:

Δcash + Δnon-cash assets = Δliabilities + Δequity

and Δcash = Δliabilities + Δequity – Δnon-cash assets.

If we buy a machine (a non-cash asset), cash goes down and non-cash assets go up. If we sell a machine or building, non-cash assets go down and cash goes up. If we borrow money, both cash and assets go up. If we issue stock or make cash profits, both cash and equity increase. If we pay dividends, retained earnings are less, so both equity and cash are less. Try to keep this framework in mind as you study the following material.

LOS 35.a: Identify the principal purposes and uses of the statement of cash flows.

The **statement of cash flows** provides information beyond that available from earnings and other financial data. This is because cash flow is essential to the continued operation of a business. The primary purpose of the statement of cash flows is to provide:

- Information about a company's cash receipts and cash payments during an accounting period.
- Information about a company's operating, investing, and financing activities.

Important information for investment decision making presented in the statement of cash flows includes whether:

- Regular operations generate enough cash to sustain the business.

- Enough cash is generated to pay off existing debts as they mature.
- The firm is likely to need additional financing.
- Unexpected obligations can be met.
- The firm can take advantage of new business opportunities as they arise.

The Financial Accounting Standards Board (FASB) states that financial statements should include information about:

- How the firm obtains and spends cash.
- The firm's borrowing and debt repayment activities.
- The firm's sale and repurchase of its ownership securities.
- The firm's dividend payments and other cash distributions to owners.
- Other factors affecting the firm's liquidity and solvency.

LOS 35.b: Compare and contrast the three major classifications (i.e., cash provided or used by operating activities, investing activities, and financing activities) in a statement of cash flows, and describe how noncash investing and financing transactions are reported.

The **statement of cash flows** provides information on cash flows from operations, investing activities, and financing activities. Information on noncash activities must also be reported along with the statement.

The statement of cash flows relates the firm's income statement to changes between the firm's beginning-of-period and end-of-period balance sheets. The objective of the statement of cash flows is to show the sources of cash and all the uses of cash during the accounting period. The statement of cash flows has the format shown in Figure 1.

Figure 1: Statement of Cash Flows for the Period 1/1/xx to 1/1/xx+1

Cash flow from operations (CFO)	+/– $xx
Cash flow from investing (CFI)	+/– $yy
Cash flow from financing (CFF)	+/– $zz
Change in the cash account	Δ cash
Beginning of period cash	+ Beginning cash
Ending cash balance	**Ending cash**

Cash flow from operations represents changes in the working capital accounts (e.g., accounts receivable, inventory, and accounts payable) and all items that flow through the income statement (e.g., cash receipts from customers, payments for good sold, wages):

- Net cash flow from operations focuses on the *liquidity* of the company rather than on profitability.
- Under Statement of Financial Accounting Standards (SFAS) 95, interest and dividend revenue and interest expense are considered operating activities, but dividends paid are considered financing activities.
- All income taxes are considered operating activities, even if some arise from financing or investing.

Cash flow from investing represents the purchase or sale of productive assets (physical assets and investments) for cash:

- Investing cash flow essentially deals with the items appearing on the lower left-hand portion of the balance sheet (fixed assets).
- Investing cash flow includes:
  - Capital expenditures for long-term assets.

- Proceeds from the sales of assets.
- Cash flow from investments in joint ventures and affiliates and long-term investment in securities.

Cash flow from financing represents acquiring and dispensing ownership funds and borrowings:

Financing cash flow deals with the lower right-hand portion of the balance sheet (long-term debt and equity). Examples include cash flows from additional debt and equity financing:

- Debt financing includes both short- and long-term financing.
- Dividends paid are a financing cash flow because dividends flow through the retained earnings statement.

Noncash investing and financing activities do not flow through the statement of cash flows because they do not require the use of cash. Examples are:

- Retiring debt securities by issuing equity securities to the lender.
- Converting preferred stock to common stock.
- Acquiring assets through a capital lease (only the initial purchase entries).
- Obtaining long-term assets by issuing notes payable to the seller.
- Exchanging one noncash asset for another noncash asset.
- The purchase of noncash assets by issuing equity or debt securities.

While these activities do not flow through the statement of cash flows, they should be disclosed in either the footnotes or on a separate schedule as investing or financing events that did not affect cash.

LOS 35.c: Calculate and analyze, using the indirect method, the net cash flow provided or used by operating activities, investing activities and financing activities.

The calculation of **cash flow from operations using the indirect method** starts with income after taxes (the bottom of the income statement) and adjusts backwards for noncash and other items. Changes in balance sheet items are used to adjust net income under the indirect method. Figure 2 identifies changes in balance sheet accounts as either sources of cash (added to net income) or uses of cash (subtracted from net income).

Figure 2: Balance Sheet Items in the Cash Flow Statement

	Increase	*Decrease*
Current assets	use of cash	source of cash
Current liabilities	source of cash	use of cash

Net income
Adjust for:

+	Noncash expenses or losses
–	Noncash revenues or gains

Adjust for changes in working capital:

+/–	Changes in operating asset accounts (e.g., *accounts receivable)*
+/–	Changes in operating liability accounts (e.g., *accounts payable)*
=	Cash flow from operations

Figure 3: Cash Flow Statement Construction

Constructing the Statement of Cash Flows
Using the Indirect Method

Calculate the change in cash

Calculate the change in all other balance sheet items

Identify changes as potential adjustments for operating,
investing, and financing activities

Determine net cash flow from operating activities

Determine financing cash flows

Determine investing cash flows

Compare cash flow from operating, investing, and
financing activities with the change in cash

Example: Statement of cash flows using the indirect method

Given the following income statement and balance sheet information, calculate the statement of cash flows using the indirect method.

Income Statement

Sales	$1,600
Cost of goods sold	(1,350)
Gross profit	250
Depreciation expense	100
Interest expense	47
Equity in earnings of investment	2
Gain on the sale of old machine	10
Income before taxes	$115
Income taxes:	
Current	35
Deferred	10
Net income after taxes	$70

Balance Sheet	1/1/end	1/1/beg	Net Change
Assets			
Cash	$292	$100	$192
Accounts receivable	280	200	80
Inventory	700	800	(100)
Property, plant, and equipment	1,020	1,000	20
Accumulated depreciation	(340)	(300)	(40)
Investments	12	10	2
Total assets	$1,964	$1,810	$154
Liabilities and Equity			
Accounts payable	$470	$450	$20
Mortgage	550	600	(50)
Bank note	100	0	100
Deferred taxes	90	80	10
Common stock	410	400	10
Retained earnings	344	280	64
Total liabilities and equity	$1,964	$1,810	$154

Additional information:

1. Dividends of $6 were paid to shareholders.

2. One new common share was sold at par value. Par is $10 per share.

3. Fixed assets were sold for $30. Original cost of these assets was $80, and $60 of accumulated depreciation has been charged to the original cost.

4. New fixed assets were purchased for $100. To pay for this acquisition, a 10-year, $100 note was issued to a bank.

5. The firm recognized a $2 gain from a subsidiary using the equity method. No cash was received.

Cash flow from operations (indirect method):

Net income		$70
Add (subtract) adjustments		
Depreciation	$100	
Deferred taxes	10	
Gain on the sale of machinery	(10)	
Equity in long-term investment	(2)	
Accounts receivable (use)	(80)	
Inventory (source)	100	
Accounts payable (source)	20	
		138
Net cash flow from operations		**$208**

Professor's Note: It is important to remember that only the current period's depreciation is considered on the statement of cash flows under the indirect method.

You might be wondering what happened to the $60 in accumulated depreciation written off when the old machine was sold. The answer is that the depreciation was entered into the cash flow computations in earlier periods.

Let's scrutinize the SCF and talk a bit about its construction:

- Depreciation and deferred taxes are noncash expenses which reduce net income. Adding them back to net income eliminates any effect on cash flows.
- The gain on the sale of machinery is equal to the market value of the machine ($30) minus the book value of the machine at the time of the sale ($80 historical cost—$60 accumulated depreciation). Observe that the full $30 is listed as a cash flow from investing, so the $10 gain is double counting and must be removed from net income when deriving CFO.
- The gain from the subsidiary is equity investment income that does not result in receipt of cash. Thus, it is eliminated from net income in deriving CFO.
- Accounts receivable and accounts payable are operating (working capital) accounts whose change is classified via sources/uses. That is, changes in accounts receivable, inventory and accounts payable are adjustments to reflect funding from customers and suppliers.

Investing Activities and Financing Activities

Determining cash flow from **investing activities** tends to be easier than calculating cash from operations. Each investing activity is classified as a cash inflow or a cash outflow. The individual items are then added together to compute cash from investing.

Continuing with our example from the previous LOS:

Investing cash flows
Purchase fixed assets (use)   ($100)
Sale of old machine (source)   __30__
Net cash flow from investing ($70)

- The purchase of fixed assets is a cash expenditure and is reflected as a cash outflow.
- The entire amount received from the sale of the old machine (fixed assets) is reflected as a cash inflow.

Cash receipts and payments from each financing activity are analyzed individually and then totaled to compute **cash flow from financing.**

Financing cash flows

10-year note (source)	$100
Sale of common stock (source)	10
Dividends paid (use)	(6)
Repayment of mortgage note (use)	(50)
Net cash flow from financing	**$54**

- The issuance of the 10-year $100 note and the sale of common stock represent cash inflows to the firm.
- Dividends paid flow through retained earnings and are classified as a financing cash outflow.
- The repayment of the mortgage note principal constitutes a use of cash.

Completed Statement of Cash Flows

Cash flow from operations (indirect method):

Net Income		$70
Add (subtract) adjustments		
Depreciation	$100	
Deferred taxes	10	
Gain on the sale of machinery	(10)	
Equity in long-term investment	(2)	
Accounts receivable (use)	(80)	
Inventory (source)	100	
Accounts payable (source)	20	
		138
Net cash flow from operations		**$208**

Investing cash flows

Purchase fixed assets (use)	($100)	
Sale of old machine (source)	30	
Net cash flow from investing		**($70)**

Financing cash flows

10-year note (source)	$100	
Sale of common stock (source)	10	
Dividends paid (use)	(6)	
Repayment of mortgage note (use)	(50)	
Net cash flow from financing		**$54**
Net cash flow		
Net increase in cash		**$192**

The net increase in cash is $192. Note that this is equal to the net increase in cash shown on the balance sheet ($292 – $100 = $192).

KEY CONCEPTS

1. The primary purpose of the statement of cash flows is to provide information about a company's cash receipts and payments as well as its sources and uses of cash from and for investing and financing activities.
2. Classifications of cash flows:
   - *Cash flow from operations* represents changes in the working capital accounts and all items that flow through the income statement.
   - *Cash flow from investing* represents the purchase or sale of assets.
   - *Cash flow from financing* represents cash expended to pay dividends, repurchase stock, or make principal payments on debt, or taken in from the sale of securities or borrowing.
3. The *indirect method* of constructing a statement of cash flows begins with income after taxes (net income) and then makes adjustments for non-cash items. Changes in balance sheet items are used to adjust net income.
4. *Cash flow from investing* is calculated by classifying each investing activity as a non-cash transaction, a cash inflow (+), or an outflow (–), and summing the individual items.
5. *Cash flow from financing* is calculated by summing the cash receipts (+) and payments (–) from each financing source.

CONCEPT CHECKERS: THE STATEMENT OF CASH FLOWS

1. The statement of cash flows is *least likely* to provide which of the following items of information for investment decision making?
    A. Whether unexpected obligations of the firm can be met.
    B. Whether the firm is likely to need additional financing.
    C. Whether the firm can take advantage of new business opportunities as they arise.
    D. Whether the firm's management has demonstrated sound fiscal management.

2. Torval Inc. retires debt securities by issuing equity securities. This is considered a:
    A. cash flow from operations.
    B. cash flow from investing.
    C. cash flow from financing.
    D. non-cash transaction.

3. Net income for Monique Inc. for the fiscal period ended December 31, 2005 is $78,000. Its accounts receivable balance at December 31, 2005 is $121,000 and it was $69,000 at December 31, 2004. Its accounts payable balance at December 31, 2005 is $72,000 and it was $43,000 at December 31, 2004. Depreciation for 2005 is $12,000 and there is an unrealized gain of $15,000 included in 2005 income from the change in value of trading securities.

    Which of the following amounts represents Monique's cash flow from operations for 2005?
    A. $52,000.
    B. $67,000.
    C. $82,000.
    D. $98,000.

4. Martin Inc. had the following transactions during 2005:
    Purchased new fixed assets for $75,000.
    Converted $70,000 worth of preferred shares to common shares.
    Received cash dividends of $12,000. Paid cash dividends of $21,000.
    Mortgage principal repayment of $17,000.

    Which of the following amounts represents Martin's cash flows from investing and cash flows from financing in 2005, respectively?

	Cash Flows From Investing	Cash Flows From Financing
A.	($5,000)	($21,000)
B.	($75,000)	($21,000)
C.	($5,000)	($38,000)
D.	($75,000)	($38,000)

ANSWERS – CONCEPT CHECKERS: THE STATEMENT OF CASH FLOWS

1. **D** "Sound fiscal management" is a very subjective term that cannot always be directly or reasonably measured from the statement of cash flows. The other three answers are important information presented in the Statement of Cash Flows.

2. **D** The exchange of debt securities for equity securities is a non-cash transaction.

3. **A**

Net income	$78,000
Add: depreciation	$12,000
Deduct: unrealized gain	($15,000)
Change in accounts receivable – use of cash	($52,000)
Change in accounts payable – source of cash	$29,000
Cash flows from operations	$52,000

4. **D** Purchased new fixed assets for $75,000 – cash <u>outflow</u> from investing
    Converted $70,000 worth of preferred shares to common shares – non-cash transaction
    Received dividends of $12,000 – cash <u>inflow</u> from operations
    Paid dividends of $21,000 – cash <u>outflow</u> from financing
    Mortgage repayment of $17,000 – cash <u>outflow</u> from financing
    CFF = –21,000 – 17,000 = –$38,000

ANALYSIS OF CASH FLOWS

EXAM FOCUS

The key to this topic review is the classification of cash flows into three categories: (1) cash flows from operations, which are cash flows related to the normal operations of a company; (2) cash flows from investing, which reflect the acquisition or retirement of assets; and (3) cash flows from financing, which are flows related to the firm's financing decisions. Some classifications are straightforward, but some are not. Know that cash interest expense, interest revenue, and dividend revenue are operating cash flows, while dividends paid are a financing cash flow. For success on the Level 1 exam, you will need to create a statement of cash flows using both the indirect and direct methods. When making adjustments to balance sheet items, memorize that there is an inverse relationship between changes in assets and cash flow, and a positive relationship between changes in liabilities and cash flow.

LOS 36.a: Classify a particular transaction or item as cash flow from 1) operations, 2) investing, or 3) financing.

Items on the cash flow statement come from two sources: (1) income statement items and (2) changes in balance sheet accounts. The cash flow statement divides cash flow into three components.

Cash flow from operations (CFO) reports the cash generated from sales and the cash used in the production process. These items essentially flow through the firm's income statement and working capital accounts. Working capital accounts are current assets and current liabilities. The key elements are:

- Cash collections from sales.
- Cash inputs into the manufacturing or retail process.
- Cash operating expenses.
- Cash interest expense.
- Cash tax payments.

Cash flow from investing (CFI) reports the cash used for property, plant, and equipment; investments; acquisitions; and the cash generated from sales of assets or businesses. These items are found in the noncurrent portion of the asset section of the balance sheet. Key elements are:

- Purchases of property, plant, and equipment.
- Investments in joint ventures and affiliates.
- Payments for businesses acquired.
- Proceeds from sales of assets.
- Investments (or sales of investments) in marketable securities.

Cash flow from financing (CFF) reports capital structure transactions. These items are found in the long-term capital section of the balance sheet and the statement of retained earnings (RE). Key elements are:

- Cash dividends paid.
- Increases or decreases in short-term borrowings.

- Long-term borrowings and repayment of long-term borrowings.
- Stock sales and repurchases.

Note that even though cash interest expense is considered to be a financing cash flow from an economic perspective, it is classified as an operating cash flow for accounting purposes.

Classifying Cash Flows

In most cases the classification of cash flows is straightforward. Items that affect cash flow are either an income statement account or a *change* in a balance sheet account. As a general rule, an increase in an asset account or a decrease in a liability account requires the use of cash and, therefore, decreases the cash flow to the firm. For example, purchasing more inventory (increase in an asset account) or retiring trade credit (decrease in a liability) results in the use of cash and a decrease in cash flow. Likewise, a decrease in an asset account or an increase in a liability account represent a source of cash or an increase in the firm's cash flow. For example, collecting accounts receivable (decrease in an asset account) or an increase in notes payable (increase in a liability) both result in cash inflows for the firm.

Operating cash flows (CFO). All items affecting income are included as a component of operating cash flow. Changes in asset or liability accounts that are a result of the sales or production process also are classified as operating cash flows.

Examples of balance sheet items that are classified as operating cash flows include changes in:

- Receivables.
- Inventories.
- Prepaid expenses.
- Taxes, interest, and miscellaneous payables.
- Deferred taxes.

Examples of income statement items that are classified as operating cash flows include:

- Cash sales.
- Cash cost of sales.
- Cash general and administrative expenses.
- Cash taxes.
- Interest paid and received.
- Dividends received.

Investing cash flows (CFI). Changes in asset accounts, typically long-term assets (and potentially corresponding liability accounts), that reflect capital investment in the company are classified as investing cash flows. Examples of items that are classified as investing cash flows include changes in:

- Most gross fixed-asset accounts.
- Marketable securities.

Financing cash flows (CFF). Changes in equity accounts, including dividends, and changes in liabilities that are part of the capital structure are classified as financing cash flows. Examples of items that are classified as financing cash flows include:

- Dividends paid to the company's shareholders.
- A change in liability accounts that represent financing (typically interest-bearing debt or deep-discount debt).
- A change in equity accounts.

Noncash transactions. Some transactions do not result in immediate cash inflows or cash outflows. These transactions are disclosed in footnotes. However, these transactions typically involve an investing and/or financing decision. For example, if a firm acquires a building and real estate by assuming a mortgage, the firm has made an investment and financing decision. Economically, this is equivalent to borrowing the purchase amount. Another example of a noncash transaction is an exchange of debt for equity. Analysts should be aware of the firm's noncash transactions and incorporate them into analysis of past and current performance, and include their effects in projections of the future.

LOS 36.b: Compute and interpret a statement of cash flows, using the direct method and the indirect method.

The statement of cash flows comprises three sections: cash flow from operating activities (CFO), investing cash flow (CFI), and financing cash flow (CFF). Under U.S. and IAS GAAP, the CFO can be presented two ways—using the *direct method* and the *indirect method*. The direct method presents more information (and requires more information to prepare) and is better for analysis. However, most firms use the indirect method for financial reporting. Thus, it is important to understand how each method presents the data used to compute CFO. An analyst must also possess the knowledge and skills to convert the indirect method to the direct method for analysis purposes.

The following is the format of the basic statement of cash flows:

Statement of Cash Flows (SCF)
for the period 1/1/2006 to 12/31/2006

	Cash flow from operations (CFO)
+	Cash flow from investing (CFI)
+	Cash flow from financing (CFF)
	Change in the cash account
+	Beginning of period cash
	Ending cash balance

Professor's Note: Throughout the discussion of the direct and indirect methods, remember the following points:

- *CFO is calculated differently, but the result is the same under both methods.*
- *The calculation of CFI and CFF is the same under both methods.*
- *There is an inverse relationship between changes in assets and changes in cash flow. In other words, an increase in an asset account (e.g., accounts receivable) is a use of cash, whereas a reduction in an asset account is a source of cash.*
- *There is a positive relationship between changes in liabilities and changes in cash flow. Said differently, an increase in a liability account is a source of cash and a decrease in a liability is a use.*
- *Sources of cash are always positive numbers in the SCF; uses of cash are always negative numbers.*

Direct method. The direct method presents operating cash flow by taking each item from the income statement and converting it to its cash equivalent by adding or subtracting the changes in the corresponding balance sheet accounts. Footnotes are often helpful in learning how inflows and outflows have affected the balance sheet accounts. The following are some common examples of operating cash flow components:

- Cash collections is the principle component of CFO. The actual amount of cash received during the period is measured with: net sales (a source), adjusted for changes in accounts receivable, and cash advances from customers.
- Cash outflows consist of cash inputs, cash operating expenses, cash interest, and cash taxes. One component of cash operating expenses is the cash used in the production of goods and services, which is measured with: cost of goods sold (COGS) adjusted for changes in inventory, changes in accounts payable, and changes in

other liabilities for inputs. Other cash operating expenses are cash expenses related to selling, administration, and research and development, adjusted for changes in related operating liabilities.

- The cash interest component only recognizes interest expense paid in cash. Accrued interest expense is not included. Cash interest is computed using interest expense (which includes noncash interest components) and removing the affect of changes in noncash interest components (such as accrued interest, the amortization of bond discounts and premia, and accretion).
- Finally, the cash tax component only recognizes taxes paid in cash. Total taxes paid are netted against changes in deferred tax accounts. Cash taxes are computed using: tax expense, changes in taxes payable, and changes in deferred taxes. Similar to our discussion of interest expense above, tax expense on the income statement includes noncash items such as taxes payable and deferred taxes.

Professor's Note: A common "trick" in direct method questions is to provide information on depreciation expense along with other operating cash flow components. When using the direct method, ignore depreciation expense—it's a noncash charge. We'll see later that we do consider depreciation expense in indirect method computations, but we do this solely because depreciation expense and other noncash expenses are embedded in net income (our starting point) and need to be "backed out" of the computation.

Investing cash flows (CFI) are calculated by finding the changes in the appropriate gross fixed-asset account. Changes in noncash fixed-asset accounts, such as accumulated depreciation and goodwill, are not included since they do not represent a cash transaction. Any gains or losses from the disposal of an asset must also be reflected in cash flow.

cash from asset disposal = decrease in asset + gain from sale

Financing cash flows are determined by measuring the cash flows occurring between the firm and its suppliers of capital. Cash flows between the firm and creditors result from new borrowings and debt repayments. Note, interest paid is technically a cash flow to the creditors but it is already accounted for in CFO. Cash flows between the firm and the shareholders or owners occur as equity issued, share repurchases, and dividends. CFF is the sum of these two measures:

net cash flows from creditors = new borrowings – principal repaid

net cash flows from owners = new equity issued – share repurchases – cash dividends

where:
cash dividends are measured using dividends paid and changes in dividends payable
CFF = net cash flows from creditors + net cash flows from owners

Finally, total cash flow is equal to the sum of cash flow from operations, cash flow from investments, and cash flow from financing. If done correctly, the total cash flow will equal the change in the cash balance from the beginning-of-period balance sheet to the end-of-period balance sheet.

Example: Direct method for computing CFO

Prepare a statement of cash flows using the direct method for a company with the following income statement and balance sheets (Figures 1 and 2). Keep track of the balance sheet items used to calculate CFO by marking them off the balance sheet. They will not be needed again when determining CFI and CFF.

Figure 1: Income Statement for 2004

Income Statement

Sales	$100,000
Expenses	
Cost of goods sold	$40,000
Wages	5,000
Depreciation	7,000
Interest	500
Total expenses	$52,000
Income from continuing operations	$47,500
Gain from sale of land	10,000
Pretax income	57,500
Provision for taxes	20,000
Net income	$37,500
Common dividends declared	$8,500

Figure 2: Balance Sheet for 2003 and 2004

Balance Sheet	2004	2003
Assets		
Current assets		
Cash	$33,000	$9,000
Accounts receivable	10,000	9,000
Inventory	5,000	7,000
Noncurrent assets		
Land	$35,000	$40,000
Gross plant and equipment	85,000	60,000
less: Accumulated depreciation	(16,000)	(9,000)
Net plant and equipment	$69,000	$51,000
Goodwill	10,000	10,000
Total assets	$162,000	$126,000
Liabilities		
Current liabilities		
Accounts payable	$9,000	$5,000
Wages payable	4,500	8,000
Interest payable	3,500	3,000
Taxes payable	5,000	4,000
Dividends payable	6,000	1,000
Noncurrent liabilities		
Bonds	$15,000	$10,000
Deferred taxes	20,000	15,000
Stockholders' equity		
Common stock	$40,000	$50,000
Retained earnings	59,000	30,000
Total liabilities & stockholders' equity	$162,000	$126,000

Answer:

Professor's Note: There are many ways to think about these calculations and lots of sources and uses and pluses and minuses to keep track of. It's likely easier if you use a "+" sign for net sales and a "–" sign for cost of goods sold and other cash expenses used as the starting points. Doing so will allow you to consistently follow the rule that an increase in assets or decrease in liabilities is a use of cash and a decrease in assets or an increase in liabilities is a source. We'll use this approach in the answer to the example. Remember, sources are always + and uses are always –.

Cash from operations:

> cash collections = net sales – increase in receivables
> = $100,000 – $1,000 = $99,000

> cash inputs = – cost of goods sold + decrease in inventory + increase in accounts payable
> = –$40,000 + $2,000 + $4,000 = –$34,000

> cash expenses = – wages – decrease in wages payable
> = –$5,000 – $3,500 = –$8,500

> cash interest = – interest expense + increase in interest payable
> = –$500 + $500 = 0

> cash taxes = – tax expense + increase in taxes payable + increase in deferred taxes
> = –$20,000 + $1,000 + $5,000 = –$14,000

Cash collections	$99,000
cash inputs	(34,000)
cash expenses	(8,500)
cash interest	0
cash taxes	(14,000)
Cash flow from operations	**$42,500**

Investing cash flow:

In this example, we have two components of investing cash flow: the sale of land and the change in gross plant and equipment (PP&E).

> cash from sale of land = decrease in asset (a source) + gain on sale (a source)
> = $5,000 + $10,000 = $15,000

Note: If the land had been sold at a loss, we would have subtracted the loss amount from the decrease in assets.

> change in gross PP&E = 2004 ending balance – 2003 ending balance
> = $85,000 – $60,000 = $25,000 (use)

Cash from sale of land	$15,000
Purchase of plant and equipment	(25,000)
Cash flow from investments	**($10,000)**

Financing cash flow:

change in bond account = 2004 ending balance – 2003 ending balance
= $15,000 – $10,000 = $5,000 (source)

change in common stock = $40,000 – $50,000 = –$10,000 (use, or a net share repurchase of $10,000)

cash dividends = – dividend + increase in dividends payable
= –$8,500* + $5,000 = –$3,500 (use)

Note: If the dividend declared/paid amount is not provided, you can calculate the amount as follows: dividends declared = beginning retained earnings + net income – ending retained earnings. Here, $30,000 + $37,500 – $59,000 = $8,500.

Sale of bonds	$5,000
Repurchase of stock	(10,000)
Cash dividends	(3,500)
Cash flow from financing	**($8,500)**

Total cash flow:

Cash flow from operations	$42,500
Cash flow from investments	(10,000)
Cash flow from financing	(8,500)
Total cash flow	**($24,000)**

The total cash flow of $24,000 is equal to the increase in the cash account. The difference between beginning cash and ending cash should be used as a check figure to ensure the total cash flow calculation is correct.

Indirect method. The three components of cash flow are equal to the same values as they were under the direct method. The only difference is that cash flow from operations is calculated in a different manner. The indirect method calculates cash flow from operations in four steps:

Step 1: Begin with net income.

Step 2: Subtract gains or add losses that result from financing or investment cash flows (such as gains from sale of land).

Step 3: Add back all noncash charges to income (such as depreciation and goodwill amortization) and subtract all noncash revenue components.

Professor's Note: Goodwill is no longer systematically amortized under U.S. GAAP and is instead subject to an "impairment determination" each year to see if any goodwill is to be written off to the income statement. Under IAS GAAP, goodwill may still be amortized.

Step 4: Add or subtract changes to operating accounts as follows:

- Increases in the balances of operating asset accounts are subtracted, while decreases in those accounts are added.
- Increases in the balances of operating liability accounts are added, while decreases are subtracted.

Cash flow from investments and cash flow from financing are calculated the same way as under the direct method. As was true for the direct method, total cash flow is equal to the sum of cash flow from operations, cash flow from investments, and cash flow from financing. If done correctly, the total cash flow will be equal to the increase in the cash balance over the period.

Example: Indirect method for computing CFO

Calculate cash flow from operations using the indirect method for the same company in the previous example.

Answer:

Step 1:   Start with net income of $37,500.

Step 2:   Subtract gain from sale of land of $10,000.

Step 3:   Add back noncash charges of depreciation of $7,000.

Step 4:   Subtract increases in receivables and inventories and add increases of payables and deferred taxes.

Net income	$37,500
− Gain from sale of land	(10,000)
+ Depreciation	7,000
Subtotal	**$34,500**
Changes in operating accounts	
− Increase in receivables	($1,000)
+ Decrease in inventories	2,000
+ Increase in accounts payable	4,000
− Decrease in wages payable	(3,500)
+ Increase in interest payable	500
+ Increase in taxes payable	1,000
+ Increase in deferred taxes	5,000
Cash flow from operations	**$42,500**

Discrepancies between the changes in accounts reported on the balance sheet and those reported in the statement of cash flows are typically due to two events: mergers and acquisitions, and changes in exchange rates.

Under SFAS 95, inventory and accounts receivable acquired in a merger or purchase of another company are treated as a component of investing activities, not operating activities. Translation gains and losses associated with exchange rate changes are excluded from CFO, CFI, and CFF. Thus, there may be some discrepancies between changes in balance sheet items (e.g., accounts receivable) and statement of cash flow items using the methodology presented here. Translation gains and losses are reported separately and can be used to reconcile any discrepancies that may exist. Differences between changes in inventory and receivables on the balance sheet and adjustment amounts on the statement of cash flows can be used to estimate the value of inventory and receivables acquired through merger or purchase of a company.

Interpretation of Cash Flows

- Operating cash flow tells an analyst how much cash is being generated by the sales activity of the company. It is the most important component of cash flow analysis.
- Cash flows can indicate problems with liquidity and solvency. Negative operating cash flows indicate that the company will have to rely on external sources of financing to fund operations.
- Trends in cash flows can be extrapolated to estimate how the company will be performing over the next few years. Trend analysis is particularly useful when compared to the trend of income over time. Discrepancies between the trends in income and cash flow can suggest that earnings trends are not reliable.

- Interrelationships between cash flow components, such as cash inputs and cash collections, can give insight similar to ratio analysis with income statement figures.

LOS 36.c: Convert an indirect statement of cash flows to a direct basis.

The only difference between the indirect and direct methods of presentation is in the cash flow from operations (CFO) section. CFO under the direct method can be computed using a combination of the income statement and a statement of cash flows prepared under the indirect method.

There are two major sections in the CFO under the direct method: cash inflows (receipts) and cash outflows (payments). We will illustrate the conversion process using commonly used accounts. Please note that the list below is for illustrative purposes and is far from all-inclusive of what may be encountered in practice. The general principal here is to begin with an income statement item and adjust the item for non-cash transactions which have been included and cash transactions that have not been included.

Cash collections from customers:

1. Begin with net sales from the income statement.

2. Deduct (add) any increase (decrease) in the accounts receivable (AR) balance as disclosed in the indirect method. If the company has sold more on credit than has been collected from customers on accounts receivable, the AR balance will have increased, and cash collected will be less than net sales.

3. Add any advances from customers. Cash received from customers when the goods or services have yet to be delivered is not included in net sales, so such advances must be added to net sales in calculating cash collections.

Cash payments for inputs:

1. Begin with cost of goods sold (COGS), a negative number, as disclosed in the income statement.

2. If depreciation and/or amortization have been included in COGS, they must be added (they reduce COGS) in computing actual cash costs of inputs.

3. Add (subtract) any increase (decrease) in the accounts payable balance as disclosed in the indirect method. If payables have increased, then more was spent on credit purchases of inputs during the period than was paid on existing payables, so cash payments are reduced by the amount of the increase in payables.

4. Subtract (add) any increase (decrease) in the inventory balance as disclosed in the indirect method. Increases in inventory are not included in COGS for the period but still represent the purchase of inputs so they increase cash payments for inputs.

5. Add any write-off of inventory value over the period. A decrease in inventory (for example from applying lower of cost or market) will reduce the ending inventory and increase COGS for the period, but no cash expenditure is associated with such a reduction in ending inventory.

Other items in a statement of cash flows under the direct method follow the same principles. Cash taxes paid, for example, can be derived from income tax expense on the income statement. Adjustment must be made for changes in related balance sheet accounts (deferred tax assets and liabilities, and income taxes payable). Cash SG&A expense is SG&A from the income statement increased (decreased) by any increase (decrease) in prepaid expenses. An increase in prepaid expenses is a cash outflow for expenses not included in SG&A for the current period.

LOS 36.d: Explain the two primary factors (i.e., acquisitions/divestitures and translation of foreign subsidiaries) that may cause discrepancies between balances of operating assets and liabilities reported on the balance sheet and those reported in the cash flow statement.

Acquisitions and Divestitures

Cash flow from operations (CFO) includes *operating* transactions and events only. The discrepancy arises when a *non-operating* transaction, such as an acquisition, results in the consolidation of the operating assets and liabilities of an existing firm to the balance sheet of the acquiring firm. Thus, the change reported in the cash flow statement in arriving at CFO will not equal the change on the balance sheet because the acquisition transaction is only reported on the balance sheet.

Translation of Foreign Subsidiaries

Translation gains and losses resulting from exchange rate fluctuations will directly flow through to the balance sheet upon translation to the reporting currency. However, given the nature of translation gains and losses as non-operating and non-cash transactions, there will be no effect on any of the three categories in the cash flow statement. The amount of the exchange rate translation effect will appear as a reconciling item in calculating the change in cash.

LOS 36.e: Describe and compute free cash flow.

Free cash flow (FCF) attempts to measure the cash available for discretionary purposes. This is the fundamental cash flow measure and is often used for valuation purposes. FCF for discretionary purposes (including growth opportunities) is operating cash flow minus those cash flows necessary to maintain the firm's present productive capacity. However, it is not practical for an analyst to determine which capital expenditures are necessary to maintain capacity and which are made to take advantage of growth opportunities. Consequently, free cash flow is often measured by:

free cash flow = operating cash flow – net capital expenditures

where:
net capital expenditures = total capital expenditures – after-tax proceeds from asset sales

When used for valuation purposes, some adjustments to free cash flow must be made. If the analyst is interested in free cash flow to the firm (all investors), after-tax interest expense must be added back $[I \times (1 - t)]$ to CFO.

LOS 36.f: Distinguish between U.S. GAAP and IAS GAAP classifications of dividends paid or received and interest paid or received for statement of cash flow purposes.

Under U.S. GAAP (SFAS 95), dividends that are paid to the company's shareholders are classified as cash from financing (CFF) and *all other interest and dividend receipts and payments are classified as CFO.*

Under IAS GAAP (IAS 7):

- Interest and dividends received may be classified as either CFO *or* CFI.
- Dividends paid to the company's shareholders and interest paid on the company's debt may be classified as either CFF *or* CFO.

KEY CONCEPTS

1. Cash flows are divided into three categories:
   - Cash flow from operations measures the cash generated from sales and the cash used in the production process.
   - Investing cash flow reports the cash used for property, plant, equipment, investments, acquisitions, and the cash generated from sales of assets or businesses.
   - Financing cash flows include dividends paid, changes in equity accounts, and changes in liabilities that are part of the capital structure.

2. The direct method calculates cash flow from operations by calculating cash collections (the cash equivalent of sales), cash inputs (the cash equivalent of cost of goods sold), cash operating expenses, cash interest expense, and cash taxes.

3. The indirect method calculates cash flow from operations by starting with net income, subtracting out gains and adding back losses resulting from financing or investment cash flows, adding back all noncash charges, and adding and subtracting changes in asset and liability balance sheet accounts that result from operations.

4. CFO under the direct method is the net of cash inflows (receipts) minus cash outflows (payments) and can be computed using a combination of the income statement and the operating cash flow portion of the statement of cash flows prepared using the indirect method.

5. The two primary factors that may cause discrepancies between balances of operating assets and liabilities reported on the balance sheet and the cash flow statement are (1) consolidations to account for acquisitions and divestitures, and (2) currency translation gains and losses related to foreign subsidiaries.

6. Free cash flow—the cash available for discretionary purposes—is equal to operating cash flow minus net capital expenditures.

7. Under U.S. GAAP, all interest and dividend cash flows are classified as CFO except for the dividends that are paid to the company's shareholders—which are classified as CFF. Under IAS GAAP (IAS 7):
   - Interest and dividends received may be classified as either CFO or CFI.
   - Dividends paid to the company's shareholders may be classified as either CFF or CFO.
   - Interest paid on the company's debt may be classified as either CFO or CFF.

CONCEPT CHECKERS: ANALYSIS OF CASH FLOWS

1. Using the following information, what is the firm's cash flow from operations?

Net income	$120
Decrease in accounts receivable	20
Depreciation	25
Increase in inventory	10
Increase in accounts payable	7
Decrease in wages payable	5
Increase in deferred taxes	15
Profit from the sale of fixed assets	2

   A. $142.
   B. $158.
   C. $170.
   D. $174.

Use the following data to answer Questions 2 through 4.

Net income	$45
Depreciation	75
Taxes paid	25
Interest paid	5
Dividends paid	10
Cash received from sale of company building	40
Sale of preferred stock	35
Repurchase of common stock	30
Purchase of machinery	20
Issuance of bonds	50
Debt retired through issuance of common	45
Paid off long-term bank borrowings	15
Profit on sale of building	20

2. The cash flow from *operations* is:
   A. $70.
   B. $100.
   C. $120.
   D. $185.

3. The cash flow from *investing activities* is:
    A. –$30.
    B. $20.
    C. $70.
    D. $50.

4. The cash flow from *financing activities* is:
    A. $30.
    B. $55.
    C. $75.
    D. $85.

5. Given the following:

Sales	$1,500
Increase in inventory	100
Depreciation	150
Increase in accounts receivable	50
Decrease in accounts payable	70
After tax profit margin	25%
Gain on sale of machinery	$30

    The cash flow from *operations* is:
    A. $25.
    B. $115.
    C. $275.
    D. $375.

Use the following data to answer Questions 6 through 15.

Balance Sheet Data

Assets	2003	2002
Cash	$290	$100
Accounts receivable	250	200
Inventory	740	800
Property, plant, & equipment	920	900
Accumulated depreciation	(290)	(250)
Liabilities		
Accounts payable	$470	$450
Interest payable	15	10
Dividends payable	10	5
Mortgage	$535	$585
Bank note	100	0
Common Stock	$430	$400
Retained earnings	350	300

Income Statement for the Year 2003	2003
Sales	$1,425
Cost of goods sold	1,200
Depreciation	100
Interest Expense	30
Gain on sale of old machine	10
Taxes	45
Net income	$60

Notes:

- Dividends declared to shareholders were $10.
- New common shares were sold at par for $30.
- Fixed assets were sold for $30. Original cost of these assets was $80, and $60 of accumulated depreciation has been charged to their original cost.
- The firm borrowed $100 on a 10-year bank note—the proceeds of the loan were used to pay for new fixed assets.
- Depreciation for the year was $100 (accumulated depreciation up $40 and depreciation on sold assets $60).

6.   The cash flow from operations, using the *indirect* method, equals:
   A. $125.
   B. $145.
   C. $165.
   D. $185.

7.   Cash collections equal:
   A. $1,250.
   B. $1,375.
   C. $1,425.
   D. $1,475.

8. Cash inputs equal:
    A. $1,000.
    B. $1,020.
    C. $1,120.
    D. $1,280.

9. Other cash expenses equal:
    A. $45.
    B. $65.
    C. $70.
    D. $75.

10. Cash flow from operations, using the *direct* method, equals:
    A. $125.
    B. $145.
    C. $165.
    D. $185.

11. Cash flow from *financing* equals:
    A. -$90.
    B. $65.
    C. $75.
    D. $85.

12. Cash flow from *investing* equals:
    A. -$80.
    B. -$70.
    C. $75.
    D. $85.

13. Total cash flow is:
    A. -$190.
    B. $100.
    C. $190.
    D. $290.

14. Free cash flow, considering flows available to shareholders, is:
    A. $115.
    B. $165.
    C. $195.
    D. $215.

15. What would be the impact on investing cash flow and financing cash flow if the company leased the new fixed assets instead of borrowing the money and purchasing the equipment?
    A. There would be no change in either type of cash flow.
    B. Investing cash flow would be higher and financing cash flow would be the same.
    C. Investing cash flow would be the same and financing cash flow would be lower.
    D. Investing cash flow would be higher and financing cash flow would be lower.

16. Which of the following items is **NOT** considered a cash flow from a financing activity in the statement of cash flows?
    A. Receipt of cash from the sale of capital stock.
    B. Receipt of cash from the sale of bonds.
    C. Payment of cash for dividends.
    D. Payment of interest on debt.

17. Which of the following would **NOT** cause a change in investing cash flow?
    A. The sale of a division of the company.
    B. The purchase of new machinery.
    C. An increase in the depreciation expense.
    D. The sale of obsolete equipment with no remaining book value.

18. Which of the following would **NOT** cause a change in cash flow from operations?
    A. A decrease in notes payable.
    B. An increase in interest expense.
    C. An increase in accounts payable.
    D. An increase in cost of goods sold.

19. Which of the following statements about the cash flow statement is **TRUE**?
    A. The change in the cash balance will always be higher than the sum of operating, financing, and investing cash flows.
    B. The calculation of cash flow under the direct and indirect methods will be identical except when the company is leasing equipment.
    C. The purchase of cars could be considered an operating cash flow for a car dealership, and could be considered an investment cash flow for a manufacturing company.
    D. Investment cash flow always is equal to the negative of operating cash flow.

20. Sales of inventory would be classified as:
    A. operating cash flow.
    B. investment cash flow.
    C. financing cash flow.
    D. no cash flow impact.

21. Sale of bonds would be classified as:
    A. operating cash flow.
    B. investment cash flow.
    C. financing cash flow.
    D. no cash flow impact.

22. Sale of land would be classified as:
    A. operating cash flow.
    B. investment cash flow.
    C. financing cash flow.
    D. no cash flow impact.

23. Increase in taxes payable would be classified as:
    A. operating cash flow.
    B. investment cash flow.
    C. financing cash flow.
    D. no cash flow impact.

24.   Increase in notes payable would be classified as:
      A. operating cash flow.
      B. investment cash flow.
      C. financing cash flow.
      D. no cash flow impact.

25.   Increase in interest payable would be classified as:
      A. operating cash flow.
      B. investment cash flow.
      C. financing cash flow.
      D. no cash flow impact.

26.   Increase in dividends payable would be classified as:
      A. operating cash flow.
      B. investment cash flow.
      C. financing cash flow.
      D. no cash flow impact.

27.   The write-off of obsolete equipment would be classified as:
      A. operating cash flow.
      B. investment cash flow.
      C. financing cash flow.
      D. no cash flow impact.

28.   Sale of obsolete equipment would be classified as:
      A. operating cash flow.
      B. investment cash flow.
      C. financing cash flow.
      D. no cash flow impact.

29.   Interest expense would be classified as:
      A. operating cash flow.
      B. investment cash flow.
      C. financing cash flow.
      D. no cash flow impact.

30.   Depreciation expense would be classified as:
      A. operating cash flow.
      B. investment cash flow.
      C. financing cash flow.
      D. no cash flow impact.

31.   Dividends paid to shareholders would be classified as:
      A. operating cash flow.
      B. investment cash flow.
      C. financing cash flow.
      D. no cash flow impact.

32.   Which of the following is *most likely* to cause discrepancies between changes in balance sheet operating assets and liabilities and those reported on the cash flow statement?
       A. Issuance of discount debt.
       B. Depreciation.
       C. Foreign currency translation gains.
       D. Accrual of liabilities.

ANSWERS – CONCEPT CHECKERS: ANALYSIS OF CASH FLOWS

1. **C** Net income – profits from sale of land + depreciation + decrease in receivables – increase in inventories + increase in accounts payable – decrease in wages payable + increase in deferred taxes = 120 – 2 + 25 + 20 – 10 + 7 – 5 + 15 = $170. Note that the profit on the sale of land should be subtracted out of net income (to avoid double counting the gain in net income and investing activities).

2. **B** Net income – profits from sale of building + depreciation = 45 – 20 + 75 = $100. Note that taxes and interest are already included in net income, and the profit on the sale of the building should be subtracted back from net income.

3. **B** Cash from sale of building – purchase of machinery = 40 – 20 = $20

4. **A** Sale of preferred + issuance of bonds – payment of bank borrowings – repurchase of common stock – dividends = 35 + 50 – 15 – 30 – 10 = $30. Note that we did not include $45 of debt retired through issuance of common stock as this was a noncash transaction. Knowing how to handle noncash transactions is important. For example, assume there was a noncash transaction where the firm acquired some PP&E assets by issuing mortgage debt. Since no cash was involved in these transactions, they should not appear on the statement of cash flows.

5. **C** Net income = $1,500 × 0.25 = $375, and cash flow from operations = net income – gain on sale of machinery + depreciation – increase in receivables – increase in inventories – decrease in accounts payable = 375 – 30 + 150 – 50 – 100 – 70 = $275.

6. **D** Net income – gain on sale of machinery + depreciation – increase in receivables + decrease in inventories + increase in accounts payable + increase in interest payable = 60 – 10 + 100 – 50 + 60 + 20 + 5 = $185.

7. **B** Sales – increase in receivables = 1,425 – 50 = $1,375

8. **C** –Cost of goods sold + decrease in inventory + increase in accounts payable = –1,200 + 60 + 20 = –$1,120. (Note that the question asks for cash inputs, so no negative sign is needed in the answer.)

9. **C** –Interest expense + increase in interest payable – tax expense = –30 + 5 – 45 = –$70. (Note that the question asks for cash expenses so no negative sign is needed in the answer.)

10. **D** The easiest way is to use the answer to Question 6, because it will be the same as cash flow from operations under the indirect method. Or you can calculate cash collections – cash inputs – cash expenses = 1,375 – 1,120 – 70 = $185.

11. **C** Sale of stock + new bank note – payment of mortgage – dividends + increase in dividends payable = 30 + 100 – 50 – 10 + 5 = $75.

12. **B** Sale of fixed assets – new fixed assets = 30 – 100 = –$70.

    Don't make this hard. We sold assets for 30 and bought assets for 100. Assets sold had original cost of 80, so (gross) PP&E only went up by 20.

13. **C** The easiest way is to simply take the change in cash from the balance sheet. However, adding the three components of cash flow will yield 185 – 70 + 75 = $190.

14. **A** Cash flow from operations – capital spending + sale of fixed assets = $185 – 100 + 30 = $115. Note that we are not asked for FCF to the firm. If we were asked about FCF to the firm, then we would have added back I(1 – t).

15. **D** The company would spend less on investments but would not have inflows from the borrowing.

16. **D** The payment of interest on debt is an *operating* cash flow.

17. **C** Depreciation does not represent a cash flow.

18. **A** Changes in notes payable represent a financing cash flow.

19. **C** Cars would be inventory to a dealership, while they would be fixed assets to most other businesses.

20. **A** Sales of inventory would be classified as operating cash flow.

21. **C** Sale of bonds would be classified as financing cash flow.

22. **B** Sale of land would be classified as investment cash flow.

23. **A** Increase in taxes payable would be classified as operating cash flow.

24. **C** Increase in notes payable would be classified as financing cash flow.

25. **A** Increase in interest payable would be classified as operating cash flow.

26. **C** Increase in dividends payable would be classified as financing cash flow.

27. **D** Write-off of obsolete equipment would be classified as no cash flow impact.

28. **B** Sale of obsolete equipment would be classified as investment cash flow.

29. **A** Interest expense would be classified as operating cash flow.

30. **D** Depreciation expense would be classified as no cash flow impact.

31. **C** Dividends would be classified as financing cash flow.

32. **C** Currency translation gains and losses do not affect cash flows but affect operating assets and liabilities. Issuance of debt and depreciation of assets do not affect operating cash flows. Increases in operating liabilities from accrual do not lead to discrepancies.

The following is a review of the Financial Statement Analysis principles designed to address the learning outcome statements set forth by CFA Institute®. This topic is also covered in:

WORLDWIDE ACCOUNTING DIVERSITY AND INTERNATIONAL STANDARDS

EXAM FOCUS

From this topic review, you should learn how the five factors listed influence accounting practices and the three primary problems caused by worldwide accounting diversity. The arguments for harmonization are that it would provide solutions to these three primary problems. Know that arguments against harmonization include nationalism, that differences among countries require different accounting practices, and that efficiently functioning global capital markets will naturally lead to the optimal amount of harmonization.

LOS 37.a: Discuss the factors influencing and leading to diversity in accounting and reporting practices throughout the world and explain why worldwide accounting diversity causes problems for capital market participants.

Meek and Saudagaran[1] identified five factors that are typically cited in the accounting literature as important in influencing the diversity of accounting and reporting practices throughout the world. The primary factors are differences among countries':

1. Legal systems.

2. Tax laws.

3. Sources of financing.

4. Inflation rates.

5. Political and economic ties.

Legal System

Countries with legal systems based on common law (primarily English-speaking countries) tend to have accounting standards that are developed by the accounting profession or other non-governmental bodies to supplement a smaller amount of statute law on the subject. The FASB in the U.S. is one (perhaps extreme) example of this model. The FASB has produced 156 Statements of Accounting Standards as of this writing which comprise U.S. Generally Accepted Accounting Principles (GAAP). This work is supplemented by voluminous guidance, clarification, and related pronouncements.

Countries which have primarily code-based legal systems typically have corporation law that lays out a basic framework for financial reporting but provides much less detail than the common law alternative discussed above. The statutes governing financial reporting originate in the national legislature rather than with a professional body.

---

1. Gary K. Meek and Sharokh M. Saudagaran, "A Survey of Research on Financial Reporting in a Transnational Context", *Journal of Accounting Literature*, 1990, 145–182.

Taxation

The important distinction between countries here is whether tax accounting and financial accounting must conform. In countries such as Germany, where conformity is the rule, corporations make accounting choices in order to minimize taxes, which lead to lower reported earnings on the firm's financial statements. The U.S. on the other hand, permits differences in accounting methods (e.g., depreciation methods) used for financial statements and for tax returns. This allows U.S. firms to increase reported earnings by making tax minimizing choices for the tax return, and to choose accounting methods that result in higher reported earnings per share when preparing financial statements in compliance with SEC requirements for reporting to shareholders.

Sources of Financing

In countries where public equity and publicly-traded debt are important sources of capital, financial reporting tends to be much more detailed. Public share ownership, especially, demands a more detailed focus on the income statement and earnings per share.

In countries where private funds and bank loans are the primary sources of corporate capital, detailed financial statements are less important. Under these circumstances, those who require financial performance information often have access to internal company information through their participation on or access to the board of directors. When bank debt financing is a primary source of financing, there tends to be more of a focus on the balance sheet and less on the income statement oriented disclosures that equity shareholders require.

Inflation Rates

In countries where very high inflation rates are, or have been typical, the problems associated with historical cost accounting are extreme. Latin American countries with a history of very high inflation rates typically have accounting rules that include inflation adjustments to historical cost.

Political and Economic Ties

Not surprisingly, former colonies of Britain and France have adopted systems of financial reporting consistent with their former colonizers. Mexico and Canada, great trading partners of the U.S., both have adopted practices similar to those of the U.S.

There is positive correlation between factors that influence accounting practices. Those countries that follow the common law tradition also tend to be those that allow differences between tax and financial reporting methods and where financing through public share offerings is more important.

Problems Caused by Worldwide Accounting Diversity

Capital markets participants encounter problems in comparing companies, even those in the same industry, when the companies are domiciled in different countries and prepare their financial statements in accordance with different accounting rules and conventions.

Companies that desire to raise capital outside their home countries can encounter problems related to accounting diversity. Foreign firms that want to list their shares on the U.S. exchanges, for example, must present results in accordance with U.S. GAAP. This can be a time consuming and expensive proposition.

Firms that do business in many countries through foreign subsidiaries face additional problems. Often, the foreign subsidiary must report in the local currency and follow local law and practices. The parent company is faced with the challenge of converting the financial statements of their subsidiaries to the accounting rules and practices of their home countries. This is in addition to problems associated with converting local currency results to the functional currency of the parent.

LOS 37.b: Discuss the importance of the hierarchical model of accounting diversity.

A **hierarchical model** of accounting diversity is one in which the accounting practices of many countries are classified, according to the various factors that drive differences in accounting practices, into successive levels or layers. The importance of such a model is that it identifies clusters of countries which are quite similar in accounting practices and it allows for conclusions about the degree of similarity (or diversity) between and among the accounting practices of different countries.

LOS 37.c: Discuss the arguments for and against harmonization and discuss the role of the International Accounting Standards Board (IASB).

Harmonization, here, refers to reducing the differences in worldwide accounting standards. The *arguments for harmonization* are essentially that it solves the problems of diversity in accounting practices. Harmonization would (1) increase the comparability of financial statements and results, (2) decrease the problems and expense of raising capital in foreign markets and reduce the cost of capital in general, and (3) decrease the problems and expense of preparing consolidated financial statements when foreign subsidiaries are subject to different accounting rules than the parent.

One argument against harmonization is that nationalism and resistance to accepting the practices of another country, or those imposed by an international body, will prevent it. Countries with great economic power may not see the value in adopting a system that incorporates foreign practices to any significant degree. Another argument against harmonization is that differences among countries in key factors, such as how capital is typically raised or inflation rates, actually require and give value to cross-border differences in accounting practices. A third argument against harmonization initiatives is that global capital markets will provide an efficient level of harmonization on their own as firms weigh the costs and benefits of both harmonization and diversity.

The International Accounting Standards Board (IASB) has 14 members from nine different countries. The IASB is responsible for issuing International Financial Reporting Standards (IFRS). Sixty-six countries require the use of IFRS for domestic company reporting, including those of the European Union. Many other countries permit the use of IFRS. In the U.S., the SEC allows foreign companies to use IFRS but requires a statement reconciling those statements to U.S. GAAP.

The IASB is and has been working with the FASB in the U.S. to work toward harmonization. In order to achieve convergence between FASB standards (U.S. GAAP) and IASB standards (IASB GAAP), both bodies are participating in projects with short-term and longer-term goals. The subjects of these projects include accounting for business combinations, performance reporting, revenue recognition, and development of a common conceptual framework.

KEY CONCEPTS:

1. Differences in accounting practices in different countries are due primarily to differences in legal systems, tax laws, financing sources, inflation rates, and political and economic ties.

2. Differences in financial reporting rules and practices (1) make it difficult to compare the financial results of firms based in different countries, (2) lead to additional effort and expense for parent companies to convert financial statements of foreign subsidiaries to their home country standards, and (3) increase the costs associated with listing shares on foreign stock exchanges.

3. A hierarchical model of accounting diversity classifies countries' accounting practices into successive layers to identify clusters of countries where the standards are similar.

4. Arguments for harmonization of global accounting practices include increasing the comparability of financial results, reducing the expense of raising capital globally, and reducing the problems multinational firms face when consolidating the results of foreign subsidiaries.

5. Arguments against harmonization stem from nationalistic resistance to accepting externally imposed standards, the value that diverse accounting practices have in addressing country differences in inflation rates and how firms are funded, and a belief that efficient global capital markets will result in an optimally efficient level of diversity in accounting regulation.

6. The IASB is working to establish a set of worldwide accounting standards and is working with the U.S. FASB on several projects designed to achieve convergence between the accounting standards of the two bodies.

CONCEPT CHECKERS: WORLDWIDE ACCOUNTING DIVERSITY AND INTERNATIONAL STANDARDS

1. All of the following are important factors in the diversity of global accounting standards EXCEPT:
    A. tax laws
    B. inflation rates.
    C. compliance costs.
    D. legal systems and political ties.

2. When an analyst classifies the accounting practices of various countries according to the factors that cause the differences between them, she is creating a:
    A. cluster model.
    B. diversity model.
    C. hierarchical model.
    D. harmonization model.

3. Which of the following problems is *least likely* to be solved by harmonization?
    A. Historical costs are less meaningful for firms in countries that have experienced high rates of inflation.
    B. Analysts should adjust earnings results when comparing global firms with U.S. firms to reflect the differences in tax laws.
    C. Multinational companies need to convert foreign subsidiaries' results to their domestic standards when they report consolidated financial statements.
    D. Before they can raise capital outside their home countries, companies must present results according to the standards of the country where they plan to issue securities.

ANSWERS – CONCEPT CHECKERS: WORLDWIDE ACCOUNTING DIVERSITY AND INTERNATIONAL STANDARDS

1. **C** Differences in legal systems, political ties, tax laws and inflation rates have all contributed to the development of diverse global practices. Compliance costs are a primary argument for harmonizing global accounting standards.

2. **C** In a hierarchical model, the accounting practices of many countries are classified into successive levels or layers by the various factors that drive differences in accounting practices. Such a model identifies clusters of countries where accounting practices are similar.

3. **A** The wide variation in different countries' historical inflation rates is one of the arguments against harmonization. In countries that have experienced rapid inflation, financial statements can better reflect economic reality if accounting standards allow price level adjustments to historical costs.

ANALYSIS OF FINANCIAL STATEMENTS

EXAM FOCUS

Financial statement analysis uses ratios calculated from a company's income statement and balance sheet to evaluate the company. These ratios are compared to ratios from previous years to assess trends in the performance of the company. Ratios are also compared to those of other firms, the overall industry, and economy-wide averages to assess the relative performance of the company. You should memorize all of the ratios discussed in this review and be ready to calculate and interpret them when analyzing a company's financial statements. You should be prepared to see ratio questions not only as part of the financial statement analysis curriculum but in other parts of the CFA® curriculum as well, such as equity analysis. Also be prepared for questions concerning DuPont analysis and questions about a company's sustainable growth rate and its implications for the company.

LOS 38.a: Interpret common-size balance sheets and common-size income statements, and discuss the circumstances under which the use of common-size financial statements is appropriate.

Common-size statements normalize balance sheets and income statements and allow the analyst to more easily compare performance across firms and for a single firm over time.

- A common-size balance sheet expresses all balance sheet accounts as a percentage of total assets.
- A common-size income statement expresses all income statement items as a percentage of sales.

In addition to the comparison of financial data across firms and time, common-size analysis is appropriate for quickly viewing certain financial ratios. For example, the gross profit margin, operating profit margin, and net profit margin are all clearly indicated within a common-size income statement.

- Common-size income statement ratios are especially useful in studying trends in costs and profit margins.

$$\text{common-size income statement ratios} = \frac{\text{income statement account}}{\text{sales}}$$

- Balance sheet accounts can also be converted to common-size ratios by dividing each balance sheet item by total assets.

$$\text{common-size balance-sheet ratios} = \frac{\text{balance sheet account}}{\text{total assets}}$$

Example: Constructing common-size statements

The common-size statements in Figure 1 show balance sheet items as percentages of assets, and income statement items as percentages of sales.

- You can convert all asset and liability amounts to their actual values by multiplying the percentages listed below by their total assets of $57,100; $55,798; and $52,071, respectively for 2006, 2005, and 2004 (data is USD millions).

- Also, all income statement items can be converted to their actual values by multiplying the given percentages by total sales, which were \$29,723; \$29,234; and \$22,922, respectively, for 2006, 2005, and 2004.

Figure 1: Common-Size Balance Sheet and Income Statement

Balance Sheet Fiscal year end	2006	2005	2004
Assets			
Cash & cash equivalents	0.38%	0.29%	0.37%
Accounts receivable	5.46%	5.61%	6.20%
Inventories	5.92%	5.42%	5.84%
Deferred income taxes	0.89%	0.84%	0.97%
Other current assets	0.41%	0.40%	0.36%
Total current assets	13.06%	12.56%	13.74%
Gross fixed assets	25.31%	23.79%	25.05%
Accumulated depreciation	8.57%	7.46%	6.98%
Net gross fixed assets	16.74%	16.32%	18.06%
Other long term assets	70.20%	71.12%	68.20%
Total assets	100.00%	100.00%	100.00%
Liabilities			
Accounts payable	3.40%	3.40%	3.79%
Short term debt	1.00%	2.19%	1.65%
Other current liabilities	8.16%	10.32%	9.14%
Total current liabilities	12.56%	15.91%	14.58%
Long term debt	18.24%	14.58%	5.18%
Other long term liabilities	23.96%	27.44%	53.27%
Total liabilities	54.76%	57.92%	73.02%
Preferred equity	0.00%	0.00%	0.00%
Common equity	45.24%	42.08%	26.98%
Total liabilities & equity	100.00%	100.00%	100.00%

Income Statement Fiscal year end	2006	2005	2004
Revenues	100.00%	100.00%	100.00%
CGS	59.62%	60.09%	60.90%
Gross profit	40.38%	39.91%	39.10%
Selling, general & administrative	16.82%	17.34%	17.84%
Depreciation	2.39%	2.33%	2.18%
Amortization	0.02%	3.29%	2.33%
Other operating expenses	0.58%	0.25%	-0.75%
Operating income	20.57%	16.71%	17.50%
Interest and other debt expense	2.85%	4.92%	2.60%
Income before taxes	17.72%	11.79%	14.90%
Provision for income taxes	6.30%	5.35%	6.17%
Net income	11.42%	6.44%	8.73%

LOS 38.b: Discuss the purposes and limitations of financial ratios and why it is important to examine a company's performance relative to the economy and its industry.

Limitations of Financial Ratios

You must be aware of the **limitations of financial ratios.** Ratios are used for internal comparisons and comparisons across firms. They are often most useful in identifying questions that need to be answered rather than for answering questions directly. Other limitations are:

- Financial ratios are not useful when viewed in isolation. They are only valid when compared to those of other firms or to the company's historical performance.
- Comparisons with other companies are made more difficult because of different accounting treatments. This is particularly important when analyzing non-U.S. firms.
- It is difficult to find comparable industry ratios when analyzing companies that operate in multiple industries.
- Conclusions cannot be made from viewing one set of ratios. All ratios must be viewed relative to one another.
- Determining the target or comparison value for a ratio is difficult—requiring some range of acceptable values.
- In conducting your analysis, you must always be aware of the limitations of ratios. Ask yourself these questions:
  - Do the firms being compared have similar accounting practices?
  - When comparing divisions within a firm, are the ratios comparable?
  - Do the ratios being used give consistent readings?
  - Do the ratios yield a reasonable figure for the industry?

A Company's Financial Ratios Relative to Its Industry, to the Aggregate Economy, and to the Company's Own Performance

The value of a single financial ratio is not meaningful by itself but must be interpreted relative to one of three factors: industry norms, overall economy norms, and the company's own historical performance.

- Comparison to industry norms is the most common type of comparison. Industry comparisons are particularly valid when the products generated by the industry are similar.

  Primarily, comparisons are made to industry averages. However, if there are wide variations within the industry, it may be more appropriate to use medians instead of means for the purposes of comparison (recall from the quantitative methods material that significant outliers can distort the mean).

  Moreover, it may be better not to use all of the firms in the industry but to use only a subset of firms with similar characteristics, including size.

  For firms that operate in multiple industries, the analyst can use cross-sectional analysis to find a group of firms that are involved in a similar mix of industries. Alternatively, the analyst can calculate composite industry averages by using a weighted average based on the proportion of the company's sales in each industry segment.

- Comparing a company to the overall economy is particularly important when overall business conditions are changing. For example, a stable profit margin might be considered good if the economy is in recession and the economy-wide average profit margin is declining. On the other hand, it might be considered problematic if a stable profit margin occurs during an economic expansion, and overall average profit margins are increasing.

- Comparing a firm with its history is very common. Analysts often conduct *time-series analysis*, which considers the trend in a ratio. Indeed, it is problematic to simply consider long-term averages of ratios without taking their trend into account.

  In most ratio comparisons it is considered desirable to be near the industry (or economy) average. For example, in all turnover ratios, a value could be considered too high or too low if it differs widely from the industry average. However, for some ratios, simply being high is considered good, even if it deviates from the industry average. This is true for most ratios involving income or cash flow. For example, most analysts would agree that having a high return on assets or high profit margin is good. An analyst would not suggest that a company with a return on assets of 15% when the industry average was 10% had an ROA that was *too high*.

  Sometimes the *goodness* of a ratio depends on the context. A high ROE that results from high profit margins or asset turnover is typically looked upon favorably. However, high ROEs that result from high levels of leverage are viewed more skeptically because of the additional risk of higher leverage.

LOS 38.c: Calculate, interpret and discuss the uses of measures of a company's internal liquidity, operating performance (i.e., operating efficiency and operating profitability), risk analysis, and growth potential.

Ratios can be used to evaluate four different facets of a company's performance and condition: (1) internal liquidity, (2) operating performance, (3) risk profile, and (4) growth potential.

Evaluating internal liquidity. Liquidity ratios are employed by analysts to determine the firm's ability to pay its short-term liabilities.

- The *current ratio* is the best-known measure of liquidity:

$$\text{current ratio} = \frac{\text{current assets}}{\text{current liabilities}}$$

  The higher the current ratio, the more likely it is that the company will be able to pay its short-term bills. A current ratio of less than one means that the company has negative working capital and is probably facing a liquidity crisis. Working capital equals current assets minus the current liabilities.

- The *quick ratio* is a more stringent measure of liquidity because it does not include inventories and other assets that might not be very liquid:

$$\text{quick ratio} = \frac{\text{cash + marketable securities + receivables}}{\text{current liabilities}}$$

  The higher the quick ratio, the more likely it is that the company will be able to pay its short-term bills.

- The most conservative liquidity measure is the *cash ratio:*

$$\text{cash ratio} = \frac{\text{cash + marketable securities}}{\text{current liabilities}}$$

  The higher the cash ratio, the more likely it is that the company will be able to pay its short-term bills.

  The current, quick, and cash ratios differ only in the assumed liquidity of the current assets that the analyst projects will be used to pay off current liabilities.

- A measure of accounts receivable liquidity is the *receivables turnover*:

$$\text{receivables turnover} = \frac{\text{net annual sales}}{\text{average receivables}}$$

Professor's Note: In most cases when a ratio compares a balance sheet account (such as receivables) with an income or cash flow item (such as sales), the balance sheet item will be the average of the account instead of simply the end-of-year balance. Averages are calculated by adding the beginning-of-year account value and the end-of-year account value, then dividing the sum by two.

It is considered desirable to have a receivables turnover figure close to the industry norm.

- The inverse of the receivables turnover times 365 is the *average collection period*, which is the average number of days it takes for the company's customers to pay their bills:

$$\text{average receivables collection period} = \frac{365}{\text{receivables turnover}}$$

It is considered desirable to have a collection period (and receivables turnover) close to the industry norm. The firm's credit terms are another important benchmark used to interpret this ratio. A collection period that is too high might mean that customers are too slow in paying their bills, which means too much capital is tied up in assets. A collection period that is too low might indicate that the firm's credit policy is too rigorous, which might be hampering sales.

- A measure of a firm's efficiency with respect to its processing and inventory management is the *inventory turnover*:

$$\text{inventory turnover} = \frac{\text{cost of goods sold}}{\text{average inventory}}$$

Professor's Note: Pay careful attention to the numerator in the turnover ratios. For inventory turnover, be sure to use cost of goods sold, not sales.

- The inverse of the inventory turnover times 365 is *the average inventory processing period*:

$$\text{average inventory processing period} = \frac{365}{\text{inventory turnover}}$$

As is the case with accounts receivable, it is considered desirable to have an inventory processing period (and inventory turnover) close to the industry norm. A processing period that is too high might mean that too much capital is tied up in inventory and could mean that the inventory is obsolete. A processing period that is too low might indicate that the firm has inadequate stock on hand, which could adversely impact sales.

- A measure of the use of trade credit by the firm is the *payables turnover ratio*:

$$\text{payables turnover ratio} = \frac{\text{cost of goods sold}}{\text{average trade payables}}$$

- The inverse of the payables turnover ratio multiplied by 365 is the *payables payment period*, which is the average amount of time it takes the company to pay its bills:

$$\text{payables payment period} = \frac{365}{\text{payables turnover ratio}}$$

- The *cash conversion cycle* is the length of time it takes to turn the firm's cash investment in inventory back into cash, in the form of collections from the sales of that inventory. The cash conversion cycle is computed from average receivables collection period, average inventory processing period, and the payables payment period.

$$\begin{array}{c}\text{cash}\\\text{conversion}\\\text{cycle}\end{array} = \left(\begin{array}{c}\text{average receivables}\\\text{collection period}\end{array}\right) + \left(\begin{array}{c}\text{average inventory}\\\text{processing period}\end{array}\right) - \left(\begin{array}{c}\text{payables payment}\\\text{period}\end{array}\right)$$

High cash conversion cycles are considered undesirable. A conversion cycle that is too high implies that the company has an excessive amount of capital investment in the sales process.

Evaluating operating performance. Performance ratios help determine how well management operates the business. They can be divided into two categories: operating efficiency ratios and operating profitability ratios. Operating efficiency ratios are comprised of the total asset turnover, net fixed asset turnover, and equity turnover ratios. These are the first three ratios presented. All of these ratios take some asset or equity account and divide it into sales to determine how efficiently the company uses assets and capital.

Operating profitability ratios include the gross profit margin, operating profit margin, net profit margin, common-size income statement, return on total capital, and return on total equity. Operating ratios compare the top of the income statement (sales) to profits. Remember that net sales is just sales net of returns, and the term 'sales' is often used to mean the same thing.

- The effectiveness of the firm's use of its total assets to create revenue is measured by the *total asset turnover:*

$$\text{total asset turnover} = \frac{\text{net sales}}{\text{average total net assets}}$$

Different types of industries might have considerably different turnover ratios. Manufacturing businesses that are capital-intensive might have asset turnover ratios near one, while retail businesses might have turnover ratios near 10. As was the case with the current asset turnover ratios discussed previously in this topic review, it is desirable for an asset turnover to be close to the industry norm. Low asset turnover ratios might mean that the company has too much capital tied up in its asset base. A turnover ratio that is too high might imply that the firm has too few assets for potential sales or that the asset base is outdated.

- The utilization of fixed assets is measured by the *net fixed asset turnover:*

$$\text{fixed asset turnover} = \frac{\text{net sales}}{\text{average net fixed assets}}$$

As was the case with the total asset turnover ratio, it is desirable to have a fixed asset turnover close to the industry norm. Low fixed asset turnover might mean that the company has too much capital tied up in its asset base. A turnover ratio that is too high might imply that the firm has obsolete equipment, or at a minimum, the firm will probably have to incur capital expenditures in the near future to increase capacity to support growing revenues.

- The *equity turnover* is a measure of the employment of owners' capital:

$$\text{equity turnover} = \frac{\text{net sales}}{\text{average equity}}$$

For this ratio, equity capital includes all preferred and common stock, paid-in capital, and retained earnings, although some analysts use only common equity, which excludes preferred stock. Analysts need to consider the capital structure of the company in evaluating this ratio because a company can increase this ratio without increasing profitability simply by using more debt financing.

Operating profitability ratios look at how good management is at turning their efforts into profits. Operating ratios compare the top of the income statement (sales) to profits. The different ratios are designed to isolate specific costs.

Know these terms:

Gross profits	= Net sales – COGS
Operating profits	= Earnings before interest and taxes = EBIT
Net income	= Earnings after taxes but before dividends
Total capital	= Long-term debt + short-term debt + common and preferred equity
Total capital	= Total assets

How they relate in the income statement:

	Net sales
–	Cost of goods sold
	Gross profit
–	Operating expenses
	Operating profit (EBIT)
–	Interest
	Earnings before taxes (EBT)
–	Taxes
	Earnings after taxes (EAT)

The *gross profit margin* is the ratio of gross profit (sales less cost of goods sold) to sales:

$$\text{gross profit margin} = \frac{\text{gross profit}}{\text{net sales}}$$

An analyst should be concerned if this ratio is too low.

- The *operating profit margin* is the ratio of operating profit (gross profit less sales, general, and administrative expenses) to sales. Operating profit is also referred to as earnings before interest and taxes (EBIT):

$$\text{operating profit margin} = \frac{\text{operating profit}}{\text{net sales}} = \frac{\text{EBIT}}{\text{net sales}}$$

Analysts should be concerned if this ratio is too low. Some analysts prefer to calculate the operating profit margin by adding back depreciation expense to arrive at earnings before interest, taxes, depreciation, and amortization (EBITDA).

- The *net profit margin* is the ratio of net income to sales:

$$\text{net profit margin} = \frac{\text{net income}}{\text{net sales}}$$

Analysts should be concerned if this ratio is too low. The net profit margin should be based on net income from continuing operations, because analysts should be primarily concerned about future expectations, and "below the line" items, such as discontinued operations, will not impact the company in the future.

- The *return on total capital* (ROTC) is the ratio of net income before interest expense to total capital:

$$\text{return on total capital} = \frac{\text{net income} + \text{interest expense}}{\text{average total capital}}$$

Analysts should be concerned if this ratio is too low. Total capital is the same as total assets. The interest expense that should be added back is gross interest expense, not net interest expense (which is gross interest expense less interest income).

An alternative method for computing ROTC is to include the present value of operating leases on the balance sheet as a fixed asset and as a long-term liability. This adjustment is especially important for firms that are dependent on operating leases as a major form of financing. Calculations related to leasing are discussed later in the accounting material.

- The *return on total equity* is the ratio of net income to total equity (including preferred stock):

$$\text{return on total equity} = \frac{\text{net income}}{\text{average total equity}}$$

Analysts should be concerned if this ratio is too low.

- A similar ratio to the return on total equity is the *return on owner's equity:*

$$\text{return on common equity} = \frac{\text{net income} - \text{preferred dividends}}{\text{average common equity}} = \frac{\text{net income available to common}}{\text{average common equity}}$$

This ratio differs from the return on total equity in that it only measures the accounting profits available to, and the capital invested by, common stockholders, instead of common and preferred stockholders. That is why preferred dividends are deducted from net income in the numerator. Analysts should be concerned if this ratio is too low.

The return on common equity is often more thoroughly analyzed using the DuPont decomposition, which is described later in this topic review.

Risk analysis. Risk analysis calculations measure the uncertainty of the firm's income flows. They can be divided into two groups, those that measure business risk and those that measure financial risk.

Business risk is the uncertainty regarding the operating income of a company and is a result of the variability of sales and production costs. The three calculations that measure business risk are business risk, sales volatility, and operating leverage.

Financial risk is the additional volatility of equity returns caused by the firm's use of debt. Financial risk can be measured using balance sheet ratios, which include the debt-to-equity ratio, the long-term debt-to-total capital ratio, and the total debt ratio; or earnings and cash flow ratios, which include the interest coverage ratio, the fixed financial charge ratio, the total fixed charge coverage ratio, the cash flow-to-interest expense ratio, the cash flow coverage ratio, the cash flow-to-long-term debt ratio, and the cash flow-to-total debt ratio.

- A general way of measuring risk of any data series is the *coefficient of variation*, which is the standard deviation of a data series divided by its mean. The calculation of *business risk* is the coefficient of variation of a company's operating income over several years:

$$\text{business risk} = \frac{\sigma \text{ of operating income}}{\text{mean operating income}} = \frac{\text{std. deviation of EBIT}}{\text{mean EBIT}}$$

Between five and ten years of data should be used to calculate the coefficient of variation, because using less data does not yield much statistical reliability and data more than ten years old is likely not relevant to the company's present situation. Analysts should be concerned if this calculation is too high.

Professor's Note: We reviewed the coefficient of variation in the quantitative methods material.

- One of the contributing sources of earnings variability is sales variability. Sales variability is the coefficient of variation of sales over several years:

$$\text{sales variability} = \left[\frac{\sigma \text{ of sales}}{\text{mean sales}} \right]$$

As was the case for business risk, between five and ten years of data should be used in this calculation. Analysts should be concerned if this calculation is too high.

- Another source of the variability of operating earnings is the firm's operating leverage, which measures how much of the company's production costs are fixed (as opposed to variable). The greater the use of fixed costs, the greater the impact of a change in sales on the operating income of a company, and, consequently, the greater the risk. The actual measurement of *operating leverage* is complex. For a given set of years, the percent change in operating earnings (%ΔOE) and the percent change in sales (%ΔS) from the previous year are calculated. Then, the average value of the absolute value of the ratio will be calculated:

$$\text{operating leverage} = \text{mean}\left[\text{absolute value}\left(\frac{\% \Delta \text{OE}}{\% \Delta \text{Sales}} \right) \right]$$

Later we will see the concept of degree of operating leverage (DOL) defined as $\dfrac{\% \Delta \text{EBIT}}{\% \Delta \text{Sales}}$

- A measure of the firm's use of fixed-cost financing sources is the *debt-to-equity ratio*:

$$\text{debt-to-equity ratio} = \frac{\text{total long-term debt}}{\text{total equity}} = \frac{\text{long-term liabilities} + \text{deferred taxes} + \left(\begin{array}{c} \text{present value of} \\ \text{lease obligations} \end{array} \right)}{\text{common} + \text{preferred equity}}$$

Some analysts exclude preferred stock and only use owner's equity. Increases and decreases in this ratio suggest a greater or lesser reliance on debt as a source of financing.

Note that for all ratios in which debt is part of the equation, the analyst has a choice of whether to include deferred taxes as part of debt. If deferred taxes are mainly a result of accelerated and straight-line depreciation differences, then the amount will likely not reverse if capital expenditures continue to grow and should not be included as part of long-term debt. The creation and analytic treatment of a deferred tax liability is covered in detail later in the financial statement analysis material.

- Another way of looking at the usage of debt is the *long-term debt-to-total capital ratio*:

$$\text{long-term debt-to-total long-term capital} = \frac{\text{total long-term debt}}{\text{total long-term capital}}$$

Total long-term capital equals all long-term debt plus preferred stock and equity. Increases and decreases in this ratio suggest a greater or lesser reliance on debt as a source of financing.

Professor's Note: Don't get confused by the apparent multitude of definitions for "total capital." In our discussion of the return on total capital above, we said that total capital equaled total assets. This statement is particularly true for companies that employ a significant amount of short-term liabilities in their capital structure. We could have just as easily analyzed the return on long-term capital, which would define total long-term capital as long-term debt plus equity (both preferred and common). On the exam, watch out for the language that is used in the question. I'm confident that CFA Institute understands this potential discrepancy and will clearly state "total capital" (which you should interpret as total assets) and "total long-term capital" (which should be interpreted as long-term debt plus equity).

- A slightly different way of analyzing debt utilization is the *total debt ratio*, which includes current liabilities in both the numerator and the denominator:

$$\text{total debt ratio} = \frac{\text{current liabilities + total long-term debt}}{\text{total debt + total equity}}$$

Total debt plus total equity is also known as total capital. As discussed in the section on the debt-to-equity ratio, total capital may or may not include deferred taxes. Increases and decreases in this ratio suggest a greater or lesser reliance on debt as a source of financing. Please note that total debt includes all liabilities—even accounts payable and deferred taxes, which are noninterest bearing accounts.

- Often, only interest bearing debt and equity are considered to be long-term capital. A further refinement excludes accounts payable and accrued expenses, which may be considered part of the firm's working capital, to get the following relationship:

$$\left(\begin{array}{c} \text{total interest-bearing debt} \\ \text{to total funded capital} \end{array} \right) = \frac{\text{total interest-bearing debt}}{\text{total capital} - \text{noninterest bearing liabilities}}$$

- The remaining risk ratios help determine the firm's ability to repay its debt obligations. The first of these is the *interest coverage ratio*:

$$\text{interest coverage} = \frac{\text{earnings before interest and taxes}}{\text{interest expense}}$$

The lower this ratio, the more likely it is that the firm will have difficulty meeting its debt payments.

- A slight variation on the interest coverage ratio is to recognize that firms that use leased facilities are in essence borrowing the capital to utilize those facilities. These lease payments are accounted for in the *fixed financial cost ratio*:

$$\text{fixed financial cost ratio} = \frac{\text{EBIT} + \text{ELIE}}{\text{gross interest expense} + \text{ELIE}}$$

where:
ELIE = estimated lease interest expense

This ratio is interpreted in the same manner as the earlier version. Higher coverage ratios suggest the firm is better able to manage its current debt levels or that the firm has unused borrowing capacity.

- A different type of variation in the coverage ratio is to use cash flow instead of income in the numerator. The basis of the cash flow measure is cash flow from operations (CFO) found in the financial statements. In this form, the cash flow measure includes depreciation expense, deferred taxes, and the impact of changes in net working capital. This version of the coverage ratio is defined as:

$$\text{cash flow coverage of fixed financial costs} = \frac{\text{CFO} + \text{interest expense} + \text{ELIE}}{\text{interest expense} + \text{ELIE}}$$

- A different way of determining the ability of a company to meet its debt obligations is to compare cash flow to the amount of long-term debt. This yields the *cash flow-to-long-term debt ratio*:

$$\text{cash flow to long-term debt} = \frac{\text{CFO}}{\text{BV of long-term debt} + \text{PV of operating leases}}$$

where:
BV of long-term debt = the book value of long-term debt
PV of operating leases = the present value of operating leases

Remember that the denominator can be computed either with or without deferred taxes. The lower this ratio, the more likely it is that the firm will have difficulty meeting its long-term debt payments.

- A slight variation on the cash flow-to-long-term debt ratio is the *cash flow-to-total debt ratio*:

$$\left(\begin{array}{c} \text{cash flow to} \\ \text{total interest-bearing debt} \end{array} \right) = \frac{\text{CFO}}{\text{total long-term debt} + \text{current interest-bearing liabilites}}$$

The lower this ratio, the more likely it is that the firm will have difficulty meeting its debt payments.

Growth analysis. Owners and creditors are interested in the firm's growth potential. Owners pay attention to growth because stock valuation is dependent on the future growth rate of the firm. The analysis of growth potential is important to the creditors because the firm's future prospects are crucial to its ability to pay existing debt obligations. If the company doesn't grow, it stands a much greater chance of defaulting on its loans. In theory, the growth rate of a firm is a function of the rate of return earned on its resources and the amount of resources (profits) retained and reinvested.

To calculate the sustainable growth rate for a firm, the rate of return on resources is measured as the return on equity capital, or the ROE. The proportion of earnings reinvested is known as the retention rate (RR).

- The formula for the *sustainable growth rate*, which is how fast the firm can grow without additional external equity issues while holding leverage constant, is:

$$g = RR \times ROE$$

- The calculation of the *retention rate* is:

$$\text{retention rate} = \left(1 - \frac{\text{dividends declared}}{\text{operating income after taxes}} \right)$$

where :

$$\frac{\text{dividends declared}}{\text{operating income after taxes}} = \text{dividend payout ratio}$$

Example: Calculating sustainable growth

Figure 2 provides data for three companies.

Figure 2: Growth Analysis Data

Company	A	B	C
Earnings per share	$3.00	$4.00	$5.00
Dividends per share	1.50	1.00	2.00
Return on equity	14%	12%	10%

Calculate the sustainable growth rate for each company.

Answer:

RR = 1 – (dividends / earnings)
        Company A: RR = 1 – (1.50 / 3.00) = 0.500
        Company B: RR = 1 – (1.00 / 4.00) = 0.750
        Company C: RR = 1 – (2.00 / 5.00) = 0.600

g = RR × ROE
        Company A: g = 0.500 × 14% = 7.0%
        Company B: g = 0.750 × 12% = 9.0%
        Company C: g = 0.600 × 10% = 6.0%

LOS 38.d: Calculate and interpret the various components of the company's return on equity using the original and extended DuPont systems and a company's financial ratios relative to its industry, to the aggregate economy, and to the company's own performance over time.

The **DuPont system of analysis** is an approach that can be used to analyze return on equity (ROE). It uses basic algebra to breakdown ROE into a function of different ratios, so an analyst can see the impact of leverage, profit margins, and turnover on shareholder returns. There are two variants of the DuPont system: the original three-part approach and the extended five-part system.

For the **original approach**, start with ROE defined as:

$$\text{return on equity} = \left(\frac{\text{net income}}{\text{equity}} \right)$$

Note that there are two subtle differences between this ROE measure and the ROE defined previously. First, the numerator does not subtract preferred dividends as our review did when ROE was first defined. Second, the common equity figure that is typically used is not average equity, but simply end-of-year equity.

Multiplying ROE by sales/sales and rearranging terms produces:

$$\text{return on equity} = \left(\frac{\text{net income}}{\text{sales}} \right) \left(\frac{\text{sales}}{\text{equity}} \right)$$

The first term is the profit margin and the second term is the equity turnover:

$$\text{return on equity} = \left(\frac{\text{net profit}}{\text{margin}} \right) \left(\frac{\text{equity}}{\text{turnover}} \right)$$

We can expand this further by multiplying these terms by assets/assets, and rearranging terms:

$$\text{return on equity} = \left(\frac{\text{net income}}{\text{sales}} \right) \left(\frac{\text{sales}}{\text{assets}} \right) \left(\frac{\text{assets}}{\text{equity}} \right)$$

Professor's Note: For the exam, remember that (net income / sales) × (sales / assets) = return on assets (ROA).

The first term is still the profit margin, the second term is now asset turnover, and the third term is now an equity multiplier that will increase as the use of debt financing increases:

$$\text{return on equity} = \left(\frac{\text{net profit}}{\text{margin}} \right) \left(\frac{\text{asset}}{\text{turnover}} \right) \left(\frac{\text{equity}}{\text{multiplier}} \right)$$

This is the original DuPont equation. It is arguably the most important equation in ratio analysis, since it breaks down a very important ratio (ROE) into three key components. If ROE is relatively low, it must be that at least one of the following is true: the company has a poor profit margin, the company has poor asset turnover, or the firm has too little leverage.

Professor's Note: Often candidates get confused and think that the DuPont method is a way to calculate ROE. While you can calculate ROE given the components of either the original or extended DuPont equations, this isn't necessary if you have the financial statements. If you have net income and equity, you can calculate ROE. The DuPont method is a way to decompose ROE to better see what changes are driving the changes in ROE.

Example: Decomposition of ROE with original DuPont

Staret Inc. has maintained a stable and relatively high ROE of approximately 18% over the last 3 years. Use traditional DuPont analysis to decompose this ROE into its three components and comment on trends in company performance.

Staret Inc. Selected Balance Sheet and Income Statement Items (Millions)			
Year	2003	2004	2005
Net Income	21.5	22.3	21.9
Sales	305	350	410
Equity	119	124	126
Assets	230	290	350

Answer:

ROE 2003: $\dfrac{21.5}{119} = 18.1\%$; 2004: $\dfrac{22.3}{124} = 18\%$; 2005: $\dfrac{21.9}{126} = 17.4\%$

DuPont 2003: 7% × 1.32 × 1.93

2004: 6.4% × 1.21 × 2.34

2005: 5.3% × 1.17 × 2.78

(some rounding in values)

While the ROE has dropped only slightly, both the total asset turnover and the net profit margin have declined. The effects of declining net margins and turnover on ROE have been offset by a significant increase in leverage. The analyst should be concerned about the net margin and find out what combination of pricing pressure and/or increasing expenses have caused this. Also, the analyst must note that the company has become more risky due to increased debt financing.

Example: Computing ROE using original DuPont

A company has a net profit margin of 4%, asset turnover of 2.0, and a debt-to-assets ratio of 60%. What is the ROE?

Answer:

Debt-to-assets = 60%, which means equity to assets is 40%; this implies assets over equity of 1 / 0.4 = 2.5

$$\text{ROE} = \left(\begin{array}{c}\text{net profit}\\\text{margin}\end{array}\right)\left(\begin{array}{c}\text{total asset}\\\text{turnover}\end{array}\right)\left(\dfrac{\text{assets}}{\text{equity}}\right) = (0.04)(2.00)(2.50) = 0.20, \text{ or } 20\%$$

The **extended DuPont equation** takes the net profit margin and breaks it down further. The numerator of the net profit margin is net income. Since net income is equal to earnings before taxes multiplied by 1 minus the tax rate $(1 - t)$, the DuPont equation can be written as:

$$ROE = \left(\frac{\text{earnings before tax}}{\text{sales}}\right)\left(\frac{\text{sales}}{\text{assets}}\right)\left(\frac{\text{assets}}{\text{equity}}\right)(1 - t)$$

Earnings before tax is simply EBIT minus interest expense. If this substitution is made, the equation becomes:

$$ROE = \left[\left(\frac{\text{EBIT}}{\text{sales}}\right)\left(\frac{\text{sales}}{\text{assets}}\right) - \left(\frac{\text{interest expense}}{\text{assets}}\right)\right]\left(\frac{\text{assets}}{\text{equity}}\right)(1 - t)$$

The first term is the operating profit margin. The second term is the asset turnover. The third term is new and is called the interest expense rate. The fourth term is the same leverage multiplier defined in the traditional DuPont equation, and the fifth term, $(1 - t)$, is called the tax retention rate. The equation can now be stated as:

$$ROE = \left[\left(\begin{array}{c}\text{operating}\\\text{profit}\\\text{margin}\end{array}\right)\left(\begin{array}{c}\text{total}\\\text{asset}\\\text{turnover}\end{array}\right) - \left(\begin{array}{c}\text{interest}\\\text{expense}\\\text{rate}\end{array}\right)\right]\left(\begin{array}{c}\text{financial}\\\text{leverage}\\\text{multiplier}\end{array}\right)\left(\begin{array}{c}\text{tax}\\\text{retention}\\\text{rate}\end{array}\right)$$

Note that in general, high profit margins, leverage, and asset turnover will lead to high levels of ROE. However, this version of the formula shows that more leverage *does not always* lead to higher ROE. As leverage rises, so does the interest expense rate. Hence, the positive effects of leverage can be offset by the higher interest payments that accompany more debt. Note that higher taxes will always lead to lower levels of ROE.

Example: Extended DuPont analysis

An analyst has gathered data from two companies in the same industry. Calculate the ROE for both companies and use the extended DuPont analysis to explain the critical factors that account for the differences in the two companies' ROEs.

Figure 3: Selected Income and Balance Sheet Data

	Company A	Company B
Revenues	$500	$900
Operating income	35	100
Interest expense	5	0
Income before taxes	30	100
Taxes	10	40
Net income	20	60
Total assets	250	300
Total debt	100	50
Owners' equity	$150	$250

Answer:

Operating margin = operating income / sales
Company A: operating margin = 35 / 500   = 7.0%
Company B: operating margin = 100 / 900 = 11.1%

Asset turnover = sales / assets
Company A: asset turnover = 500 / 250 = 2.0
Company B: asset turnover = 900 / 300 = 3.0

Interest expense rate = interest expense / assets
Company A: interest expense rate = 5 / 250 = 2.0%
Company B: interest expense rate = 0 / 300 = 0%

Financial leverage = assets / equity
Company A: financial leverage = 250 / 150 = 1.67
Company B: financial leverage = 300 / 250 = 1.2

Income tax rate = taxes / pretax income
Company A: income tax rate = 10 / 30   = 33.3%
Company B: income tax rate = 40 / 100 = 40.0%

$$ROE = \left[\left(\begin{array}{c}\text{operating}\\\text{profit}\\\text{margin}\end{array}\right)\left(\begin{array}{c}\text{total}\\\text{asset}\\\text{turnover}\end{array}\right) - \left(\begin{array}{c}\text{interest}\\\text{expense}\\\text{rate}\end{array}\right)\right]\left(\begin{array}{c}\text{financial}\\\text{leverage}\\\text{multiplier}\end{array}\right)\left(\begin{array}{c}\text{tax}\\\text{retention}\\\text{rate}\end{array}\right)$$

Company A: ROE = (7.0% × 2.0 – 2.0%) × 1.67 × (1 – 33.3%) = 13.4%
Company B: ROE = (11.1% × 3.0 – 0%) × 1.2 × (1 – 40%) = 24.0%

Asset turnover for Company B is much higher, which is the main reason that its ROE is higher. Profit margin is also a contributing factor. Company B's ROE is higher despite the fact that it is using less leverage.

Professor's Note: There are other variants of the DuPont system. Candidates would be wise to forget about them for testing purposes. The two variants presented here are the equations that candidates will be expected to remember for the exam.

Example: Ratio computation and analysis

Figure 4 shows a balance sheet for a company for this year and the previous year. Figure 5 shows its income statement for the current year.

Figure 4: Sample Balance Sheet

Year	Current year	Previous year
Assets		
Cash	$105	$95
Receivables	205	195
Inventories	310	290
Total current assets	620	580
Gross property, plant, and equipment	$1,800	$1,700
Accumulated depreciation	$360	340
Net property, plant, and equipment	1,440	1,360
Total assets	$2,060	**$1,940**
Liabilities		
Payables	$110	$90
Short-term debt	160	140
Current portion of long-term debt	55	45
Current liabilities	$325	$275
Long-term debt	$610	$690
Deferred taxes	105	95
Common stock	300	300
Additional paid in capital	400	400
Retained earnings	320	180
Common shareholders equity	1,020	880
Total liabilities and equity	$2,060	**$1,940**

Figure 5: Sample Income Statement

Year	Current year
Sales	$4,000
Cost of goods sold	3,000
Gross profit	$1,000
Operating expenses	650
Operating profit	350
Interest expense	50
Earnings before taxes	300
Taxes	100
Net income	200
Common dividends	$60

Using the company information in Figures 4, 5, and 6, calculate the current year ratios. Discuss how these ratios compare with the company's performance last year and with the industry's performance.

Figure 6: Financial Ratio Template

	Current Year	Last Year	Industry
Current ratio		2.1	1.5
Quick ratio		1.1	0.9
Receivables collection period		18.9	18.0
Inventory turnover		10.7	12.0
Total asset turnover		2.3	2.4
Equity turnover		4.8	4.0
Gross profit margin		27.4%	29.3%
Net profit margin		5.8%	6.5%
Return on capital		13.3%	15.6%
Return on common equity		24.1%	19.8%
Debt-to-equity		78.4%	35.7%
Interest coverage		5.9	9.2
Cash flow-to-long-term debt		35.1%	45.3%
Retention rate		50.0%	43.6%
Sustainable growth rate		12.0%	8.6%

Answer:

- Current ratio = $\dfrac{\text{current assets}}{\text{current liabilities}}$

  current ratio $= \dfrac{620}{325} = 1.9$

The current ratio indicates lower liquidity levels when compared to last year and more liquidity than the industry average.

- Quick ratio = $\dfrac{\text{cash + receivables}}{\text{current liabilities}}$

  quick ratio $= \dfrac{(105 + 205)}{325} = 0.95$

The quick ratio is lower than last year and is in line with the industry average.

- Average collection period = $\dfrac{365}{\text{sales}/\text{average receivables}}$

  average collection period = $\dfrac{365}{4{,}000 / [(205 + 195)/2]} = 18.25$

The average collection period is a bit lower relative to the company's past performance but slightly higher than the industry average.

- Inventory turnover = $\dfrac{\text{cost of goods sold}}{\text{average inventories}}$

$$\text{inventory turnover} = \frac{3,000}{(310 + 290) / 2} = 10.0$$

The inventory turnover is much lower than last year and the industry average. This suggests that the company is not managing inventory efficiently and may have obsolete stock.

- Total asset turnover = $\dfrac{\text{sales}}{\text{average assets}}$

$$\text{total asset turnover} = \frac{4,000}{(2,060 + 1,940) / 2} = 2.0$$

The total asset turnover is slightly lower than last year and the industry average.

- Equity turnover = $\dfrac{\text{sales}}{\text{average equity}}$

$$\text{equity turnover} = \frac{4,000}{(1,020 + 880) / 2} = 4.2$$

The equity turnover is lower than last year, but still above the industry average.

- Gross profit margin = $\dfrac{\text{gross profit}}{\text{net sales}}$

$$\text{gross profit margin} = \frac{1,000}{4,000} = 25.0\%$$

The gross profit margin is lower than last year and much lower than the industry average.

- Net profit margin = $\dfrac{\text{net income}}{\text{net sales}}$

$$\text{net profit margin} = \frac{200}{4,000} = 5.0\%$$

The net profit margin is lower than last year and much lower than the industry average.

- Return on capital = $\dfrac{\text{net income + interest expense}}{\text{average total capital}}$

$$\text{return on capital} = \frac{200 + 50}{(2,060 + 1,940) / 2} = 12.5\%$$

The return on capital is below last year and below the industry average. This suggests a problem stemming from the low asset turnover and low profit margin.

- Return on common equity = $\dfrac{\text{net income} - \text{preferred dividends}}{\text{average owners' equity}}$

return on common equity = $\dfrac{200}{(1{,}020 + 880) / 2} = 21.1\%$

The return on equity is lower than last year but better than the industry average. The reason it is higher than the industry average is probably because of greater use of leverage.

- Debt-to-equity ratio = $\dfrac{\text{long-term debt (not including deferred taxes)}}{\text{total equity}}$

debt-to-equity ratio = $\dfrac{610}{1{,}020} = 59.8\%$

Note that this calculation assumes that deferred taxes are not part of long-term debt.

The debt-to-equity ratio is lower than last year but still much higher than the industry average. This suggests the company is trying to get its debt level more in line with the industry.

- Interest coverage = $\dfrac{\text{net income} + \text{income taxes} + \text{interest expense}}{\text{interest expense}}$

interest coverage = $\dfrac{200 + 100 + 50}{50} = 7.0$

The interest coverage is better than last year but still worse than the industry average. This, along with the slip in profit margin and return on assets, might cause some concern.

- Cash flow-to-long-term debt =

$$\dfrac{\left(\begin{array}{c}\text{net}\\\text{income}\end{array}\right) + \text{depreciation} + \left(\begin{array}{c}\text{increase in}\\\text{deferred taxes}\end{array}\right) - \left(\begin{array}{c}\text{increase in}\\\text{receivables}\end{array}\right) - \left(\begin{array}{c}\text{increase in}\\\text{inventories}\end{array}\right) + \left(\begin{array}{c}\text{increase in}\\\text{payables}\end{array}\right)}{\text{long-term debt (not including deferred taxes)}}$$

cash flow-to-long-term debt = $\dfrac{200 + 20 + 10 - 10 - 20 + 20}{610} = 36.1\%$

The cash flow to long-term debt ratio is better than last year but much worse than the industry average. This should concern an analyst.

- Retention rate = $1 - \dfrac{\text{dividends}}{\text{earnings}}$

retention rate = $1 - \dfrac{60}{200} = 70\%$

The retention rate is much higher than last year and much higher than the industry. This might suggest that the company is aware of its cash flow and earnings issues and is reinvesting cash into the company to improve the ratios.

• ROE = $\dfrac{\text{net income}}{\text{equity}}$

  ROE = $\dfrac{200}{1,020}$ = 0.196, or 19.6%

• Sustainable growth rate, g = retention rate × ROE

  sustainable growth rate = 0.7 × 0.196 = 0.137, or 13.7%

With the high retention rate and good ROE, the company is positioned to grow at a faster rate than last year and faster than the rest of the industry.

Summary: The company has average liquidity. However, performance figures suggest that earnings have declined, and turnover has worsened. Coverage ratios have slipped a bit, which might cause some concern, particularly for lenders.

Professor's Note: We used the end-of-year equity to calculate ROE when calculating the sustainable growth rate. Be aware that the ROE is calculated by different analysts and for different purposes using NI divided by beginning, ending, or average equity. On the CFA exam you will likely be given guidance on which to use if the choice affects the answer.

KEY CONCEPTS

1. A common-size balance sheet expresses all balance sheet accounts as a percentage of total assets. A common-size income statement expresses all income statement items as a percentage of sales.
2. Ratios are valid only in a relative context—when compared to other firms, industry averages, economic averages, or the firm's ratios from prior periods.
3. Ratios can be divided into four types—internal liquidity, operating performance, risk analysis, and growth potential.
   • Internal liquidity ratios indicate the company's ability to pay its short-term obligations. An average amount for balance sheet accounts is used in the denominator.
   • Operating performance ratios include two categories: operating efficiency ratios (various turnover ratios) and operating profitability (various margin ratios).
   • Risk analysis ratios address two types of risk: business risk (resulting from variability in sales and operating costs) and financial risk (volatility resulting from the use of debt).
   • Growth analysis ratios indicate the company's ability to pay future obligations. The calculation of the sustainable growth rate is g = RR × ROE, where RR = retention rate = 1 – (dividends declared / after-tax operating income) and ROE is return on equity.
4. The original DuPont equation is:

   $$\text{return on equity} = \left(\frac{\text{net income}}{\text{sales}}\right)\left(\frac{\text{sales}}{\text{assets}}\right)\left(\frac{\text{assets}}{\text{equity}}\right)$$

   The extended DuPont equation is:

   $$\text{ROE} = \left[\left(\frac{\text{EBIT}}{\text{sales}}\right)\left(\frac{\text{sales}}{\text{assets}}\right) - \left(\frac{\text{interest expense}}{\text{assets}}\right)\right]\left(\frac{\text{assets}}{\text{equity}}\right)(1-t)$$

CONCEPT CHECKERS: ANALYSIS OF FINANCIAL STATEMENTS

1. To study trends in a firm's cost of goods sold (COGS), the analyst should standardize the cost of goods sold numbers to a common-sized basis by dividing COGS by:
   A. assets.
   B. sales.
   C. net income.
   D. the prior year's COGS.

2. A company's current ratio is 1.9. If some of the accounts payable are paid off from the cash account, the:
   A. numerator and the current ratio would remain unchanged.
   B. numerator would decrease more than the denominator, resulting in a lower current ratio.
   C. denominator would decrease more than the numerator, resulting in a higher current ratio.
   D. numerator and denominator would decrease proportionally, leaving the current ratio unchanged.

3. A company's quick ratio is 1.2. If inventory were purchased for cash, the:
   A. numerator and the quick ratio would remain unchanged.
   B. numerator would decrease more than the denominator, resulting in a lower quick ratio.
   C. denominator would decrease more than the numerator, resulting in a higher quick current ratio.
   D. numerator and denominator would decrease proportionally, leaving the current ratio unchanged.

4. All other things held constant, which of the following transactions will *increase* a firm's current ratio if the ratio is greater than one?
   A. Accounts receivable are collected and the funds received are deposited in the firm's cash account.
   B. Fixed assets are purchased from the cash account.
   C. Accounts payable are paid with funds from the cash account.
   D. Inventory is purchased on account.

5. RGB, Inc.'s income statement indicates cost of goods sold of $100,000. The balance sheet shows an average accounts payable balance of $12,000. What is RGB's payables payment period?
   A. 28 days.
   B. 37 days.
   C. 44 days.
   D. 52 days.

6. RGB, Inc. has a gross profit of $45,000 on sales of $150,000. The balance sheet shows average total assets of $75,000 with an average inventory balance of $15,000. What are RGB's total asset turnover and inventory turnover?

	Asset Turnover	Inventory Turnover
A.	7.00 times	2.00 times
B.	2.00 times	7.00 times
C.	0.50 times	0.33 times
D.	10.00 times	0.60 times

7. If RGB, Inc. has annual sales of $100,000, average accounts payable of $30,000, and average accounts receivable of $25,000, what is RGB's receivables turnover and average collection period?

	Receivables Turnover	Average Collection Period
A.	1.8 times	203 days
B.	2.1 times	174 days
C.	3.3 times	111 days
D.	4.0 times	91 days

8. RGB, Inc.'s receivable turnover is 10 times, the inventory turnover is 5 times, and the payables turnover is 9 times. RGB's cash conversion cycle is:
   A. 69 days.
   B. 104 days.
   C. 150 days.
   D. 170 days.

9. RGB, Inc.'s income statement shows sales of $1,000, cost of goods sold of $400, pre-interest operating expense of $300, and interest expense of $100. RGB's interest coverage ratio is:
   A. 1 times.
   B. 2 times.
   C. 3 times.
   D. 4 times.

10. Return on equity using the traditional DuPont formula equals:
    A. (net profit margin) (interest component) (solvency ratio).
    B. (net profit margin) (total asset turnover) (tax retention rate).
    C. (net profit margin) (total asset turnover) (financial leverage multiplier).
    D. (tax rate) (interest expense rate) (financial leverage multiplier).

11. RGB, Inc. has a net profit margin of 12%, a total asset turnover of 1.2 times, and a financial leverage multiplier of 1.2 times. RGB's return on equity is:
    A. 12.0%.
    B. 14.2%.
    C. 17.3%.
    D. 18.9%.

12. Use the following information for RGB, Inc.:
    • EBIT/sales = 10%
    • Tax retention rate = 60%
    • Sales/assets = 1.8 times
    • Current ratio = 2 times
    • Interest/assets = 2%
    • Assets/equity = 1.9 times

    What is RGB, Inc.'s return on equity?
    A. 10.50%.
    B. 11.32%.
    C. 12.16%.
    D. 18.24%.

13. All of the following equations represent return on equity EXCEPT:
    A. (net profit margin)(equity turnover).
    B. (net profit margin)(total asset turnover)(assets/equity).
    C. (ROA)(interest burden)(tax retention rate).
    D. [(operating profit margin)(total asset turnover) – interest expense rate)]
       (financial leverage multiplier)(tax retention rate).

14. The percentage change in operating earnings divided by the percentage change in sales is referred to as the:
    A. coefficient of variation of operating income.
    B. coefficient of variation of sales.
    C. operating leverage.
    D. gross profit margin.

15. A firm has a dividend payout ratio of 40%, a net profit margin of 10%, an asset turnover of 0.9 times, and a financial leverage multiplier of 1.2 times. The firm's sustainable growth rate is *closest* to:
    A. 5.5%.
    B. 6.5%.
    C. 7.5%.
    D. 8.0%.

Use the following data to answer Questions 16 through 22. (Answers may be rounded off.)

Alpha Company	
Sales	$5,000
Cost of goods sold	2,500
Average	
Inventories	$600
Accounts receivable	450
Working capital	750
Cash	200
Accounts payable	500
Fixed assets	4,750
Total assets	$6,000
Annual purchases	$2,400

16. Alpha's inventory turnover is:
    A. 3.1 times.
    B. 4.2 times.
    C. 6.3 times.
    D. 8.4 times.

17. Alpha's average inventory processing period is:
    A. 37 days.
    B. 44 days.
    C. 65 days.
    D. 88 days.

18. Alpha's receivables turnover is:
    A. 11.11 times.
    B. 12.12 times.
    C. 13.50 times.
    D. 15.00 times.

©2007 Schweser

19.   Alpha's average collection period:
        A. 25 days.
        B. 30 days.
        C. 33 days.
        D. 45 days.

20.   Alpha's payables turnover is:
        A. 4.0 times.
        B. 4.8 times.
        C. 5.0 times.
        D. 10.0 times.

21.   Alpha's average days payable is:
        A. 37 days.
        B. 62 days.
        C. 73 days.
        D. 76 days.

22.   Alpha's cash conversion cycle is:
        A. 33 days.
        B. 127 days.
        C. 48 days.
        D. 19 days.

Use the following data to answer Questions 23 through 26.

Beta Co. has a loan covenant requiring it to maintain a current ratio of 1.5 or better. As Beta approaches year-end, current assets are $20 million ($1 million in cash, $9 million in accounts receivable and $10 million in inventory) and current liabilities are $13.5 million.

23.   Beta's current ratio is *closest* to:
        A. 0.675 times.
        B. 1.480 times.
        C. 1.500 times.
        D. 0.740 times.

24.   Beta's quick ratio is *closest* to:
        A. 0.675 times.
        B. 0.740 times.
        C. 0.810 times.
        D. 1.480 times.

25.   What can Beta Co. do to meet its loan covenant?
        A. Sell $1 million in inventory and deposit the proceeds in the company's checking account.
        B. Borrow $1 million short term and deposit the funds in their checking account.
        C. Sell $1 million in inventory and pay off some of its short-term creditors.
        D. Do nothing at all.

26.   If Beta sells $2 million in inventory on credit, the current ratio will:
       A.   increase, and if Beta sells $1 million in inventory and pays off accounts payable, the quick ratio will
             remain the same.
       B.   remain the same, and if Beta sells $1 million in inventory for cash and uses it to reduce accounts
             payable, the quick ratio will decrease.
       C.   remain the same, and if Beta sells $1 million in inventory for cash and uses it to reduce accounts
             payable, the quick ratio will increase.
       D.   increase, and if Beta sells $1 million in inventory and pays off accounts payable, the quick ratio will
             increase.

27.   Paragon Co. has an operating profit margin (EBIT/S) of 11%; an asset turnover (S/A) of 1.2; a financial
       leverage multiplier (A/E) of 1.5 times; an average tax rate of 35%; and an interest expense rate (I/A) of
       4%. Which number is *closest* to Paragon's return on equity?
       A.   0.09.
       B.   0.10.
       C.   0.11.
       D.   0.12.

28.   Paragon Co. has the following information:
       • Interest expense ratio (I/assets) of 10%.
       • Current ratio of 1.8.
       • Tax retention rate $(1 - t)$ of 70%.
       • Effective tax rate of 30%; a leverage ratio (A/E) of 2 times.
       • Debt-to-equity ratio of 1.
       • Total asset turnover of 1.2 times.
       • Operating profit margin of 12%.

       What is Paragon's return on equity?
       A.   5.7%.
       B.   6.2%.
       C.   6.7%.
       D.   3.0%.

29.   In 1993, RGB, Inc.'s operating profit margin (EBIT/S) was 15%; total asset turnover (S/A)
       was 1 times; financial leverage multiplier (A/E) was 2 times; tax retention rate was 70%; and interest
       expense rate (I/A) was 7%. In 2003, RGB's operating profit margin was 10%; total asset turnover was 1.5
       times; financial leverage multiplier was 2 times; tax retention rate was 70%; interest expense rate was 7%.
       Which statement is **TRUE**?
       A.   Return on equity increased because the firm's asset turnover increased.
       B.   Return on equity fell because the firm's profit margin fell.
       C.   Return on equity remained constant because the fall in profits offset the increase in sales.
       D.   Return on equity remained constant because the increase in profits offset the decrease in sales.

30.   Given the following ten ratios:
      1. Debt-to-equity   6. Interest-to-assets
      2. 1 – t   7. EBT-to-EBIT
      3. EAT-to-EBT   8. EBT-to-EAT
      4. CA-to-CL   9. EBIT-to-sales
      5. Assets-to-equity   10. Sales-to-assets

Using their corresponding numbers, which combination of five will give the firm's ROE?
A. [(9)(4) + (7)](5)(6).
B. [(1 + 3 + 5)(7)] – (9).
C. [(9)(10) – (6)](5)(2).
D. (3)(5)(6)(9)(10).

ANSWERS – CONCEPT CHECKERS: ANALYSIS OF FINANCIAL STATEMENTS

1. **B** With a common-size income statement, all income statement accounts are divided by sales.

2. **C** CR = (cash + AR + inv) / AP. If cash and AP decrease by the same amount and the CR is > 1, then the denominator falls faster than the numerator and the current ratio increases.

3. **B** Quick ratio = (cash + AR) / AP. If cash decreases, the quick ratio will also decrease. The denominator is unchanged.

4. **C** Current ratio = current assets/current liabilities. If CR is > 1, then if CA and CL both fall, the overall ratio will increase.

5. **C** Payables turnover = (COGS / avg. AP) = 100 / 12 = 8.33. Payables payment period = 365 / 8.33 = 43.8 days

6. **B** TAT = (sales / total assets) = 150 / 75 = 2 times

    inventory turnover = (COGS / avg. inventory) = (150 – 45) / 15 = 7 times

7. **D** RT = (S / avg. AR) = 100 / 25 = 4

    CP = 365 / 4 = 91.25 days

8. **A** (365 / 10 + 365 / 5 – 365 / 9) = 69 days

9. **C** ICR = EBIT / I = (1000 – 400 – 300) / 100 = 3 times

10. **C** This is the correct formula for the three-ratio DuPont model for ROE.

11. **C** return on equity = $\left(\dfrac{\text{net income}}{\text{sales}}\right)\left(\dfrac{\text{sales}}{\text{assets}}\right)\left(\dfrac{\text{assets}}{\text{equity}}\right)$ = (0.12)(1.2)(1.2) = 0.1728 = 17.28%

12. **D** ROE = [(EBIT / S)(S / A) – (I / A)](A / EQ)(1 – t) = [(0.1)(1.8) – (0.02)](1.9)(0.6) = 0.1824 = 18.24%

13. **C** (ROA)(interest burden)(tax retention rate) is not one of the DuPont models for calculating ROE.

14. **C** The percentage change in operating earnings divided by the percentage change in sales is referred to as the operating leverage.

15. **B** g = (retention rate)(ROE), return on equity = $\left(\dfrac{\text{net profit}}{\text{margin}}\right)\left(\dfrac{\text{asset}}{\text{turnover}}\right)\left(\dfrac{\text{equity}}{\text{multiplier}}\right)$ = (0.1)(0.9)(1.2) = 0.108,

    g = (1 – 0.4)(0.108) = 6.5%

16. **B** inventory turnover = COGS / avg. inventory = 2500 / 600 = 4.167 times

17. **D** average inventory processing period = 365 / inventory turnover = 365 / 4.167 = 87.6 days

18. **A** receivables turnover = sales / avg. account receivable = 5,000 / 450 = 11.11 times

19. **C** average collection period = 365 / receivables turnover = 365 / 11.11 = 32.85 days

20. **C** payables turnover = COGS / avg. payables = 2,500 / 500 = 5 times

21. **C** average days payable = 365 / payables turnover = 365 / 5 = 73 days

22. C $\dfrac{\text{cash}}{\text{conversion}} = \left(\dfrac{\text{average receivables}}{\text{collection period}}\right) + \left(\dfrac{\text{average inventory}}{\text{processing period}}\right) - \left(\dfrac{\text{payables}}{\text{payment}}\right)$ = 33 + 88 – 73 = 48 days

23. B $\text{current ratio} = \dfrac{\text{current assets}}{\text{current liabilities}}$ = [(1 + 9 + 10) / 13.5] = 20 / 13.5 = 1.48 times

24. B $\text{quick ratio} = \dfrac{\text{cash} + \text{marketable securities} + \text{receivables}}{\text{current liabilities}}$ = (1 + 9) / 13.5 = 10 / 13.5 = 0.74 times

25. C This transaction would increase the current ratio: (20 – 1)/(13.5 – 1) = 19 / 12.5 = 1.52. Selling $1 million in inventory and depositing the proceeds in the company's checking account would leave the ratio unchanged: (20 + 1 – 1) / 13.5 = 1.48. Borrowing $1 million short term and depositing the funds in their checking account would decrease the current ratio: (20 + 1) / (13.5 + 1) = 21 / 14.5 = 1.45.

26. C If inventory goes down and receivables rise by the same amount, the numerator would be unchanged. QR = (cash + AR) / AP. AP will decrease without any change to the numerator, thus increasing the overall ratio.

27. A ROE = [(EBIT / S)(S / A) – (I / A)](A / E)(1 – t) = [(0.11)(1.2) – (0.04)](1.5)(0.65) = 0.0897

28. B ROE = [(0.12)(1.2) – (0.1)](2)(0.7) = 0.0616 = 6.16%

29. C 1993 ROE = [(0.15)(1) – (0.07)](2)(0.7) = 0.112 and 2003 ROE = [(0.10)(1.5) – (0.07)](2)(0.7) = 0.112

30. C The correct formula for the extended DuPont model for calculating ROE is: [(EBIT / sales)(sales / assets) – (I / assets)](assets / equity)(1 – t)

The following is a review of the Financial Statement Analysis principles designed to address the learning outcome statements set forth by CFA Institute®. This topic is also covered in:

DILUTIVE SECURITIES AND EARNINGS PER SHARE

EXAM FOCUS

The amount of income a company earns for every share of common stock it has outstanding, or EPS, is the standard for reporting company earnings. Companies with a complex capital structure have securities such as warrants or convertible bonds that can increase the number of shares of common stock a firm has outstanding without changing earnings, therefore decreasing, or diluting, EPS. Firms with a complex structure will report both basic EPS, which does not consider dilutive securities, and diluted EPS, which considers dilutive securities. For the Level 1 exam, prepare for basic and diluted EPS calculations. Know how to compute the weighted average number of common shares outstanding, recognize that stock splits and stock dividends do not change the owner's proportionate claim on earnings, and be able to differentiate between dilutive and antidilutive securities.

LOS 39.a: Differentiate between simple and complex capital structures for purposes of calculating earnings per share (EPS), describe the components of EPS, and calculate a company's EPS in a simple capital structure.

Earnings per share (EPS) is one of the most commonly used corporate profitability performance measures for publicly traded firms (nonpublic companies are not required to report EPS data).

EPS is only reported for shares of common stock. The disclosure requirements are set forth in SFAS 128 and SFAS 129. Basically, a company must:

- Report EPS for all components of net income.
- Reconcile basic EPS and diluted EPS numerators and denominators.

A company may have either a simple or complex capital structure:

- A **simple capital structure** is one that contains *no* potentially dilutive securities. A simple capital structure contains only common stock, nonconvertible debt, and preferred stock.
- A **complex capital structure** contains *potentially dilutive securities* such as options, warrants, or convertible securities.

All firms with complex capital structures must report both *basic* and *diluted* EPS. Firms with simple capital structures report only basic EPS.

Companies that report intermediate components of income (e.g., income from continuing operations, income before extraordinary items) must report EPS amounts for these components in either the income statement or in the notes to the financial statements.

The Components of EPS and Calculating a Company's EPS in a Simple Capital Structure

The basic EPS calculation *does not* consider the effects of any dilutive securities in the computation of EPS.

$$\text{basic EPS} = \frac{\text{net income} - \text{preferred dividends}}{\text{weighted average number of common shares outstanding}}$$

The current year's preferred dividends are subtracted from net income because EPS refers to the per-share earnings *available to common shareholders*. Net income minus preferred dividends is the income available to common stockholders. Common stock dividends are *not* subtracted from net income because they are a part of the net income available to common shareholders.

LOS 39.b: Calculate a company's weighted average number of shares outstanding.

The **weighted average number of common shares** is the number of shares outstanding during the year weighted by the portion of the year they were outstanding.

Example: Effect of stock dividends

During 2006, R & J, Inc., had net income of $100,000, paid dividends of $50,000 to its preferred stockholders, and paid $30,000 in dividends to its common shareholders. R & J's common stock account showed the following:

01/01/06	Shares issued and outstanding at the beginning of the year	10,000
04/01/06	Shares issued	4,000
07/01/06	10% stock dividend	
09/01/06	Shares repurchased for the treasury	3,000

Compute the weighted average number of common shares outstanding during 2006, and compute EPS.

Answer:

Step 1: Adjust the number of pre-stock dividend shares to their post-stock dividend units to reflect the 10% stock dividend by multiplying all share numbers prior to the stock dividend by 1.1. Shares issued or retired after the stock dividend are not affected.

01/01/06	Initial shares adjusted for the 10% dividend	11,000
04/01/06	Shares issued adjusted for the 10% dividend	4,400
09/01/06	Shares of treasury stock repurchased (no adjustment)	–3,000

Step 2: Compute the weighted average number of post-stock dividend shares:

Initial shares	(11,000)(12 months outstanding)	132,000
Issued shares	(4,400)(9 months outstanding)	39,600
Retired treasury shares	(−3,000)(4 months retired)	−12,000
Total share-month		159,600
Average shares	159,600 / 12	13,300

Step 3: Compute basic EPS:

$$\text{basic EPS} = \frac{\text{net income} - \text{pref div}}{\text{wt. avg. shares of common}} = \frac{\$100,000 - \$50,000}{13,300} = \$3.76$$

Things to know about the weighted average shares outstanding:

- The weighting system is days outstanding divided by the number of days in a year, but on the exam the monthly approximation method will probably be used.
- Shares issued enter into the computation from the date of issuance.
- Reacquired shares are excluded from the computation from the date of reacquisition.
- Previously reported EPS data is restated to reflect stock splits and dividends.
- Shares sold or issued in a purchase of assets are included from the date of issuance.

Example: Weighted average shares and basic EPS

Johnson Company has net income of $10,000 and paid $1,000 cash dividends to its preferred shareholders and $1,750 cash dividends to its common shareholders. At the beginning of the year, there were 10,000 shares of common stock outstanding. 2,000 new shares were issued on July 1. Assuming a simple capital structure, what is Johnson's basic EPS?

Answer:

Calculate Johnson's weighted average number of shares.

Shares outstanding all year = 10,000(12) = 120,000
Shares outstanding 1/2 year = 2,000(6) = 12,000
Weighted average shares = 132,000 / 12 = 11,000 shares

$$\text{Basic EPS} = \frac{\text{net income} - \text{pref div}}{\text{wt. avg. shares of common}} = \frac{\$10,000 - \$1,000}{11,000} = \$0.82$$

Professor's Note: Remember, the payment of a (cash) common stock dividend is not considered in the calculation of EPS.

LOS 39.c: Determine the effect of stock dividends and stock splits on a company's weighted average number of shares outstanding.

A stock dividend is the distribution of additional shares to each shareholder in an amount proportional to their current number of shares. If a 10% stock dividend is paid, the holder of 100 shares of stock would receive 10 additional shares.

A stock split refers to the division of each "old" share into a specific number of "new" (post-split) shares. The holder of 100 shares will have 200 shares after a 2-for-1 split or 150 shares after a 3-for-2 split.

The important thing to remember is that each shareholder's proportional ownership in the company is unchanged by either of these events. Each shareholder has more shares but the same percentage of the total shares outstanding.

The weighted average number of common shares is the number of shares outstanding during the year weighted by the portion of the year they were outstanding.

- In computing weighted average number of shares, stock dividends and stock splits are considered to be changes in the number of common shares outstanding, *not* changes in the ownership of earnings. Stock dividends and splits do not change an owner's proportionate claim on the firm's earnings.
- A stock split or dividend is applied to all shares issued prior to the split and to the beginning of period weighted average shares. The split or dividend is *not* applied to any shares that are issued or repurchased after the dividend or split date. One way to keep this clear is to think about shares before the split or stock dividend as "old" shares and shares issued or repurchased after the split or stock dividend date as "new" shares. Since end-of-period shares for calculation of EPS are "new" shares, the retroactive adjustment of all share numbers prior to the split or stock dividend date is translating numbers of "old" shares into their equivalent number of "new" shares.

LOS 39.d: Distinguish between dilutive and antidilutive securities and calculate a **company's basic** and diluted EPS in a complex capital structure, and describe and determine the effects **of convertible** securities, options and warrants on a company's EPS.

Before calculating EPS you need to understand the following terms:

- **Dilutive securities** are stock options, warrants, convertible debt, or convertible preferred stock that would *decrease EPS* if exercised or converted to common stock.
- **Antidilutive securities** are securities that would *increase EPS* if exercised or converted to common stock.

The Effects of Convertible Securities, Options, and Warrants on a Company's EPS

The numerator of the basic EPS equation contains income available to common shareholders (net income less preferred dividends). In the case of dilutive EPS, if there are dilutive securities (e.g., convertible preferred stock, convertible bonds, or warrants) that will cause the weighted average common shares to change, then the numerator must be adjusted for the following:

- If convertible preferred stock is dilutive (meaning EPS will fall if stock is converted), the convertible preferred dividends must be added back to the previously calculated income from continuing operations less preferred dividends.
- If convertible bonds are dilutive, then the bonds' after-tax interest expense would not be considered as an interest expense for diluted EPS. Hence, interest expense multiplied by $(1 - t)$ must be added back to the numerator.

The denominator contains the number of shares of common stock issued, weighted by the days that the shares have been outstanding. A share outstanding all year is counted as one share. But a share outstanding for only a third of a year is counted as a third of a share.

The basic EPS denominator is the weighted average number of shares. When considering dilutive securities, the denominator is the basic EPS denominator adjusted for the equivalent number of common shares created by the conversion of all outstanding dilutive securities (convertible bonds, convertible preferred shares, warrants, and options). If a dilutive security was issued during the year, the increase in the weighted average number of shares for diluted EPS is based on only the portion of the year the dilutive security was outstanding.

Dilutive stock options and/or warrants increase the number of common shares outstanding in the denominator for diluted EPS. There is no adjustment to net income in the numerator.

- Stock options and warrants are dilutive only when their exercise price is less than the average market price of the stock over the year.
- Use the *treasury stock method* (discussion follows) to calculate the adjustment to the number of shares in the denominator.
- If there are restrictions on the proceeds received when warrants are exercised (e.g., must be used to retire debt), then dilutive EPS calculations must reflect the results of those agreements.

The Treasury Stock Method

- The treasury stock method assumes that the hypothetical funds received by the company from the exercise of the options are used to purchase shares of the company's common stock in the market at the average market price.
- The treasury stock method reduces the total increase in shares created from the hypothetical exercise of the options into common stock.
- The net increase in the number of shares outstanding (the adjustment to the denominator) will be the number of shares created by exercising the options less the number of shares repurchased with the proceeds of exercise.

The **diluted EPS equation** (assuming convertible securities are dilutive) is:

$$\text{diluted EPS} = \frac{\text{adjusted income available for common shares}}{\text{weighted-average common and potential common shares outstanding}}$$

where adjusted income available for common shares is:

$$
\begin{array}{l}
\quad \text{Net income} - \text{preferred dividends} \\
+ \ \text{Dividends on convertible preferred stock} \\
+ \ \text{After-tax interest on convertible debt} \\
\hline
\quad \text{Adjusted income available for common shares}
\end{array}
$$

Therefore, diluted EPS is:

$$\text{diluted EPS} = \frac{\left[\text{net income} - \dfrac{\text{preferred}}{\text{dividends}}\right] + \left[\begin{array}{c}\text{convertible}\\\text{preferred}\\\text{dividends}\end{array}\right] + \left(\begin{array}{c}\text{convertible}\\\text{debt}\\\text{interest}\end{array}\right)(1-t)}{\left(\begin{array}{c}\text{weighted}\\\text{average}\\\text{shares}\end{array}\right) + \left(\begin{array}{c}\text{shares from}\\\text{conversion of}\\\text{conv. pfd. shares}\end{array}\right) + \left(\begin{array}{c}\text{shares from}\\\text{conversion of}\\\text{conv. debt}\end{array}\right) + \left(\begin{array}{c}\text{shares}\\\text{issuable from}\\\text{stock options}\end{array}\right)}$$

Remember, each potentially dilutive security must be examined separately to determine if it is actually dilutive (would reduce EPS if converted to common stock). The effect of conversion to common is only included in the calculation of diluted EPS for a given security if it is in fact dilutive.

Sometimes in an acquisition there will be a provision that the shareholders of the acquired company will receive additional shares of the acquiring firm's stock if certain performance targets are met. These *contingent shares* should be included in the calculation of diluted EPS if the target has been met as of the end of the reporting period.

Basic and Diluted EPS in a Complex Capital Structure

Example 1: EPS with convertible debt

During 2006, ZZZ Corp. reported net income of $115,600 and had 200,000 shares of common stock outstanding for the entire year. ZZZ also had 1,000 shares of 10%, par $100 preferred stock outstanding during 2006. During 2005, ZZZ issued 600, $1,000 par, 7% bonds for $600,000 (issued at par). Each of these bonds is convertible to 100 shares of common stock. The tax rate is 40%. Compute the 2006 basic and diluted EPS.

Answer:

Step 1:   Compute 2006 basic EPS:

$$\text{basic EPS} = \frac{\$115,600 - \$10,000}{200,000} = \$0.53$$

Step 2:   Calculate diluted EPS:

- Compute the increase in common stock outstanding if the convertible debt is converted to common stock at the beginning of 2006:

  shares issuable for debt conversion = (600)(100) = 60,000 shares

- If the convertible debt is considered converted to common stock at the beginning of 2006, then there would be no interest expense related to the convertible debt. Therefore, it is necessary to increase ZZZ's after-tax net income for the after-tax effect of the decrease in interest expense:

  increase in income = [(600)($1,000)(0.07)] (1 − 0.40) = $25,200

- Compute diluted EPS as if the convertible debt were common stock:

$$\text{diluted EPS} = \frac{\text{net inc} - \text{pref div} + \text{convert int } (1-t)}{\text{wt. avg. shares} + \text{convertible debt shares}}$$

$$\text{diluted EPS} = \frac{\$115,600 - \$10,000 + \$25,200}{200,000 + 60,000} = \$0.50$$

- Check to make sure that *diluted EPS is less than basic EPS*. [$0.50 < $0.53]. If diluted EPS is more than the basic EPS, the convertible bonds are *antidilutive* and should not be treated as common stock in computing diluted EPS.

A quick way to determine whether the convertible debt is antidilutive is to calculate its per share impact by:

$$\frac{\text{convertible debt interest } (1-t)}{\text{convertible debt shares}}$$

If this per share amount is greater than basic EPS, the convertible debt is antidilutive and the effects of conversion should not be included when calculating diluted EPS.

If this per share amount is less than basic EPS, the convertible debt is dilutive and the effects of conversion should be included in the calculation of diluted EPS.

For ZZZ:

$$\frac{\$25,200}{60,000} = \$0.42$$

The company's basic EPS is $0.53, so the convertible debt is dilutive and the effects of conversion should be included in the calculation of diluted EPS.

Example 2: EPS with convertible preferred stock

During 2006, ZZZ reported net income of $115,600 and had 200,000 shares of common stock and 1,000 shares of preferred stock outstanding for the entire year. ZZZ's 10%, $100 par value preferred-stock shares are each *convertible* into 40 shares of common stock. The tax rate is 40%. Compute basic and diluted EPS.

Answer:

Step 1:   Calculate 2006 basic EPS:

$$\text{basic EPS} = \frac{\$115,600 - \$10,000}{200,000} = \$0.53$$

Step 2:   Calculate diluted EPS:

- Compute the increase in common stock outstanding if the preferred stock is converted to common stock at the beginning of 2006: (1,000)(40) = 40,000 shares.
- If the convertible preferred stock were converted to common stock, there would be no preferred dividends paid. Therefore, you should add back the convertible preferred dividends that had previously been subtracted out.
- Compute diluted EPS as if the convertible preferred stock were converted into common stock:

$$\text{diluted EPS} = \frac{\text{net inc} - \text{pref div} + \text{convert pref dividends}}{\text{wt. avg. shares} + \text{convert pref common shares}}$$

$$\text{diluted EPS} = \frac{\$115,600 - \$10,000 + \$10,000}{200,000 + 40,000} = \$0.48$$

- Check to see if diluted EPS is less than basic EPS ($0.48 < $0.53). If the answer is yes, the preferred stock is dilutive and must be included in diluted EPS as computed above. If the answer is no, the preferred stock is antidilutive and conversion effects are not included in diluted EPS.

Example 3: EPS with stock options

During 2006, ZZZ reported net income of $115,600 and had 200,000 shares of common stock outstanding for the entire year. ZZZ also had 1,000 shares of 10%, par $100 preferred stock outstanding during 2006. ZZZ has 10,000 stock options (or warrants) outstanding the entire year. Each option allows its holder to purchase 1 share of common stock at $15 per share. The average market price of ZZZ's common stock during 2006 is $20 per share. Compute the diluted EPS.

Answer:

Number of common shares created if the options are exercised:	10,000 shares
Cash inflow if the options are exercised ($15/share)(10,000):	$150,000
Number of shares that can be purchased with these funds is: $150,000 / $20	7,500 shares
Net increase in common shares outstanding from the exercise of the stock options	2,500 shares

$$\text{diluted EPS} = \frac{\$115{,}600 - \$10{,}000}{200{,}000 + 2{,}500} = \$0.52$$

Professor's Note: A quick way to calculate the net increase in common shares from the potential exercise of stock options or warrants when the exercise price is less than the average market price is:

$$\left[\frac{AMP - EP}{AMP}\right] \times N$$

where :
AMP = average market price over the year
EP   = exercise price of the options or warrants
N   = number of common shares that the options or warrants can be converted into

$$\textit{For ZZZ: } \frac{\$20 - \$15}{\$20} \times 10{,}000 \textit{ shares} = 2{,}500 \textit{ shares}$$

Example 4: EPS with convertible bonds, convertible preferred, and options

During 2006, ZZZ reported net income of $115,600 and had 200,000 shares of common stock outstanding for the entire year. ZZZ had 1,000 shares of 10%, $100 par convertible preferred convertible into 40 shares each outstanding for the entire year. ZZZ also had 600, 7%, $1,000 par value convertible bonds, convertible into 100 shares each outstanding for the entire year. Finally, ZZZ had 10,000 stock options outstanding during the year. Each option is convertible into one share of stock at $15 per share. The average market price of the stock for the year was $20. What are ZZZ's basic and diluted EPS? (Assume a 40% tax rate.)

Answer:

Step 1:   From Examples 1, 2, and 3, we know that the convertible preferred stock, convertible bonds, and stock options are all dilutive. Recall that basic EPS was calculated as:

$$\text{basic EPS} = \frac{\$115{,}600 - \$10{,}000}{200{,}000} = \$0.53$$

Step 2: Review the number of shares created by converting the convertible securities and options (the denominator):

Converting the convertible preferred shares	40,000 shares
Converting the convertible bonds	60,000 shares
Exercising the options	2,500 shares

Step 3: Review the adjustments to net income (the numerator):

Converting the convertible preferred shares	$10,000
Converting the convertible bonds	$25,200
Exercising the options	$0

Step 4: Compute ZZZ's diluted EPS:

$$\text{diluted EPS} = \frac{\$115,600 - 10,000 + 10,000 + 25,200}{200,000 + 40,000 + 60,000 + 2,500} = \$0.47$$

Example 5: Treasury stock method

Baxter Company has 5,000 shares outstanding all year. Baxter had 2,000 outstanding warrants all year, convertible into one share each at $20 per share. The year-end price of Baxter stock was $40, and the average stock price was $30. If Baxter had net income of $10,000 of the year, what is Baxter's basic and diluted EPS?

Answer:

Calculate the effect of the warrants using the treasury stock method.

$$\left[\frac{\$30 - \$20}{\$30} \right] \times 2,000 \text{ shares} = 667 \text{ shares}$$

Basic EPS = $10,000 / 5,000 shares = $2 per share
Diluted EPS = $10,000 / (5,000 + 667 shares) = $1.76 per share

LOS 39.e: Compare and contrast the requirements for EPS reporting in simple versus complex capital structures.

With a **simple capital structure**, only basic EPS is reported. If a firm has a **complex capital structure**, it must report both basic EPS and diluted EPS. If the firm is reporting discontinued operations, extraordinary items, or cumulative effects of an accounting change (all reported below the line net of tax), per-share values of these items must be reported as well. The following shows the format for a company with a complex capital structure that reports a loss from discontinued operations.

Basic earnings per share	
Income before discontinued operations	$2.40
Discontinued operations	0.35
Net income	$2.05

Diluted earnings per share	
Income before discontinued operations	$1.95
Discontinued operations	0.28
Net income	$1.67

KEY CONCEPTS

1. A simple capital structure is one that contains no potentially dilutive securities, while a complex capital structure contains potentially dilutive securities such as options, warrants, or convertible securities.

2. The basic EPS calculation (the only EPS for firms with a simple capital structure) is:

$$\text{basic EPS} = \frac{\text{net income} - \text{preferred dividends}}{\text{weighted average number of common shares outstanding}}$$

3. Calculating the weighted average number of common shares outstanding:
   - Stock splits and dividends result in the additional shares being considered outstanding from the beginning of the year for the purpose of this computation.
   - Shares issued enter into the computation from the date of issuance.
   - Reacquired shares are excluded from the computation from the date of reacquisition.
   - Shares sold or issued in a purchase of assets are included from the date of issuance.

4. Dilutive securities are stock options, warrants, convertible debt, or convertible preferred stock that decrease EPS if exercised or converted to common stock. Antidilutive securities are those that would increase EPS if exercised or converted to common stock.

5. Calculating diluted EPS with a complex capital structure:

$$\text{diluted EPS} = \frac{\left[\text{net income} - \dfrac{\text{preferred}}{\text{dividends}}\right] + \left[\begin{array}{c}\text{convertible}\\\text{preferred}\\\text{dividends}\end{array}\right] + \left(\begin{array}{c}\text{convertible}\\\text{debt}\\\text{interest}\end{array}\right)(1-t)}{\left(\begin{array}{c}\text{weighted}\\\text{average}\\\text{shares}\end{array}\right) + \left(\begin{array}{c}\text{shares from}\\\text{conversion of}\\\text{conv. pfd. shares}\end{array}\right) + \left(\begin{array}{c}\text{shares from}\\\text{conversion of}\\\text{conv. debt}\end{array}\right) + \left(\begin{array}{c}\text{shares}\\\text{issuable from}\\\text{stock options}\end{array}\right)}$$

6. Warrants and options are potentially dilutive; in the diluted EPS calculation, the number of shares is adjusted by adding $\dfrac{\text{AMP} - \text{EP}}{\text{AMP}} \times N$ shares whenever AMP > EP.

7. A company with a complex capital structure must report both basic and diluted EPS.

CONCEPT CHECKERS: DILUTIVE SECURITIES AND EARNINGS PER SHARE

1. Which of the following securities would NOT be found in a simple capital structure?
    A. 7%, $100 par value nonconvertible preferred.
    B. 8%, $1,000 par value callable mortgage bond.
    C. 3%, $100 par value convertible preferred.
    D. 6%, $5,000 par value general obligation bond.

2. Which of the following actions requires an adjustment to the number of shares outstanding at the beginning of the year?
    A. New issuance of common stock for cash.
    B. Stock repurchases.
    C. Issuance of common stock in a purchase of assets.
    D. A stock split.

3. Previously reported earnings per share calculations must be restated for which of the following events?
    A. Conversion of a bond into common stock.
    B. A stock split.
    C. Share repurchase.
    D. Issuance of new common shares.

4. At the beginning of this year, Evans Corporation had 400,000 shares of common stock outstanding. Evans paid a 10% stock dividend on March 31 of this year. Evans issued 90,000 new common shares on June 30 of this year and repurchased 12,000 shares on December 1. The number of shares Evans should use in computing basic EPS at the end of the year is:
    A. 475,000.
    B. 476,000.
    C. 484,000.
    D. 490,500.

5. The Hall Corporation had 100,000 shares of common stock outstanding at the beginning of the year. Hall issued 30,000 shares of common on May 1. On July 1, the company issued a 10% stock dividend. On September 1, Hall issued 1,000, 10% bonds, each convertible into 21 shares of stock. What is the weighted average number of shares to be used in computing basic and diluted EPS, assuming the convertible bonds are dilutive?

	Basic	Dilutive
A.	130,000	132,000
B.	132,000	139,000
C.	132,000	146,000
D.	139,000	146,000

Use the following data to answer Questions 6 through 8.

An analyst gathered the following information about a company:

*   Net income was $800,000 for the year.
*   At the beginning of the year, there were 70,000 common shares outstanding.
*   There are 30,000 shares of 8%, $100 par cumulative nonconvertible preferred outstanding.
*   In the past year, the company has had the following common stock transactions:
    *   March 30: declared a 10% stock dividend.
    *   March 31: issued 10,000 shares for cash.

©2007 Schweser

6. How many common shares should be used in computing the company's EPS?
    A. 70,000.
    B. 82,750.
    C. 84,500.
    D. 85,250.

7. The company's capital structure would be classified as:
    A. simple.
    B. complex.
    C. one sided.
    D. limited.

8. What is the company's EPS?
    A. $4.98.
    B. $6.63.
    C. $9.47.
    D. $11.43.

9. Given the following information, how many shares should be used in computing diluted EPS?
    •   300,000 shares outstanding.
    •   100,000 warrants exercisable at $50 per share.
    •   Average share price is $55.
    •   Ending share price is $60.
    A. 9,091.
    B. 90,909.
    C. 309,091.
    D. 390,909.

Use the following data to answer Questions 10 and 11.

An analyst gathered the following information about a company:

•   2,500,000 shares outstanding at the beginning of the year.
•   2,000,000 weighted average number of shares outstanding for the year.
• $40 average stock price for the period.
• $50 ending stock price.
•   1,000,000 warrants outstanding exercisable at $30 per share.
•   100,000, 7%, $1,000 par value convertible bonds (conversion ratio 15 to 1) issued two years ago.
• $5,000,000 net after tax income for the year.
•   30% tax rate.

10. Basic EPS is:
    A. $2.10.
    B. $2.22.
    C. $2.50.
    D. $2.64.

11. Diluted EPS is:
    A. $1.33.
    B. $2.22.
    C. $2.33.
    D. $3.64.

12. An analyst gathered the following information about a company:
    - 100,000 common shares outstanding all year.
    - Earnings of $125,000.
    - 1,000, 7% $1,000 par bonds convertible into 40 shares each outstanding all year.
    - The tax rate is 40%.

    What is the company's diluted EPS?
    A. $1.09.
    B. $1.19.
    C. $1.23.
    D. $1.25.

13. Antidilutive common stock equivalents should:
    A. be used in calculating basic EPS per share but not diluted EPS.
    B. be used in calculating diluted EPS per share but not basic EPS.
    C. be used in calculating basic EPS only.
    D. not be used in calculating diluted EPS.

14. An analyst gathered the following information about a company:
    - 100,000 common shares outstanding from the beginning of the year.
    - Earnings of $125,000.
    - 1,000, 7% $1,000 par bonds convertible into 25 shares each outstanding as of the beginning of the year.
    - The tax rate is 40%.

    What is the company's diluted EPS?
    A. $1.22.
    B. $1.25.
    C. $1.34.
    D. $1.42.

15. An analyst gathered the following information about a company:
    - 50,000 common shares outstanding from the beginning of the year.
    - Warrants outstanding all year on 50,000 shares, exercisable at $20 per share.
    - Stock is selling at year end for $15.
    - The average price of the company's stock for the year was $25.

    How many shares should be used in calculating the company's diluted EPS?
    A. 10,000.
    B. 50,000.
    C. 60,000.
    D. 90,000.

16. An analyst has gathered the following information about a company:
   - 50,000 common shares outstanding from the beginning of the year.
   - Warrants outstanding all year on 50,000 shares, exercisable at $20 per share.
   - Stock is selling at year end for $25.
   - The average price of the company's stock for the year was $15.

   How many shares should be used in calculating the company's diluted EPS?
   A. 16,667.
   B. 33,333.
   C. 50,000.
   D. 66,667.

COMPREHENSIVE PROBLEMS: DILUTIVE SECURITIES AND EARNINGS PER SHARE

1. The following is the share information for Alcorp Products last year:

1/1	2,400,000 common shares outstanding
4/1	400,000 new shares issued
6/1	3-for-2 stock split
10/1	300,000 shares repurchased

   What is the weighted average number of common shares for the year?

2. The capital structure of Beta Corp. for the past year is as follows:

2,500,000	shares common stock
1,000,000	shares 5% preferred stock—par value $30
500,000	4% convertible preferred—par value $50, convertible into 500,000 sh. common
$10,000,000	face value 3.5% bond maturing in 10 years convertible to common stock at 35 sh. per $1,000 face value
100,000	warrants for 5 shares each with an exercise price of $22/sh.

   - The firm's marginal tax rate is 35%, and its average tax rate is 32%.
   - The firm's common stock was valued at $20/sh at year end and had an average price of $23 over the year.
   - The firm's operating earnings were $7,200,000, and it had no interest charges other than the outstanding bond.
   - The common stock pays a dividend of $0.40 per share.

   A. What are basic earnings per share?

   B. What are diluted earnings per share?

ANSWERS – CONCEPT CHECKERS: DILUTIVE SECURITIES AND EARNINGS PER SHARE

1. C The convertible preferred is potentially dilutive and therefore would not be found in a simple capital structure.

2. D A stock split is treated as if it were done at the beginning of the accounting period.

3. B Previously reported EPS must be restated when a stock split occurs so that comparisons of EPS over time are not misleading.

4. C Remember that the effects of stock dividends are applied retroactively to the beginning of the year.

$$\frac{(440,000 \times 12) + (90,000 \times 6) - (12,000 \times 1)}{12} = 484,000$$

5. B The new stock is weighted by 8 / 12. The bonds are weighted by 4 / 12 and are not affected by the stock dividend.

{[100,000 × (12 / 12)] + [30,000 × (8 / 12)]} × 1.10 = 132,000

132,000 + [21,000 × (4 / 12)] = 139,000

6. C 70,000 × 1.1 = 77,000

77,000 + [10,000 × (9 / 12)] = 84,500

7. A Because there are no potentially dilutive securities, the company has a simple capital structure.

8. B Don't forget to subtract the preferred stock dividends!

$$\frac{800,000 - 240,000}{84,500} = \$6.63$$

9. C Since the exercise price of the warrants is less than the average share price, the warrants are dilutive. Using the treasury stock method to determine the denominator impact:

$$\frac{\$55 - \$50}{\$55} \times 100,000 \text{ shares} = 9,091 \text{ shares}$$

Thus, the denominator will increase by 9,091 shares to 309,091 shares. The question asks for the total, not just the impact of the warrants.

10. C $5,000,000 / 2,000,000 = $2.50

11. **B**   The warrants are dilutive because the exercise price is less than the average stock price. Next, check if the convertible bonds are dilutive.

numerator impact = [(100,000 × 1,000 × 0.07 × (1 – 0.3)] = $4,900,000

denominator impact = (100,000 × 15) = 1,500,000

per share impact = $4,900,000 / $1,500,000 = $3.27

Since this is greater than the basic EPS calculated in the previous question, the bonds are antidilutive. Thus, diluted EPS includes only the warrants.

$$\frac{\$40 - \$30}{\$40} \times 1,000,000 \text{ shares} = 250,000 \text{ shares}$$

Thus, the denominator will increase by 250,000 shares to 2,250,000 shares

Diluted EPS = $5,000,000 / 2,250,000 = $2.22

12. **B**   First calculate basic EPS = 125,000 / 100,000 = $1.25. Then check to see if the bonds are dilutive.

Numerator impact = [(1,000 × 1,000 × 0.07 × (1.0 – 0.40)] = $42,000

Denominator impact = (1,000 × 40) = 40,000 shares.

$$\frac{\$42,000}{40,000} = \$1.05$$

Since this is less than basic EPS, the bonds are dilutive and diluted EPS is $1.19 = $\frac{\$125,000 + \$42,000}{100,000 + 40,000}$.

13. **D**   Antidilutive common stock equivalents should not be used in calculating either basic or diluted EPS.

14. **B**   First, calculate basic EPS = $\frac{125,000}{100,000} = \$1.25$. Next, check if the convertible bonds are dilutive:

numerator impact = (1,000 × 1,000 × 0.07) × (1 – 0.4) = $42,000

denominator impact = (1,000 × 25) = 25,000 shares

$$\text{per share impact} = \frac{\$42,000}{25,000 \text{ shares}} = \$1.68$$

Since $1.68 is greater than the basic EPS of $1.25, the bonds are antidilutive. Thus, diluted EPS = basic EPS = $1.25.

15. **C**   Since the exercise price of the warrants is less than the average share price, the warrants are dilutive.

$$\left[\frac{\$25 - \$20}{\$25} \right] \times 50,000 \text{ shares} = 10,000 \text{ shares}$$

Thus, the denominator will increase by 10,000 shares to 60,000 shares.

16. **C**   The warrants in this case are antidilutive. The average price per share of $15 < strike price $20. (The year-end price per share is not used.) Don't use the treasury stock method. The denominator consists of only the common stock.

ANSWERS – COMPREHENSIVE PROBLEMS: DILUTIVE SECURITIES AND EARNINGS PER SHARE

1. First adjust for the stock split and weight by months outstanding:

$$
\begin{array}{rcccccccl}
 & 2,400,000 & \times & 3/2 & \times & 12 & = & 43,200,000 \\
+ & 400,000 & \times & 3/2 & \times & 9 & = & 5,400,000 \\
- & 300,000 & & & \times & 3 & = & -900,000 \\
\hline
 & & & & & & = & 47,700,000
\end{array}
$$

Then divide by 12: $\dfrac{47,700,000}{12} = 3,975,000.$

2. Since EBIT is $7,200,000 and interest on the bond is $10,000,000 (0.035) = $350,000, pre-tax earnings are $7,200,000 − $350,000 = $6,850,000. With an average tax rate of 32%, net income is 6,850,000 (1 − 0.32) = $4,658,000.

The dividends on the two preferred stocks are:

1,000,000 × $30 × 0.05 = $1,500,000 and 500,000 × $50 × 0.04 = $1,000,000

Net income available to common is $4,658,000 − $1,500,000 − $1,000,000 = $2,158,000.

$$\text{basic EPS} = \frac{\$2,158,000}{2,500,000} = \$0.86$$

Dividing the total dividends on the convertible preferred by the number of common shares if converted gives us

$\dfrac{\$1,000,000}{500,000} = \$2 \text{ sh} > \$0.86$. The convertible preferred is antidilutive.

The after-tax bond interest is $10,000,000 (0.035) (1 − 0.35) = $227,500, and the number of shares if converted is 350,000 (note the use of the *marginal* tax rate).

$\dfrac{\$227,500}{350,000} = \$0.65 < \$0.86$, so the convertible bonds are dilutive.

The exercise price of the warrants is $22, which is less than the average price of $23, and the number of new shares using the treasury stock method is $\dfrac{23-22}{23}(100,000)(5) = 21,739$ sh.

$$\text{diluted EPS} = \frac{\$2,158,000 + \$227,500}{2,500,000 + 350,000 + 21,739} = \$0.83$$

ANALYSIS OF INVENTORIES

EXAM FOCUS

This topic review discusses specific analytical processes for inventory. The complication in analyzing inventory is that firms can use three different methods to account for inventory—FIFO, LIFO, and average cost. You should memorize the basic inventory relationship, EI = BI + P − COGS, and be able to algebraically convert this equation to solve for its other components (i.e., solve for COGS given the other three). You should also know how to calculate inventory balances and COGS using all three methods and how to convert inventory or COGS data derived from FIFO into LIFO and from LIFO into FIFO. Finally, you should know and be able to explain why LIFO accounting produces a better measure of COGS and why FIFO accounting produces a better measure of inventory value.

INVENTORY ACCOUNTING

The choice of accounting method used to account for inventory affects the firm's income statement, balance sheet, and related financial ratios. More importantly, the choice of inventory accounting method affects cash flow because taxes paid by the firm are affected by the choice of inventory method. Unlike depreciation methods, inventory accounting methods must be the same for taxes as for financial reporting.

U.S. Generally Accepted Accounting Principles (GAAP) require inventory valuation on the basis of *lower of cost or market* (LCM). If replacement cost is rising, the gains in the value of inventory are ignored, and the inventory is valued at cost. However, losses in the value of inventory due to obsolescence, deterioration, etc., are recognized, and inventory is written down to its new market value. Remember, LCM is applied regardless of the inventory costing method used.

In general, *cost* represents reasonable and necessary costs to get the asset in place and ready to use.

- Merchandise inventories include costs of purchasing, transportation, receiving, inspecting, etc.
- Manufactured inventories include costs of direct materials, direct labor, and manufacturing overhead (i.e., all other indirect costs).

A basic inventory formula relates the beginning balance, purchases, and cost of goods sold (COGS) to the ending balance. Memorize and understand the relationships in the following equation:

ending inventory = beginning inventory + purchases − COGS

This equation is rearranged for several purposes, such as:

purchases = ending inventory − beginning inventory + COGS

or COGS = purchases + beginning inventory − ending inventory

or COGS + ending inventory = beginning inventory + purchases

LOS 40.a: Compute ending inventory balances and cost of goods sold using the LIFO, FIFO, and average cost methods to account for product inventory and explain the relationship among and the usefulness of inventory and cost of goods sold data provided by the LIFO, FIFO, and average cost methods when prices are 1) stable or 2) changing.

Three methods of inventory accounting are:

First In, First Out (FIFO):

- The cost of inventory first acquired (beginning inventory and early purchases) is assigned to the cost of goods sold for the period.
- The cost of the most recent purchases is assigned to ending inventory.

Last In, First Out (LIFO):

- The cost of inventory most recently purchased is assigned to the cost of goods sold for the period.
- The costs of beginning inventory and earlier purchases go to ending inventory.
- Note that in the U.S., companies using LIFO for tax purposes must also use LIFO in their financial statements.

Average cost:

Under the average cost method, cost per unit is calculated by dividing cost of goods available by total units available. This average cost is used to determine both cost of goods sold and ending inventory.

Figure 1: Inventory Method Comparison

Method	Assumption	Cost of goods sold consists of...	Ending inventory consists of...
FIFO	The items first purchased are the first to be sold.	first purchased	most recent purchases
LIFO	The items last purchased are the first to be sold.	last purchased	earliest purchases
Weighted average cost	Items sold are a mix of purchases.	average cost of all items	average cost of all items

Example: Inventory costing

Use the inventory data in Figure 2 to calculate the cost of goods sold and ending inventory under each of the three methods.

Figure 2: Inventory Data

January 1 (beginning inventory)	2 units @ $2 per unit =	$4
January 7 purchase	3 units @ $3 per unit =	9
January 19 purchase	5 units @ $5 per unit =	25
Cost of goods available	10 units	$38
Units sold during January		7 units

Answer:

FIFO cost of goods sold (value the seven units sold at unit cost of first units purchased). Start with the earliest units purchased and work down as illustrated in Figure 3.

Figure 3: FIFO COGS Calculation

From beginning inventory	2 units @ $2 per unit =	$4
From first purchase	3 units @ $3 per unit =	9
From second purchase	2 units @ $5 per unit =	10
FIFO cost of goods sold	7 units	$23
Ending inventory	3 units @$5 =	$15

LIFO cost of goods sold (value the seven units sold at unit cost of last units purchased). Start with the most recently purchased units and work up as illustrated in Figure 4.

Figure 4: LIFO COGS Calculation

From second purchase	5 units @ $5 per unit	$25
From first purchase	2 units @ $3 per unit	6
LIFO cost of goods sold	7 units	$31
Ending inventory	2@$2 + 1@$3	$7

Average cost of goods sold (value the seven units sold at the average unit cost of goods available).

Figure 5: Weighted Average COGS Calculation

Average unit cost	$38 / 10	$3.80 per unit
Weighted average cost of goods sold	7 units @ $3.80 per unit	$26.60
Ending inventory	3 units @ $3.80 per unit	$11.40

Figure 6: Summary

Inventory system	COGS	Ending Inventory
FIFO Costing	$23.00	$15.00
LIFO Costing	$31.00	$7.00
Average Costing	$26.60	$11.40

Note that prices and inventory levels were rising over the period and that the costs of purchases during the period are the same for all costing methods.

The Relationship Between LIFO and FIFO

During periods of rising prices, LIFO cost of goods sold is greater than FIFO cost of goods sold. Therefore, LIFO net income will be less than FIFO net income. Consistently, LIFO inventory is less than FIFO inventory because items remaining in inventory are taken to be those acquired earlier at lower prices. Average cost methods yield COGS, net income, and balance sheet inventory values between the other two.

This should make intuitive sense because during periods of rising prices, the last units purchased are more expensive. Under LIFO, the last in (more costly) is the first out (to cost of goods sold). This results in LIFO profitability ratios being smaller than under FIFO. When prices are rising, LIFO inventory is smaller than under FIFO, the firm's current ratio will be lower and inventory turnover will be higher.

If financial statements are compared for firms using different cost flow assumptions, then adjustments have to be made to achieve comparability. Consider the following diagram in Figure 7 to help you visualize the FIFO-LIFO difference during periods of *rising prices* and growing inventory levels. Remember, it's not that older or newer inventory items are being sold. The difference is only in the costs we assign to the units sold and those remaining in inventory.

Figure 7: LIFO and FIFO Diagram—Rising Prices and Growing Inventory Balances

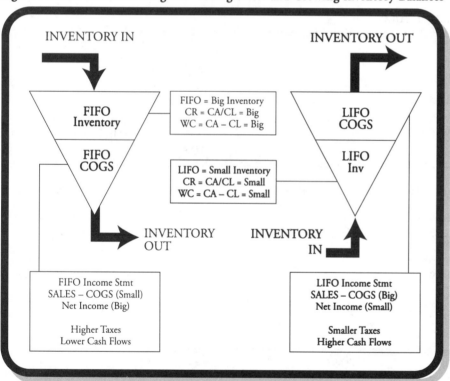

During periods of rising prices, LIFO results in higher COGS, lower net income, and lower inventory levels. This decreases the current ratio (CA / CL) and increases inventory turnover (COGS / average inventory). If prices do not change, then the different inventory valuation methods do not affect the financial statements.

Professor's Note: For the exam, you should understand that if prices are decreasing (deflation), then the opposite relationships between FIFO and LIFO hold. Also, when you are finished with this review, please take the time to look at these graphs and relationships again to solidify the concepts in your mind.

By decreasing inventory to levels below normal levels, thus dipping into the old "cheap" inventory, a firm's management can increase profits for the period under LIFO. When this strategy is employed, COGS under LIFO will be lower and profits higher than if more inventory were purchased and inventory levels not drawn down. This is called a **LIFO liquidation**.

If there is LIFO liquidation (e.g., the firm sells more items than it purchased during the period), LIFO, COGS and, hence, income are distorted. COGS does not reflect current costs.

Most U.S. firms use LIFO on their statements because the Internal Revenue Code states that if firms use LIFO on their tax returns, they must use LIFO on their general-purpose statements. (This is an exception to the general rule that firms can use different methods in computing tax and financial income.) During the last forty years of rising prices, firms have saved money by using LIFO on their tax returns, since their reported net income is lower than if they had used FIFO. This results in the peculiar situation where *lower income is associated with a higher cash flow from operations.*

Usefulness of Inventory and Cost-of-Goods-Sold Data Provided by the LIFO, FIFO, and Average Cost Methods

Professor's Note: The presumption in this section is that inventory quantities are stable or increasing.

During periods of stable prices, all three inventory valuation processes will yield the same results for inventory, COGS, and earnings. During periods of changing prices, the key point to remember is that *FIFO will provide the most useful estimate of the inventory value and LIFO will provide the most useful estimate of the cost of goods sold.* This is a crucial point.

Inventory Value

When prices are changing, FIFO inventory costing provides the best balance sheet information on the value of inventory. If prices are steadily rising, FIFO inventory is valued at the more recent purchase prices, which are higher and provide a better estimate of the replacement value of the inventory. If prices are steadily falling, FIFO inventory valuation is still preferred from a balance sheet perspective, since the value of existing inventory is based on the new, lower replacement cost.

U.S. GAAP require that inventory be valued at the lower of cost or market (LCM), where "market" is usually taken to mean replacement cost. If replacement cost is falling, the usefulness of LIFO-based carrying values for inventory is improved by applying LCM. Without LCM and with price declines, LIFO inventory values will be high compared to economic value or replacement cost. When the LCM method is also applied, units of inventory acquired earlier, at higher cost, are revalued downward, reducing the overstatement in LIFO inventory carrying values. Since inventory carrying values are not revalued upward for changes in replacement cost, the usefulness of LIFO-based inventory values is not improved by the LCM adjustment during periods of rising prices. LCM cannot be used for tax purposes if the firm is using LIFO.

Cost of Goods Sold

By the same logic applied in the previous section, LIFO provides the better measure of the cost of goods sold when prices are either rising or falling. Viewing the firm as an ongoing concern, the economic profit is best approximated by using the replacement cost of inventory items. While LIFO inventory costing may fall short of this goal, it provides a better estimate of the replacement cost of goods sold than does FIFO. If prices are falling, inventory replacement cost is falling, and the most recently acquired inventory items will be closer to replacement cost than items purchased earlier. For calculating earnings, the FIFO cost of goods sold will overstate replacement cost. The same logic holds if prices are rising. LIFO costing will produce a cost of goods sold much closer to replacement cost than FIFO costing, which will understate the replacement cost and overstate income.

FIFO, LIFO, and average cost inventory accounting will all produce the same inventory value and COGS when prices are stable. When prices are changing, the average cost method will produce values of COGS and ending inventory between those of FIFO and LIFO.

The previous discussion assumes the value for purchases is known, but this too may be affected by management choice. For example, in a manufacturing business with raw materials, work in process, and finished goods inventories, the allocation of overhead such as rent, depreciation, supervisor salaries, maintenance expenses, and utilities to various classes of inventory is subject to management discretion.

At higher production levels, less of a particular fixed cost (such as factory rent) is allocated to each unit produced. However, if more units are produced than sold, then some of the allocated overhead ends up in ending inventory. If all the units produced were sold, then all of the fixed costs would be in COGS and expensed in the current period.

Firms may choose different inventory methods for different product lines, business segments, or geographical locations. FIFO inventory accounting is the primary method outside the United States. Information about inventory accounting methods should be available in the footnotes to financial statements and information is available that allows the analyst to restate financial statements using an alternative inventory accounting method.

LOS 40.b: Analyze the financial statements of companies using different inventory accounting methods to compare and describe the effect of the different methods on cost of goods sold and inventory balances, discuss how a company's choice of inventory accounting method affects other financial items such as income, cash flow, and working capital, and compute and describe the effects of the choice of inventory method on profitability, liquidity, activity, and solvency ratios.

Often, an analyst wants to compare a company to other companies in the same industry. When two companies use different methods of accounting for inventory, one of the firms' inventories must be adjusted in order to make the comparison relevant. There are two types of conversion: LIFO to FIFO and FIFO to LIFO.

The LIFO to FIFO conversion is relatively simple because U.S. GAAP require all companies that use LIFO to also report a **LIFO reserve**, which is the difference between what ending inventory would have been under FIFO accounting and its value under LIFO.

Figure 8: LIFO Reserve

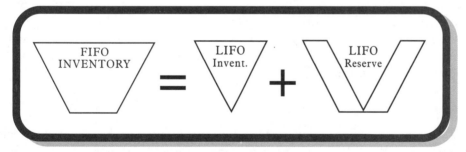

current cost of inventory (FIFO) = LIFO inventory + LIFO reserve

If you add the LIFO reserve to the LIFO inventory, you will get the FIFO inventory. An alternative expression is:

LIFO reserve = FIFO inventory – LIFO inventory

The LIFO reserve is typically shown in the footnotes to the financial statements.

To convert LIFO inventory balances to a FIFO basis, simply add the LIFO reserve to the LIFO inventory:

$Inv_F = Inv_L + LIFO$ reserve

To convert COGS from LIFO to FIFO use the formula:

$$COGS_{FIFO} = COGS_{LIFO} - \text{change in the LIFO reserve}$$

$$= COGS_{LIFO} - (\text{LIFO reserve}_{ENDING} - \text{LIFO reserve}_{BEGINNING})$$

Remember that during a period of rising prices $COGS_{FIFO}$ is too low (below replacement costs). Also the LIFO reserve is increasing when prices are rising. This increase in the LIFO reserve is exactly the difference between $COGS_{LIFO}$ and $COGS_{FIFO}$. During a period of falling prices we would still subtract the change in the LIFO reserve from $COGS_{LIFO}$ to get $COGS_{FIFO}$, but the change is a negative number and $COGS_{FIFO}$ will be the larger of the two measures.

We can derive the above relation by using the basic inventory equation:

$$COGS_{FIFO} = \text{purchases} + BEG\ INV_{FIFO} - END\ INV_{FIFO}$$

We know the relation between FIFO and LIFO inventory balances is:

$$BEG\ INV_{FIFO} = BEG\ INV_{LIFO} + \text{LIFO Reserve}_{BEG}$$

$$END\ INV_{FIFO} = END\ INV_{LIFO} + \text{LIFO Reserve}_{END}$$

Substituting we get:

$$COGS_{FIFO} = [\text{purchases} + BEG\ INV_{LIFO} - END\ INV_{LIFO}] - [\text{LIFO Reserve}_{END} - \text{LIFO Reserve}_{BEG}]$$

Which is:

$$COGS_{FIFO} = [COGS_{LIFO}] - [\text{change in LIFO reserve}], \text{ as previously shown}$$

Example: Converting from LIFO to FIFO

Sipowitz Company, which uses LIFO, reported end-of-year inventory balances of $500 in 2005 and $700 in 2006. The LIFO reserve was $200 for 2005 and $300 for 2006. COGS during 2006 was $3,000. Convert 2006 ending inventory and COGS to a FIFO basis.

Answer:

Inventory:

$$Inv_F = Inv_L + \text{LIFO reserve} = \$700 + \$300 = \$1,000$$

COGS:

$$COGS_F = COGS_L - (\text{LIFO reserve}_E - \text{LIFO reserve}_B)$$
$$= \$3,000 - (\$300 - \$200) = \$2,900$$

FIFO to LIFO conversions are typically not done for inventory, since inventory under LIFO is not a reflection of current value. However, it may be useful to consider what COGS would be under LIFO. The adjustment process is completely different than the process of converting COGS from LIFO to FIFO. There is no precise calculation; an analyst must estimate what the costs would have been under LIFO.

The estimate of COGS is equal to:

$$COGS_L = COGS_F + (BI_F \times \text{inflation rate})$$

The inflation rate should not be a general inflation rate for the economy but should be an inflation rate appropriate for the firm or industry. It can be determined two ways:

- Industry statistics.
- The increase in the LIFO reserve for another company in the same industry divided by that company's beginning inventory level converted to FIFO accounting.

An analyst can also estimate what the COGS would have been under the LIFO method for a company that uses the average cost method. The logic is that because the average cost method always reports inventory values and costs of goods sold *between* values reported under LIFO and FIFO, the adjustment for the COGS estimate should be half of the adjustment used for FIFO accounting:

$$COGS_L = COGS_W + 1/2 \times (BI_W \times \text{inflation rate})$$

where:
$COGS_W$ = the COGS under the average cost method
BI_W = the beginning inventory under the average cost method

Example: FIFO to LIFO conversion

Logan Company is in the same industry as Sipowitz Company from the previous example. Logan uses FIFO accounting and has COGS of $2,000, ending inventory of $500, and beginning inventory of $350. Estimate Logan's COGS under LIFO accounting.

Answer:

First estimate the inflation rate using data from Sipowitz. The increase in the LIFO reserve for Sipowitz is $300 – $200 = $100. The beginning inventory converted to FIFO is $500 + $200 = $700. That means the inflation rate is $100 / $700 = 14.3%.

Now the estimate of COGS can be calculated as:

$$COGS_L = COGS_F + (BI_F \times \text{inflation rate}) = \$2,000 + (\$350 \times 14.3\%) = \$2,050$$

How a Company's Choice of Inventory Accounting Method Affects Other Financial Items

Professor's Note: The presumption in this section is that prices are rising and inventory quantities are stable or increasing. The implications when inventories or prices decline will be discussed later.

In the absence of taxes, there would be no difference in cash flow between LIFO and FIFO. With taxes, however, the higher LIFO COGS causes reported income to be lower, causing taxes (a cash cost) to also be lower. This causes cash flow to be higher. The U.S. tax code requires the same method of inventory accounting to be used in both GAAP and tax accounting. The results in periods of rising prices and stable or increasing inventory quantities are shown in Figure 9.

Figure 9: LIFO and FIFO Comparison—Rising Prices and Stable or Increasing Inventories

LIFO results in...	*FIFO results in...*
higher COGS	lower COGS
lower taxes	higher taxes
lower net income (EBT and EAT)	higher net income (EBT and EAT)
lower inventory balances	higher inventory balances
lower working capital (CA – CL)	higher working capital (CA – CL)
higher cash flows (less taxes paid out)	lower cash flows (more taxes paid out)

- With rising prices, LIFO is the best choice because it increases after-tax cash flow.
- LIFO firm liquidity measures are misleading because of the understatement of working capital (inventory too low).
- The analyst must be aware that FIFO firms will show higher net income (all else the same).

The effect of taxes is a real effect so that, during a period of rising prices, the choice of LIFO can increase firm value, although lower net income will be reported. In general, when prices are changing, an analyst should use *LIFO-based values for income statement items* and ratios, and *FIFO-based values for balance sheet items* and ratios because of the distortions described in the previous LOS.

The following example illustrates the difference between net income under the FIFO and LIFO methods.

Example: FIFO vs. LIFO and net income

Consider the assumptions in Figure 10.

Figure 10: Assumptions

				Suggestion: Keep track of the number of units	
Beginning inventory	50 units @ $1.00	= $50		Beginning	50
Purchases:	100 purchased @ $2.00	= $200 + 450 = $650		Purchased	+ 100
	150 purchased @ $3.00			Purchased	+ 150
Ending inventory	200 units			Sold	− 100
Sales	100 units @$7			Ending	200

The COGS and inventory balances under FIFO and LIFO are shown in Figure 11.

Figure 11: COGS and Inventory

	Cost of goods sold	*Inventory*
FIFO	50 units @ $1 + 50 @ $2 = $150	50 @ $2 + 150 @ $3 = $550
LIFO	100 @ $3 = $300	50 @ $1 + 100 @ $2 + 50 @ $3 = $400

Net income is calculated as shown in Figure 12.

Figure 12: Net Income Under FIFO and LIFO

	FIFO	LIFO	LIFO lower by ...
Sales	$700	$700	$0
Cost of goods sold	$150	$300	$(150)
Income before tax	$550	$400	$150
Tax @ 40%	$220	$160	$60
Net income	$330	$240	$90 ⇐LIFO produces lower income.

With taxes $60 higher under FIFO, cash flow will be $60 lower.

Choice of Inventory Method and Profitability, Liquidity, Activity, and Solvency Ratios

Professor's Note: The presumption in this section is that prices are rising and inventory quantities are stable or increasing. The implications when inventories or prices decline are discussed later.

Since the choice of inventory accounting method has an impact on income statement and balance sheet items, it will have an impact on ratios as well. In general, *an analyst should use LIFO values when examining profitability or cost ratios and FIFO values when examining asset or equity ratios.*

Profitability
Compared to FIFO, LIFO produces COGS balances that are higher and are a better measure of true economic cost. Consequently, we have seen that LIFO produces income values that are lower than FIFO, and LIFO figures are a better measure of future profitability. Profitability ratios, such as gross margin and net profit margin, are lower under LIFO than under FIFO, and ratios calculated using LIFO figures are better for comparison purposes. For firms that use FIFO, income ratios should be recalculated using estimates of what COGS would be under LIFO.

Liquidity
Compared to LIFO, FIFO produces inventory figures that are higher and are a better measure of economic value. LIFO inventory figures use prices that are outdated and have less relevance to the economic value of inventory. Liquidity ratios, such as the current ratio, are higher under FIFO than under LIFO, and ratios calculated using FIFO figures are better for comparison purposes. For firms that use LIFO, liquidity ratios should be recalculated using inventory balances that have been restated using the LIFO reserve.

Activity
Inventory turnover makes little sense for firms using LIFO due to the mismatching of costs (the numerator is largely influenced by current or recent past prices, while the denominator is largely influenced by historical prices). Using LIFO when prices are rising causes the inventory turnover ratio to trend higher even if physical turnover does not change. FIFO-based inventory ratios are relatively unaffected by price changes and are a better approximation of actual turnover. However, the ratio itself can still be misleading because the numerator does not reflect COGS as well as LIFO accounting does. The preferred method of analysis is to use LIFO COGS and FIFO average inventory. In this way, current costs are matched in the numerator and denominator. This method is called the *current cost method*.

Some firms use an economic order quantity (EOQ) model to determine optimal inventory ordering policies. For these firms the level of sales will greatly influence inventory turnover; the lower the sales, the lower turnover will be. Some firms are adopting just-in-time inventory policies and keep no inventory (at most, very little) on hand. This results in very large inventory turnover ratios. For these firms, there would be virtually no differences due to the choice between the LIFO and FIFO methods.

LIFO firms tend to carry larger quantities of inventory than comparable FIFO firms. This can most likely be explained by the tax advantages (i.e., lower taxes due to higher COGS) of LIFO.

Solvency

FIFO produces higher inventory values that are more relevant than LIFO inventory values. To reconcile the balance sheet, stockholders' equity must also be adjusted by adding the LIFO reserve. Solvency ratios such as the debt ratio and debt-to-equity ratio will be lower under FIFO because the denominators are larger. For firms that use LIFO, equity, and therefore assets, should be increased by adding the LIFO reserve.

Professor's Note: It may seem inconsistent to use LIFO figures for net income and FIFO figures for stockholders' equity. Nonetheless, that is exactly what an analyst should do.

Example: Converting LIFO to FIFO

Figure 13 shows a balance sheet for a company for 2005 and 2006, along with its income statement for 2006.

Figure 13: Sample Balance Sheet

Year	2006	2005
Assets		
Cash	$105	$95
Receivables	205	195
Inventories	310	290
Total current assets	620	580
Gross property, plant, and equipment	$1,800	$1,700
Accumulated depreciation	360	340
Net property, plant, and equipment	1,440	1,360
Total assets	$2,060	**$1,940**
Liabilities		
Payables	$110	$90
Short-term debt	160	140
Current portion of long-term debt	55	45
Current liabilities	$325	$275
Long-term debt	$610	$690
Deferred taxes	105	95
Common stock	300	300
Additional paid in capital	400	400
Retained earnings	320	180
Common shareholders equity	1,020	880
Total liabilities and equity	$2,060	**$1,940**

Year	2006
Sales	$4,000
Cost of goods sold	3,000
Gross profit	$1,000
Operating expenses	650
Operating profit	350
Interest expense	50
Earnings before taxes	300
Taxes	100
Net income	200
Common dividends	$60

* **Footnote:** The company uses the LIFO inventory cost-flow assumption to account for inventories. As compared to FIFO, inventories would have been $100 higher in 2006 and $90 higher in 2005.

Part A: Convert inventory for 2005 and 2006 and COGS for 2006 into FIFO.

Part B: Calculate the net profit margin, current ratio, inventory turnover, and long-term debt-to-equity ratio using the accounting figures that are most appropriate to compare to industry norms.

Answer:

Part A:

2005: $\text{Inv}_F = \text{Inv}_L + \text{LIFO reserve} = 290 + 90 = 380$
2006: $\text{Inv}_F = \text{Inv}_L + \text{LIFO reserve} = 310 + 100 = 410$
$\text{COGS}_F = \text{COGS}_L - (\text{LIFO reserve}_E - \text{LIFO reserve}_B) = 3,000 - (100 - 90) = 2,990$

Part B:

$$\text{net profit margin} = \frac{\text{net income under LIFO}}{\text{sales}} = \frac{200}{4,000} = 5.0\%$$

$$\text{current ratio} = \frac{\text{current assets under FIFO}}{\text{current liabilities}} = \frac{\text{current assets under LIFO} + \text{LIFO reserve}}{\text{current liabilities}} = \frac{620 + 100}{325} = 2.2$$

$$\text{inventory turnover} = \frac{\text{COGS under LIFO}}{\text{average inventory under FIFO}} = \frac{3,000}{(380 + 410)/2} = 7.6$$

$$\text{debt-to-equity} = \frac{\text{long-term debt}}{\text{equity under FIFO}} = \frac{\text{long-term debt}}{\text{equity under LIFO} + \text{LIFO reserve}} = \frac{610}{1,020 + 100} = 54.5\%$$

When calculating FIFO equity, we have added the entire LIFO reserve without any adjustment for taxes. Note the difference between the questions: What would retained earnings (COGS, net income) have been if the company had used FIFO instead of LIFO? and, How should an analyst adjust retained earnings (assets, equity) for a firm using LIFO to get more meaningful ratios for analysis? In the first case (assuming rising prices), if the firm had used FIFO, then earnings before tax, taxes, net income and retained earnings would all have been higher. In the second case, we are not asking the effects of a different inventory accounting method, but are adjusting ratios to make them more meaningful. The fact that the LIFO firm has an artificially low inventory value is corrected by adding the LIFO reserve to both inventory and retained earnings (equity). Unless there is a reason to believe the firm will actually have a LIFO liquidation, there is no reason to subtract taxes that have been avoided in adjusting the inventory value, retained earnings, and stockholders' equity of LIFO firms.

LOS 40.c: Discuss the reasons that a LIFO reserve might decline during a given period and discuss the implications of such a decline for financial analysis.

The analysis above assumed that prices and inventory were stable or rising. Stable or rising prices and stable or increasing inventory quantities are a typical situation for a business. In these cases, the LIFO reserve will not decline. However, the *LIFO reserve will decline if*:

- Inventory quantity is falling.
- Prices are falling.

A **LIFO liquidation** refers to a declining inventory balance for a company using LIFO (i.e., units available for sale are declining). In this case, the prices for goods being sold are no longer recent prices and can be many years out of date. This would make COGS appear to be very low and gross and net profits to be artificially high. An analyst must adjust COGS for the decline in the LIFO reserve that is caused by the decline in inventory quantity. This amount is typically listed in the footnotes of the financial statements.

If *prices decline*, the differences in the values of inventory and COGS under LIFO and FIFO are the opposite of what was stated before. Specifically:

- If prices are declining, the value of inventory under FIFO will be lower than the value of inventory under LIFO (more recently purchased goods have a lower value relative to goods purchased earlier).
- If prices are declining, the COGS under LIFO will be lower than the COGS under FIFO.

However, even when prices decline, FIFO still provides a more accurate estimate of the economic value of inventory, and LIFO still provides a more accurate estimate of the economic COGS. The decline in the LIFO reserve does *not* mean COGS has to be adjusted if it occurs because of a price decline.

LOS 40.d: Discuss how inventories are reported in the financial statements and how the lower of cost or market principle is used and applied.

U.S. GAAP requires that inventories be reported on the financial statements using the lower of historical cost or market (LCM) principle. This is consistent with the broader accounting concept of conservatism as it will prevent the overstatement of inventories on the balance sheet (and the related income statement effects). Under normal circumstances, inventories are reported at historical cost, and even if market value is higher than historical cost, inventory is not written up above the historical cost. However, if the realizable market value or cost to replace inventory is less than historical cost, a writedown is required.

Inventory gains are not realized until items are sold, but losses prior to sale may be realized on the financial statements as they occur.

Cost is calculated using the actual purchase prices of the items, and the calculation follows one of the three cost-flow assumptions (FIFO, LIFO, or weighted-average) that were discussed earlier.

Market is calculated using the replacement cost of the inventory at a particular point in time. However, the replacement cost must fall within a range of values. The higher end of the range is the **net realizable value** (NRV). NRV is generally equal to the selling price of the inventories less the selling costs. The lower end is NRV less normal profit margin.

So if replacement cost is greater than NRV, then market = net realizable value. If replacement cost is less than NRV less a normal profit margin, then market = net realizable value minus normal profit margin.

Professor's Note: Think of lower of cost or "market" where market cannot be outside a range of values. That range is from net realizable value less a normal profit margin to net realizable value. So the size of this range is normal profit margin in dollars. "Net" means net of the selling costs.

KEY CONCEPTS

1. The three methods of accounting for inventory are FIFO, LIFO, and average cost, and the basic formula for inventory calculations is:

    ending inventory = beginning inventory + purchases – COGS.

2. When prices are changing, FIFO provides the more useful estimate of inventory and balance sheet information, while LIFO provides the more useful estimate of COGS and operating income.

3. Adjusting LIFO inventory balances to FIFO balances requires adding the LIFO reserve to inventory; adjusting LIFO COGS to FIFO requires subtracting the difference between the ending and beginning LIFO reserve.

4. Adjusting FIFO COGS to LIFO requires estimating the inflation rate for the firm and adding the product of the inflation rate and the beginning inventory to the reported FIFO COGS.

5. In periods of rising prices and stable or increasing inventory quantities, LIFO and FIFO result in the following:

LIFO results in:	FIFO results in:
higher COGS	lower COGS
lower taxes	higher taxes
lower net income (EBT and EAT)	higher net income (EBT and EAT)
lower inventory balances	higher inventory balances
lower working capital	higher working capital
higher cash flows (less taxes paid out)	lower cash flows (more taxes paid out)
lower net and gross margins	higher net and gross margins
lower current ratio	higher current ratio
higher inventory turnover	lower inventory turnover
D/A and D/E higher	D/A and D/E lower

6. The LIFO reserve may decline because:
   - Inventory is falling (a LIFO liquidation)—adjust COGS for decrease in LIFO reserve.
   - Prices are declining—no need to adjust COGS for LIFO firms—FIFO still provides a better estimate of inventory value.

7. Under U.S. GAAP, inventory values are written down to replacement cost when that is lower than historical cost, or to NRV if that is lower than replacement cost, but not to less than NRV minus a normal profit margin in any case.

CONCEPT CHECKERS: ANALYSIS OF INVENTORIES

1. The choice of inventory accounting method has cash flow effects because it affects:
   A. purchases.
   B. sales.
   C. taxes.
   D. the turnover ratio.

2. An analyst gathered the following information about a company:
   • Beginning inventory $40,000
   • Purchases over the accounting period $55,000
   • COGS $60,000

   Ending inventory will be:
   A. $35,000.
   B. $45,000.
   C. $50,000.
   D. cannot determine without knowing inventory method.

3. An analyst gathered the following information about a company:
   • Beginning inventory $2.8 million
   • Purchases $11.2 million
   • Ending inventory $3.0 million

   COGS is:
   A. $5.4 million.
   B. $5.8 million.
   C. $11 million.
   D. $14 million.

4. If COGS is overstated by $2,000, and purchases and beginning inventory are correct, ending inventory will be:
   A. unaffected.
   B. understated by $2,000.
   C. overstated by $2,000.
   D. cannot determine without knowing inventory method.

5. If beginning inventory is overstated by $2,000 and ending inventory is understated by $3,000, the firm's before tax income will be:
   A. overstated by $1,000.
   B. overstated by $5,000.
   C. understated by $1,000.
   D. understated by $5,000.

6.   An analyst gathered the following information about a firm:
     • Beginning inventory $15,000
     • Net purchases $25,000
     • Ending inventory $17,000

     COGS is:
     A. $15,000.
     B. $23,000.
     C. $25,000.
     D. $27,000.

7.   When a firm uses first in, first out (FIFO) accounting, COGS reflects the cost of items purchased:
     A. first and ending inventory reflects the value of the items purchased first.
     B. first and ending inventory reflects the cost of the most recent purchases.
     C. most recently and ending inventory reflects the cost of items purchased most recently.
     D. most recently and ending inventory reflects the cost of items purchased first.

Use the following data to answer Questions 8 through 13.

Purchase	Sales
40 units at $30	13 units at $35
20 units at $40	35 units at $45
90 units at $50	60 units at $60

Assume beginning inventory was zero.

8.   Inventory value at the end of the period using FIFO is:
     A. $1,200.
     B. $2,100.
     C. $2,400.
     D. $6,000.

9.   Inventory value at the end of the period using LIFO is:
     A. $1,200.
     B. $1,280.
     C. $2,100.
     D. $2,400.

10. Using LIFO and information for the entire period, gross profit at the end of the period is:
     A. $360.
     B. $410.
     C. $990.
     D. $1,230.

11. Using FIFO and information for the entire period, gross profit is:
     A. $360.
     B. $410.
     C. $990.
     D. $1,230.

12. Inventory value at the end of the period using the weighted average method is:
    A. $1,540.
    B. $1,820.
    C. $2,100.
    D. $4,680.

13. Using the weighted average cost method for the entire period, gross profit at the end of period is:
    A. $950.
    B. $1,230.
    C. $2,100.
    D. $3,810.

14. During periods of rising prices and stable or increasing inventory levels:
    A. LIFO COGS > weighted average COGS > FIFO COGS.
    B. LIFO COGS < weighted average COGS < FIFO COGS.
    C. LIFO COGS = weighted average COGS = FIFO COGS.
    D. weighted average COGS > LIFO COGS > FIFO COGS.

15. During periods of falling prices:
    A. LIFO income > weighted average income > FIFO income.
    B. LIFO income < weighted average income < FIFO income.
    C. LIFO income = weighted average income = FIFO income.
    D. LIFO COGS < weighted average COGS > FIFO COGS.

16. From an analyst's perspective, inventories based on:
    A. LIFO are preferable since they reflect historical cost.
    B. FIFO are preferable since they reflect current cost.
    C. weighted averages are preferable since they reflect normal results.
    D. all three methods are equivalent because the equity account is unaffected by the accounting method.

17. From an analyst's perspective:
    A. LIFO provides a better measure of current income because it allocates recent costs to COGS.
    B. FIFO provides a better measure of current income because it allocates historical costs to COGS.
    C. weighted average is best because it allocates average costs to COGS and requires no flow assumptions.
    D. any method provides the same value because the equity account is unaffected by the accounting method.

18. In periods of rising prices and stable or increasing inventory quantities, LIFO (as compared to FIFO) results in:
    A. lower COGS, higher taxes, lower net income, and lower cash flows.
    B. lower COGS, higher taxes, lower inventory, and higher COGS.
    C. higher COGS, lower taxes, lower inventory, and lower cash flows.
    D. higher COGS, lower taxes, lower inventory, and higher cash flows.

19. If prices are rising and two firms are identical except for inventory methods, the firm using FIFO will have:
    A. higher net income.
    B. lower inventory.
    C. lower net income.
    D. higher total cash flow.

20. Which of the following is *likely* to occur under a LIFO liquidation?
    A. An increase in the gross profit margin.
    B. A sharp increase in inventory.
    C. A sharp increase in accounts receivable.
    D. All of the above.

21. In periods of falling prices, firms using FIFO will:
    A. report higher earnings than equivalent firms using LIFO.
    B. report lower earnings than equivalent firms using LIFO.
    C. report identical earnings as equivalent firms using LIFO.
    D. cannot tell without knowing the timing of the price decline.

22. Which of the following statements about inventory accounting is **FALSE**?
    A. If a U.S. firm uses LIFO for tax reporting, it must use LIFO for financial reporting.
    B. During periods of rising prices, LIFO income will be lower than FIFO income.
    C. During periods of rising prices, LIFO cash flows will be higher than FIFO cash flows.
    D. During periods of rising prices, FIFO-based current ratios will be smaller than LIFO-based current ratios.

23. An analyst is evaluating a company after a period of time when prices have fallen. The company uses LIFO accounting. Which of the following is **TRUE**?
    A. The analyst must restate COGS because it is lower than what it would be under FIFO accounting.
    B. Income will be lower than it would have been under FIFO accounting.
    C. Inventory need not be restated because the LIFO reserve will have decreased.
    D. COGS need not be restated because LIFO COGS is always an accurate measure of current cost as long as inventory quantity does not decline.

24. Assuming no LIFO layer liquidation, a LIFO firm reports higher net income than an otherwise identical FIFO firm. Prices must be:
    A. steady.
    B. rising.
    C. falling.
    D. falling first and then rising.

25. In periods of rising prices and stable or increasing inventory levels, compared to FIFO accounting for inventories, LIFO accounting will give:
    A. lower profitability ratios.
    B. lower inventory levels.
    C. a lower current ratio.
    D. all of the above.

26. If all else holds constant in periods of rising prices and inventory levels, which of the following statements is **TRUE**?
    A. FIFO firms have higher debt-to-equity ratios than LIFO firms.
    B. LIFO firms have higher gross profit margins than FIFO firms.
    C. FIFO firms will have greater stockholder's equity than LIFO firms.
    D. LIFO firms will have greater current asset balances than FIFO firms.

©2007 Schweser

27.	A firm uses LIFO for inventory accounting and reports the following:
- COGS $125,000
- Beginning inventory $25,000
- Ending inventory $27,000
- Footnotes to the financial statements reveal a beginning LIFO reserve of $12,000 and an ending LIFO reserve of $15,000.

    The COGS on a FIFO basis is:
    A. $122,000.
    B. $125,000.
    C. $128,000.
    D. $140,000.

Use the following data to answer Questions 28 through 32.

The beginning of period LIFO reserve is $50,000, and the ending period LIFO reserve is $60,000. The firm's tax rate is 40%.

28.	To adjust end-of-period LIFO inventory to FIFO inventory:
    A. add $10,000.
    B. subtract $10,000.
    C. add $60,000.
    D. subtract $60,000.

29.	To adjust end-of-period owner's equity in order to calculate the debt-to-equity ratio, an analyst should:
    A. make no adjustment.
    B. add $10,000.
    C. add $36,000.
    D. add $60,000.

30.	To adjust end-of-period accounts payable from LIFO based to FIFO based:
    A. make no adjustment.
    B. add $24,000.
    C. add $36,000.
    D. subtract $36,000.

31.	To adjust COGS from LIFO to FIFO, an analyst should adjust the LIFO COGS by:
    A. increasing it by $60,000.
    B. decreasing it by $60,000.
    C. increasing it by $10,000.
    D. decreasing it by $10,000.

32.	The effect on after-tax income of using FIFO instead of LIFO would be to:
    A. increase it by $6,000.
    B. decrease it by $6,000.
    C. increase it by $10,000.
    D. decrease it by $10,000.

33. Which of the following statements concerning a firm using FIFO is **FALSE**?
    A. There is no reason to convert inventory to LIFO because LIFO inventory is less reflective of current value.
    B. It is impossible to estimate COGS on a LIFO basis.
    C. If prices are rising and inventory levels are stable, the firm will have higher inventory than a firm using LIFO.
    D. If prices have been rising and the firm is located in the U.S., taxes would be lower under LIFO than under FIFO.

34. A firm's financial statements were prepared using LIFO. What accounts should be adjusted when the financial statements are restated for the purpose of comparing ratios to industry averages?
    A. Net income.
    B. Accounts receivable.
    C. Long-term debt.
    D. Stockholders' equity.

35. Three analysts are debating about the inflation rate that should be used to adjust a firm's COGS, which was reported using FIFO, to a LIFO basis. The first states that they should use the inflation rate for the economy. The second states that they should use an inflation rate derived from a competitor's LIFO reserve calculations. The third states that they should use figures derived for the industry by a trade association. Which of the three are valid?
    A. First only.
    B. Third only.
    C. First and the third.
    D. Second and the third.

36. Kamp Inc. sells specialized bicycle shoes. At year-end, due to a sudden increase in manufacturing costs, the replacement cost per pair of shoes is $55. The historical cost is $43, and the current selling price is $50. The normal profit margin is 10% of the selling price, and the selling costs are $3 per pair.

    At which of the following amounts should each pair of shoes be recorded on Kamp's year-end balance sheet?
    A. $42.
    B. $43.
    C. $47.
    D. $55.

ANSWERS – CONCEPT CHECKERS: ANALYSIS OF INVENTORIES

1. **C** The choice of inventory accounting method flows through the income statement to ultimately affect taxes.

2. **A** Beginning inventory + purchases – COGS = $40,000 + $55,000 – $60,000 = $35,000

3. **C** Purchases + beginning inventory – ending inventory = $11.2 + $2.8 – $3 = $11

4. **B** If COGS is overstated, ending inventory must be understated.

5. **D** Overstated beginning inventory coupled with understated ending inventory implies that COGS is overstated by $5,000. If COGS is overstated, income will be understated.

6. **B** Purchases + beginning inventory – ending inventory = $25,000 + $15,000 – $17,000 = $23,000

7. **B** COGS reflects the items purchased first in FIFO accounting. Remember, first in, first out.

8. **B** 108 units were sold (13 + 35 + 60), and 150 units were available for sale (beginning inventory of 0 plus purchases of 40 + 20 + 90), so there are 150 – 108 = 42 units in ending inventory. Under FIFO, units from the last batch purchased would remain: 42 × $50 = $2,100.

9. **B** Under LIFO, the first 42 units purchased would be in inventory: (40 × $30) + (2 × $40) = $1,280.

10. **B** Revenue = (13 × $35) + (35 × $45) + (60 × $60) = $5,630
    Purchases = (40 × $30) + (20 × $40) + (90 × $50) = $6,500
    COGS = purchases + beginning inventory – ending inventory = 6,500 + 0 – 1,280 = $5,220
    Gross profit = $5,630 – $5,220 = $410

11. **D** COGS = purchases + beginning inventory – ending inventory = 6,500 + 0 – 2,100 = $4,400
    Gross profit = $5,630 – $4,400 = $1,230

12. **B** The average cost of inventory is [(40 × $30) + (20 × $40) + (90 × $50)] / (40 + 20 + 90) = $43.33
    Inventory value = $43.33 × 42 units = $1,820

13. **A** COGS = 43.33 × 108 = 4,680
    Gross profit = $5,630 – $4,680 = $950

14. **A** Weighted average COGS will be always be in the middle of FIFO and LIFO whether prices are rising or falling. If prices are rising, LIFO COGS will be the highest because the most recent goods produced go to COGS.

15. **A** LIFO COGS will be the lowest of the three methods when prices are falling. That means LIFO income will be the highest.

16. **B** With FIFO, older inventory is sold first, so current inventory is a better reflection of the current cost it would take to replace that inventory.

17. **A** Analysts prefer LIFO for the income statement because the COGS is current.

18. **D** With rising prices, LIFO results in higher COGS. Higher costs mean lower income; lower income means lower taxes; and lower taxes mean higher cash flow.

19. **A** Firms using FIFO will have lower COGS, which means they will have higher net income when compared to a firm using LIFO when prices are rising.

20. **A** COGS per unit decline and profit margins increase.

21. **B** Falling prices for a firm using FIFO mean older, more expensive goods are going to COGS, thus lowering net income.

22. **D**   If prices are rising, FIFO inventories will be higher. Because inventory is a current asset, this will result in a higher current ratio than firms using LIFO.

23. **D**   LIFO COGS is the better measure of economic cost as long as inventory levels have not declined.

24. **C**   If the LIFO firm is reporting higher net income, prices must be falling.

25. **D**   With rising prices, all of the answers apply to LIFO compared to FIFO.

26. **C**   All else equal, the FIFO firm has a higher level of assets due to the higher inventory. Since liabilities are assumed to be equal to total assets, the FIFO must have higher equity to finance those assets.

27. **A**   FIFO COGS = LIFO COGS – (ending LIFO reserve – beginning LIFO reserve) = $125,000 – ($15,000 – $12,000) = $122,000

28. **C**   LIFO inventory is lower than FIFO, so add the LIFO reserve.

29. **D**   Retained earnings must be increased by LIFO reserve, $60,000. No tax adjustment is necessary here.

30. **A**   Accounts payable are not affected by inventory accounting methods.

31. **D**   Decrease LIFO COGS by the change in the LIFO reserve.

32. **A**   Because costs decrease by $10,000, pretax income would increase by $10,000, and after-tax net income would increase by $6,000. The change in LIFO reserve, +$10,000, times (1 – 0.4) = $6,000.

33. **B**   Costs can be estimated by adding the inflation rate multiplied by the beginning inventory.

34. **D**   Inventory would increase, which means assets would increase, which means equity would increase to keep the balance sheet in balance.

35. **D**   Either the change in a competitor's LIFO reserve as a percentage of BI_{FIFO} or industry statistics can be used to estimate the inflation rate.

36. **B**   Market is equal to the replacement cost subject to replacement cost being within a specific range. The upper bound is net realizable value (NRV), which is equal to selling price ($50) less selling costs ($3) for an NRV of $47. The lower bound is NRV ($47) less normal profit (10% of selling price = $5) for a net amount of $42. Since replacement cost ($55) is greater than NRV ($47), market equals NRV ($47). Additionally, we have to use the lower of cost ($43) or market ($47) principle, so the shoes should be recorded at the cost of $43.

The following is a review of the Financial Statement Analysis principles designed to address the learning outcome statements set forth by CFA Institute®. This topic is also covered in:

LONG-TERM ASSETS

EXAM FOCUS

Long-term assets have a useful life of greater than one year and are used for production of the company's goods or services. The key to this topic review is recognizing how costs for long-term assets are allocated according to the matching principle (reporting expenses in the same period as the revenues earned as a result of those expenses). Depreciation, the process of allocating the cost of an asset to expense over time, can be done in a number of different ways depending on how rapidly or slowly a company wants to write off the asset's cost. For the Level 1 exam, candidates should be prepared for questions requiring depreciation of an asset using any of the different methods.

LOS 41.a: Describe the factors that distinguish long-term assets from other assets and identify the common types of long-term assets and how carrying value is determined on the balance sheet.

A **long-term asset** is an asset that is typically employed in the production process of the firm and has a useful life of greater than one year. Long-term assets are not made available for sale to the firm's customers (i.e., they do not represent inventory for sale).

Long-term assets are classified in three main categories:

- *Tangible assets* have a physical existence. Examples include land, buildings, and equipment. The process of allocating the cost of a tangible asset over its useful life is called *depreciation*.
- *Natural resources* are purchased for the economic value that can be taken from the Earth and used up over time. Examples include oil fields, timberland, and mines. The process of allocating the cost of a natural resource according to its use (e.g., cutting timber, pumping oil) is called *depletion*.
- *Intangible assets* have no physical existence, but have a value that is based on rights or advantages that are conferred to the owner. Examples include copyrights, patents, trademarks, franchises, and goodwill. The cost of most intangible assets is allocated to the periods over which it provides benefits through a process called *amortization*.

Professor's Note: Goodwill is an intangible asset that is not amortized under U.S. GAAP. We will discuss accounting for goodwill later in this topic review.

Long-term assets are generally reported at their **carrying value or book value** (that is, historical cost less accumulated depreciation or depletion). If, however, the asset has lost its revenue-generating ability, its book value may be reduced. This is referred to as *asset impairment*, in which case the amount of the write-down is recorded as a loss.

The decision to acquire long-term assets is based on some type of present value analysis in which the present value of the asset's cash inflows is compared to the present value of the asset's cash outflows (e.g., initial outlay).

The following are accounting issues pertaining to long-term assets:

- How to spread the cost over the useful life.
- How to represent the remaining value of the asset each period on the balance sheet.

PROPERTY, PLANT, AND EQUIPMENT (PP&E)

A *plant asset* is a tangible asset that is fixed or permanent. Property, plant, and equipment (PP&E) assets are long-lived tangible assets *used in the production or sale of other assets*.

- PP&E versus other assets:
- PP&E assets' long lives distinguish them from prepaid expenses and other current assets. PP&E assets are used and not sold (like inventory) during the business's regular course of operations.
- PP&E assets are not ultimately sold as would be done with interest or dividend-generating investments. PP&E assets' tangible physical existence differentiates them from intangible assets.
- The primary difference between plant assets and inventory is that plant assets are held to be used in operations, whereas inventory is held to be sold.
- The primary difference between plant assets and current assets, in general, is their useful lives.
- The primary difference between plant assets and long-term investments is that plant assets are used in the operations of the business.

LOS 41.b: Determine the costs that are capitalized to property, plant and equipment and determine which costs are expensed as incurred.

The **cost of plant assets** includes all expenditures (e.g., transportation of the asset, insurance while the asset is transported, installation cost, search cost, broker cost, and legal fees to transfer title) that are necessary to acquire the assets and ready them for use. All these expenditures are made prior to (and are necessary for) placing the asset in service.

If the plant is constructed, capitalized costs (added to the purchase cost of the asset) include materials, labor, reasonable amounts of overhead, interest cost during the construction period, and architectural fees.

Included in the cost of land are expenditures such as search cost, real estate commissions, title transfer fees, back property taxes paid, surveying, and landscaping costs.

Examples of costs that would be expensed as incurred, rather than capitalized and depreciated over time are:

- Cost to repair damage during installation.
- Cost to train employees to operate new equipment.
- Interest costs related to the *purchase*, rather than construction, of an asset (these are operating costs).
- Routine and normal maintenance.
- Items of little cost, such as a stapler or coffee pot, will be expensed as "supplies."

LOS 41.c: Explain depreciation accounting (including the reasons for depreciation), calculate depreciation using the straight-line, production (also known as units-of-production), and declining-balance methods, and calculate depreciation after revising the estimated useful life of an asset.

Depreciation is used to allocate the cost of an asset over a period of time. *Depreciation expense* is the amount of this allocation for a given period.

Land represents space for production facilities (real estate) and is not depreciated. Land remains valued at its original cost.

Plant and equipment, however, have limited lives due to wear and tear and/or obsolescence. Because of this, plant and equipment costs must be allocated to expense over the plant and equipment's estimated economic life.

The **straight-line method** allocates the depreciable cost of an asset evenly over the asset's estimated useful economic life. The following is an example of the straight-line method of calculating depreciation.

- A machine has a historical cost of $12,000.
- The estimated useful life is ten years.
- After ten years, the machine will have an estimated salvage value of $2,000.
- Cost less salvage value equals the depreciable value ($12,000 – $2,000 = $10,000).

The straight-line depreciation method results in equal depreciation expense each year over the equipment's 10-year life:

$$\frac{\text{straight-line}}{\text{depreciation}} = \frac{\text{cost} - \text{salvage value}}{\text{useful life}} = \frac{\$12,000 - 2,000}{10} = \$1,000 \text{ per year}$$

After three years of use (accumulated depreciation is $3,000), the determination is made that the machine can only be used for two more years. To revise the depreciation schedule, the net book value of the machine ($12,000 – $3,000 = $9,000) less the salvage value of $2,000 will be depreciated over the remaining two years of useful life:

$$\frac{\text{straight-line}}{\text{depreciation}} = \frac{\text{net book value} - \text{salvage value}}{\text{useful life}} = \frac{\$9,000 - 2,000}{2} = \$3,500 \text{ per year}$$

The production (units-of-production) method allocates the depreciable cost of the asset as a function of the asset's use rather than time. The following is an example of the units-of-production method of calculating depreciation.

- A truck costs $920,000.
- It has an estimated life of 300,000 miles.
- Salvage value is $20,000.
- Cost of the truck per mile driven is:

$$\text{depreciation} = \frac{\text{cost} - \text{salvage value}}{\text{estimated miles}} = \frac{\$920,000 - 20,000}{300,000} = \$3.00 \text{ per mile}$$

If the truck is driven for 50,000 miles in year 1, the units-of-production depreciation expense is:

$$\text{depreciation} = (\text{miles driven})(\text{depreciation per mile}) = (50,000 \text{ miles})(\$3.00 \text{ per mile}) = \$150,000$$

Accelerated depreciation speeds up the recognition of depreciation expense in a systematic way so that more depreciation expense is recognized in the earlier years of the asset's life and less is recognized later in the asset's life. Total depreciation expense, however, over the life of the asset will be the same as with straight-line depreciation.

The **declining balance method** (DB) is a method that requires applying a constant rate to a declining book value. The most common declining balance method is the *double declining balance method* (DDB), which uses 200% of the straight-line rate as the rate applied against the declining balance. If an asset's life is 10 years, the straight-line rate is 1/10 or 10%. The DDB rate for this asset is 2/10 or 20%.

$$\text{DDB depreciation} = \left(\frac{2}{\text{useful life}}\right)(\text{cost} - \text{accumulated depreciation})$$

DB does not explicitly use the salvage value in calculations, but depreciation expense will be halted when the cost less salvage value has been depreciated.

The following is an example of declining balance depreciation.

- A machine is purchased on January 1 of year 1 for a cost of $12,000.
- The estimated useful life is five years.
- Estimated salvage value is $2,000.

The depreciation expense using the double declining balance method is:

- Year 1:(2 / 5)($12,000 – 0)= $4,800.00
- Year 2:(2 / 5)($12,000 – $4,800)= $2,880.00
- Year 3:(2 / 5)($12,000 – $7,680)= $1,728.00

In years 1 through 3, the company has recognized cumulative depreciation expense of $9,408. Since the total depreciation expense is $10,000 ($12,000 – $2,000 salvage value), the depreciation in year 4 is limited to $592, rather than the (2 / 5)($12,000 – $9,408) = $1,036.80 using the DDB formula.

Year 5: Depreciation expense is $0 since the asset is fully depreciated to salvage value.

Note that the rate of depreciation is doubled (2/5) from straight-line, and the only thing that changes from year to year is the base amount upon which depreciation is calculated.

Professor's Note: We've been discussing the "double" declining balance method, which uses a factor of 2 times the straight-line rate. The general method is that of declining balance, and you can compute declining balance depreciation based on any factor, double, 1.5, triple, etc.

LOS 41.d: Describe how to account for the sale, exchange, or disposal of depreciable assets, and determine whether a gain or loss is recorded.

Assets that are worn out or no longer useful may be discarded, sold, or exchanged for another asset.

When an **asset is sold or discarded**, its market value at the time of sale or disposal will most likely be different from the asset's *book value*. The book value of an asset is equal to its original historical cost minus all accumulated depreciation (including depreciation for partial years) on that asset.

- *Discarded assets* are simply disposed of and the firm receives nothing in return. The market value for the asset is zero. If the asset has been depreciated to zero before being discarded, no gain or loss is recorded. However, if the asset has any remaining book value at the time of disposal, the book value amount is recognized as a *realized loss* on the income statement. When the asset is disposed of, all records of the asset must be removed from the balance sheet.
- When an *asset is sold*, the firm receives a cash payment in exchange for the asset. The asset's book value is compared to the sale price and any difference is recognized as a *realized gain or loss* on the income statement. Please note that realized gains and losses are *always* posted to the income statement.

Example: Asset sold for cash

The Toft Company purchased an automobile three years ago for $20,000, and its accountants have booked $12,000 of depreciation against the auto (i.e., using straight-line depreciation methods with zero assumed salvage value, the accountants recorded depreciation expense of $4,000 each year and increased accumulated depreciation by that same amount). Today, the *book value* of the auto is $8,000 = $20,000 – $12,000.

The Toft Company decides to sell this automobile and is able to get $10,000 for it. The entries that take place upon the sale of the asset are an increase in cash of $10,000, the removal of accumulated depreciation on the asset (reduced by $12,000), and the reduction of PPE by the $20,000 historical asset cost. The $2,000 excess of the sale price ($10,000) over the net book value ($8,000) is recorded as a gain and added to income as "other revenues and expenses."

Firms also dispose of assets by **exchanging assets** for credit toward the purchase of other (typically newer) assets. If the trade-in allowance received is greater than the book value of the asset being disposed of, the result is a gain; if the trade-in allowance is less than the book value, the result is a loss.

The key to accounting for asset exchanges is whether the asset is being exchanged for a *similar asset* (e.g., a new model of a printing press), or a *dissimilar asset* (e.g., exchanging a printing press for a grain silo).

For financial accounting purposes:

- For exchanges of dissimilar assets, both gains and losses are recognized on the income statement.
- For similar assets, only losses are recognized. If a "gain" results from the exchange of similar assets, the book value of the old asset (which is lower than the trade-in allowance) is added to the cash paid to determine the recorded cost of the new asset. This will result in a lower cost basis than would have been recorded for the new asset if the whole trade-in allowance was added to cash paid. The "gain" is thus effectively postponed until the new asset is sold or disposed of.

For income tax purposes:

- For exchanges of dissimilar assets, both gains and losses are recognized on the income statement.
- For exchanges of similar assets, no gains or losses are recognized. Gains or losses are effectively postponed to future periods.

LOS 41.e: Identify assets that should be classified as natural resources, determine their carrying values on the balance sheet and calculate depletion.

Natural resources, also known as *wasting assets*, are assets such as timberlands, oil fields, and mineral deposits. Natural resource assets become inventory through the process of cutting timber, pumping oil, or mining for ore. As the resource is extracted from the asset, the carrying value of the asset should be reduced proportionately.

The cost of natural resources is allocated based on units-of-production and is referred to as *depletion*. The amount of depletion in a given period is determined using the units-of-production method.

Example: Depletion

Suppose a firm acquired mineral rights for $1.5 million. And suppose that it is estimated that the mineral deposits will produce 100,000 tons of ore. If 10,000 tons were extracted during the period, 1/10 of the cost is allocated to this period. The entries to record the depletion are the recognition of depletion expense of $150,000 on the income statement and an increase of $150,000 in accumulated depletion on the balance sheet. The carrying value is simply cost minus accumulated depreciation. $1,500,000 − $150,000 = $1,350,000 is the carrying value after one year.

LOS 41.f: Identify the types of intangible assets and describe how the accounting treatment for goodwill under U.S. GAAP differs from the accounting treatment for other intangible assets.

Intangible assets have no physical existence, but legal rights confer benefits to the assets' owners. Intangible assets are distinguished from other assets that are classified as current assets (e.g., receivables) because intangibles are investments that are used in operations (e.g., produce products or provide services).

Examples of intangible assets include:

- Trademarks or brand names.
- Copyrights.
- Patents.
- Licenses or franchises.
- Leaseholds or leasehold improvements.
- Technology.
- Non-compete covenants.

Typically, intangible assets are only recorded on the balance sheet when they are purchased from another firm. All costs for developing intangible assets internally are expensed as incurred.

When a company acquires an intangible asset (e.g., buys a patent), an asset is created by debiting the asset account for the acquisition cost. The cost of intangible assets is allocated over the life of the asset (e.g., as prescribed by law) or an estimated life—which typically does not exceed 40 years. This allocation process is referred to as *amortization*. Amortization of intangibles uses the straight-line method.

Example: Amortization of intangibles

Suppose a firm acquired a patent for $1.5 million. And suppose that the patent was determined to have a useful life of 15 years. The entries to record the amortization are an amortization expense of $100,000 on the income statement and an increase of $100,000 in accumulated amortization on the balance sheet.

Professor's Note: Internally developed computer software is an exception to the rule that only intangible assets purchased from another firm are recognized on the balance sheet. Once the software is determined to be technologically feasible, development costs are recorded as an asset and amortized over the software's economic life.

Goodwill is created when a firm purchasing another business pays more than the fair market value of the business's assets if they were purchased individually. If the excess purchase price cannot be attributed to patents, brands, copyrights, or other intangible assets, it is recorded as goodwill. Goodwill reflects the factors that enable a company to earn an above average rate of return such as strong management, manufacturing efficiency, and customer approval.

The process of **accounting for goodwill** is different from the process for other intangible assets. According to U.S. GAAP, goodwill is not amortized, but is subject to an *annual impairment review.* Each year, a company must estimate the fair market value of its goodwill. If the fair market value is less than the carrying value on the balance sheet, the goodwill is said to be *impaired*. If impairment occurs, the carrying value of the goodwill account is reduced to its fair market value and an impairment charge is recorded on the income statement.

Key Concepts

1. Long-term assets are used to produce items for resale and have a useful life of greater than one year.
2. The cost of plant assets includes all expenditures necessary to place the asset into service that are made prior to placing the asset in service.
3. The cost of an asset is allocated over time through depreciation. Three main methods are straight-line, units-of-production, and declining-balance.
4. When assets are sold or discarded, a realized gain or loss may result. The gain or loss is equal to sale proceeds minus book (carrying) value.
5. For natural resources, the units-of-production method is the most appropriate method to use because natural resources are depleted as used.
6. Intangible assets do not have a physical existence but they do produce benefits to the assets' owners.

CONCEPT CHECKERS: LONG-TERM ASSETS

1. A trademark is an example of a(n):
    A. capital asset.
    B. intangible asset.
    C. natural resource.
    D. tangible asset.

2. Which of the following items is NOT included in the cost of purchased plant assets?
    A. Broker fees.
    B. Installation costs.
    C. Title transfer charges.
    D. Allocated overhead amounts.

3. Rocco Inc. purchases a manufacturing capital asset for a cost of $170,000. Included in the cost is an amount of $10,000 relating to the installation. The useful life of the asset is 10 years and the estimated salvage value at the end of 10 years is $20,000.

    Which of the following amounts represents the *difference* between the straight-line and the double-declining methods with regard to calculating Rocco's depreciation expense for the asset in the first year?
    A. $15,000.
    B. $17,000.
    C. $19,000.
    D. $20,000.

4. Sicsic Music Studios purchased a high-end copier/scanner at a total cost of $30,000. Estimated useful life and salvage value are 10 years and $6,000, respectively. After exactly four years, the machine was sold for $17,000 cash. Sicsic uses the straight-line method of depreciation.

    Which of the following amounts represents the gain or loss that Sicsic should record on the exchange?
    A. Loss of $1,000.
    B. Gain of $1,000.
    C. Loss of $3,400.
    D. Gain of $3,400.

5. Slocan Inc. acquired logging rights at a cost of $2 million five years ago. The rights allow Slocan to cut down a total of 1 million trees. Slocan has been cutting down trees at a steady rate of 50,000 trees per year.

    With regards to the logging rights, which of the following financial statement accounts and amounts is **CORRECT**?
    A. Accumulated depletion or depreciation = $1.5 million.
    B. Depletion expense for the year = $0.5 million.
    C. Depreciation expense for the year = $0.5 million.
    D. Natural resources = $1.5 million.

6.   Three years ago, Nora Inc. developed a breakthrough pharmaceutical drug to treat stroke patients. At that time, it obtained a patent for the drug, which had a legal life of 17 years. However, management at Nora was well aware that the useful life of the patent was five years. Total development costs were $3.4 million.

According to U.S. GAAP, which of the following is the amount at which Nora should carry the development costs for the patent on its balance sheet?
A. $0.
B. $1.36 million.
C. $2.04 million.
D. $2.8 million.

7.   Apex Gold has purchased mining rights for $3 million on a property that it estimates has 6,000 tons of recoverable ore. In the third year of operation Apex removes 800 tons of ore, bringing the total ore extraction to 4,000 tons. The depletion in the third year and carrying value of the mineral rights asset at the end of the third year are closest to:

	Depletion	Carrying Value
A.	$315,000	$2,600,000
B.	$315,000	$1,000,000
C.	$400,000	$2,600,000
D.	$400,000	$1,000,000

ANSWERS – CONCEPT CHECKERS: LONG-TERM ASSETS

1. **B** Intangible assets are those that cannot be seen or touched (have no physical existence). The value of them is based on rights or advantages conferred to the owner. A trademark (e.g., CFA) clearly demonstrates those qualities so it is a good example of an intangible asset.

2. **D** Allocated overhead amounts are only considered in the cost if the plant assets are *constructed*. They are not included in the cost of plant assets that are purchased.

3. **C** Depreciation expense under the straight-line method: (170,000 – 20,000) / 10 = $15,000

    Depreciation expense under the double declining-balance method: (2/10) x 170,000 = $34,000

    Difference = 34,000 – 15,000 = $19,000

4. **C** Annual depreciation = (30,000 – 6,000) / 10 = $2,400

    Accumulated depreciation for four years = 4 × 2,400 = $9,600

    Book value after four years = 30,000 – 9,600 = $20,400

    Sale proceeds = $17,000

    Loss = Sale proceeds – Book value = 17,000 – 20,400 = ($3,400)

5. **D** Annual depletion = 50,000 / 1,000,000 = 5%

    Depletion expense for the year = 5% × 2,000,000 = $100,000

    Accumulated depletion for five years = 5 × 100,000 = $500,000

    Natural resources = cost – accumulated depletion = 2,000,000 – 500,000 = $1,500,000

6. **A** The patent in this situation is an example of an internally-generated intangible asset. Therefore, all costs for the development should be expensed as incurred so that nothing is recorded on the balance sheet. The actual expenditures for legally registering the patent can be capitalized.

7. **D** Third year depletion is: $\dfrac{800}{6,000} \times 3$ million $= \$400,000$

    Carrying value is: 3 million $(1 - \dfrac{4,000}{6,000}) = \$1.0$ million

ANALYSIS OF LONG-LIVED ASSETS: PART I – THE CAPITALIZATION DECISION

Study Session 9

EXAM FOCUS

Firms must decide to either expense (write off immediately) or capitalize (place on the balance sheet) the costs of acquiring an asset. The decision is typically based on the longevity of the asset in accordance with the matching principle discussed earlier. For the Level 1 exam, know that the expensing versus capitalizing decision affects financial statement components and ratios. Typically, firms that capitalize costs will have smoother net income, higher profitability in early years (lower in later years), higher cash flows from operations, lower cash flows from investing, and lower leverage ratios. Candidates should understand the circumstances and financial statement effects of capitalizing expenses in general, interest costs during construction, and intangible assets.

LOS 42.a: Compute and describe the effects of capitalizing versus expensing on net income, shareholders' equity, cash flow from operations, and financial ratios including the effect on the interest coverage ratio (times interest earned) of capitalizing interest costs.

The costs (cash price plus all necessary expenditures made before an asset is ready for use) of acquiring resources that provide services over more than one operating cycle are capitalized and carried as assets on the balance sheet. The decision to **capitalize** or **expense** some items depends on management choices, and is subject to manipulation. These choices may affect the balance sheet, income statement, cash flow statement, and related financial ratios for the current period as well as over the life of the asset. When correctly employed, capitalization of expenses allows better matching of revenues with the expenses incurred to generate those revenues.

Issues that arise in capitalization include:

- Which components of cost are capitalized (e.g., interest charges, R&D).
- What method should be used to determine the amount capitalized.

Statement of Financial Accounting Concepts (SFAC) 6 defines accounting assets as those assets that provide probable future economic benefits. However, for the purpose of analysis the term "asset" may represent:

- The initial investment outlays.
- Those parts of a firm that represent "wealth."
- One of the inputs in the production function.

Depending on the purpose of the analysis, the firm's assets may be evaluated by looking at:

- Profitability [by return on assets (ROA)].
- Solvency (protection for creditors).
- Operating efficiency and operating leverage.

Different types of analysis may require asset definitions different from those found in the accounting rules. For example, machinery acquired under an operating lease is not recognized as an asset on the balance sheet, but its recognition as an asset may be appropriate in security analysis. Research and development and advertising expenditures may provide future services, but are expensed when incurred and not recognized as an asset under accounting practices.

How Capitalization Affects Financial Statements and Ratios

The effects of capitalizing expenses on financial statements and ratios stem from the fact that capitalizing reduces current period expenses by the amount capitalized. The amount of capitalized expenses is added to assets, and the related cash flow is treated as an investing cash flow rather than an operating cash flow. The decision to capitalize expenses does not affect debt. Capitalizing expenses will increase equity, by increasing net income and retained earnings in the current period, and increase assets, because of the addition of the capitalized amount. The asset created by capitalizing expenses will be amortized—that is, the capitalized expenses will be spread over a period of years. The asset value is reduced by amortization each year, similar to depreciation of plant and equipment.

Financial statement effects. Although it may make no operational difference, the choice between capitalizing or expensing will affect reported income, cash flow from operations, and leverage ratios. Companies that capitalize expenses will show higher asset balances, greater cash flow from operations and lower cash flow from investing. The capitalized expense is classified as an investing cash flow, rather than as an operating cash flow.

Income variability. Firms that capitalize costs and depreciate them over time *will show smoother reported income.* Firms that expense costs will tend to have greater variance in reported income. The expenditures that are candidates for capitalization are large in magnitude and tend to vary widely from year to year. When these amounts are expensed instead of capitalized, their variability causes a high degree of variability in net income.

Profitability. In the year in which an expense is capitalized, companies that capitalize expenses have higher profitability measures than expensing companies. When a company expenses large purchases, this decreases income. In later years, net income, ROA and ROE will be lower for a company that capitalizes, because profits in later years will be lower than for expensing firms due to continuing depreciation, and because assets will be higher by the capitalized amount. Firms that expense have lower asset levels (and because of this, lower equity levels), so ROA and ROE will typically be higher over time than for firms that capitalize.

Cash flow from operations. Although *net* cash flows are not affected by the choice of capitalization or expensing (ignoring tax effects), the components of cash flow are affected. Because a firm that capitalizes outlays classifies those expenditures as investing cash flows, *cash flow from operations will be higher* and *investing cash flows will be lower* than that of a firm that expenses.

Leverage ratios. Capitalizing firms have higher asset and equity levels, while expensing firms report lower assets and equity levels. Therefore, *debt to equity and debt to asset ratios will appear worse for expensing firms* than for capitalizing firms.

These financial implications of capitalizing versus expensing are summarized in Figure 1:

Figure 1: Financial Statement Impacts: Capitalizing vs. Expensing

	Capitalizing	*Expensing*
Income variability	Lower	Higher
Profitability—early years (ROA & ROE)	Higher	Lower
Profitability—later years (ROA & ROE)	Lower	Higher
Total cash flows	Same	Same
Cash flow from operations	Higher	Lower
Cash flow from investing	Lower	Higher
Leverage ratios (debt/equity & debt/assets)	Lower	Higher

Example: Effect of capitalization

Figure 2 is a balance sheet for Soprano Company for 2005 and 2006 and its income statement for 2006.

Figure 2: Soprano Company Balance Sheet and Income Statement

Balance Sheet

	2006	2005
Assets		
Current assets		
Cash	$105	$95
Receivables	205	195
Inventories	310	290
Total current assets	$620	$580
Noncurrent assets		
Gross property, plant, and equipment	$1,800	$1,700
Accumulated depreciation	(360)	(340)
Net property, plant, and equipment	$1,440	$1,360
Total assets	$2,060	$1,940
Liabilities		
Current liabilities		
Payables	$110	$90
Short-term debt	160	140
Current portion of long-term debt	55	45
Total current liabilities	$325	$275
Noncurrent liabilities		
Long-term debt	$610	$690
Deferred taxes	105	95
Stockholders' equity		
Common stock	$300	$300
Additional paid in capital	400	400
Retained earnings	320	180
Common shareholders' equity	1,020	880
Total liabilities & equity	$2,060	$1,940

Figure 2: Soprano Company Balance Sheet and Income Statement (Continued)

Income Statement	2006
Sales	$4,000
Cost of goods sold	$3,000
Gross profit	1,000
Operating expense	650
Operating profit	350
Interest expense	50
Earnings before taxes	300
Taxes	100
Net income	$200
Common dividends	$60

During 2006, the company discovered that $150 of its operating expenses should have been capitalized, which would also have increased depreciation expense by $20.

Complete the table in Figure 3, *assuming that there will be no impact on taxes:*

Figure 3: Soprano Company Answer Template

	Before Capitalization	After Capitalization
Net income	$200	_____
Profit margin	5.0%	_____
Return on capital	12.5%	_____
Cash flow from operations	220	_____
Cash flow from investing	(100)	_____
Total cash flow	10	_____
Debt/equity	59.8%	_____

Answer:

Net income: Cash operating expense decreases by $150, but depreciation increases by $20. New net income will be 200 + (150 − 20) = $330.

Profit margin: net income/sales = 330 / 4,000 = 8.3%. This ratio increased because the numerator, or net income, increased and the denominator remained constant.

Return on capital: 2006 total assets will increase by $150 less the depreciation of $20. New total assets = 2,060 + 150 − 20 = $2,190. Return on total capital = (net income + interest expense) / average total capital = (330 + 50) / [(2,190 + 1,940) / 2] = 18.4%. This ratio also increased. As will usually be the case, the relative net income (numerator) effect of the decreased expense was greater than the relative increase in average total capital (equity).

Cash flow from operations: Cash operating expense decreases by $150, so cash flow from operations will be 220 + 150 = $370. This is an increase.

Cash flow from investing: Outflows will increase by $150, so cash flow from investments will be −100 − 150 = −$250. This is a decrease, or a higher outflow.

Total cash flow will not change and will remain at $10.

Note: These cash flow calculations ignore any tax impact.

Debt-to-equity: Assets increased by $130, so equity will now increase by $130. New equity = 1,020 + 130 = $1,150. The debt-to-equity ratio = long-term debt / total equity = 610 / 1,150 = 53.0%. This ratio decreased because equity (the denominator) increased by the amount of the capitalized asset, and debt (the numerator) remained unchanged.

CAPITALIZED INTEREST

Capitalized interest is the interest incurred during the construction of long-lived assets. It is included in the initial cost of the asset on the balance sheet instead of being charged off as interest expense on the income statement.

The argument for interest capitalization is that the cost of the self-constructed asset should be identical to the cost of the asset purchased after completion. The argument against the capitalization of interest is that the interest expense is the result of a *financing* decision and not an *operating* or *investment* decision. Internationally, capitalization of interest is optional.

Computation of capitalized interest. In the U.S., Statement of Financial Accounting Standards (SFAS) 34 requires the capitalization of interest costs incurred during the construction period.

- Interest incurred on borrowed funds during construction must be capitalized (i.e., included in cost of asset) and not expensed (SFAS 34), and the amount capitalized must be disclosed.
- If no specific borrowing is identified, the interest is estimated using the weighted average interest rate on outstanding debt up to the amount of the investment. Capitalized interest cannot exceed actual interest paid in any case.

When a firm constructs its own operating facilities (e.g., machinery or a building), then interest costs incurred during the period of construction are capitalized by adding that interest cost to the cost of the facility. To be capitalized, the interest must actually be paid by the firm (no opportunity costs are capitalized). The capitalized interest cost is based upon the average cost of the partially completed facility, first using the interest rate associated with borrowings to directly finance construction. Then the average interest rate of the firm's outstanding debt is applied to the excess of the investment in the project over these project-specific borrowings, if any. Thus, during construction, interest expense is total interest paid less capitalized interest.

Example: Capitalizing interest

During the current year, a firm has been constructing a building to be used for its production facility. The average cost of the building in process is $1,000,000. The firm has borrowed $500,000 at 5% interest to finance this construction. It has $3,000,000 of 10% debentures outstanding. Calculate the amount of interest that should be capitalized and the amount that should be expensed.

Answer:

Interest on construction debt: [$500,000 (0.05)]	$25,000
Interest on debentures [$500,000 (0.10)]	$50,000
Total capitalized interest	$75,000

$$\text{Total interest expense} = \text{total interest paid} - \text{capitalized interest}$$
$$= \$25,000 + \$300,000 - \$75,000$$
$$= \$250,000$$

Note: If the firm's only debt were the $500,000, 5% construction loan, then only the interest paid on that debt ($25,000) would be capitalized.

The Effects of Capitalizing Interest Costs

- During the current year, **capitalized interest decreases interest expense and increases net income.** For analysis purposes, capitalized interest should be added to interest expense and taken out of the fixed asset. When the capitalized interest is removed from fixed assets, depreciation expense will be reduced when that asset is placed in operations.
- **Capitalized interest distorts the classification of cash flows.** Interest capitalized as part of fixed assets is reported as a cash flow from investing (CFI), not a cash flow from operations (CFO). So CFO is overstated and CFI is understated. Therefore, cash flows should be adjusted by adding the capitalized interest back to the CFI and deducting it with the other interest payments from the CFO.
- For firms in an expansion phase, **capitalization of interest may result in a gain in earnings over an extended period** of time because the amount of interest amortized will not catch up with the amount of interest capitalized in the current period. Net income will be overstated.

Professor's Note: Although the LOS for this topic does not explicitly state that you should understand potential analyst adjustments for capitalized interest, many analysts "undo" the effects of capitalized interest when analyzing and comparing firms.

An analyst should adjust income statements and balance sheets to reverse the impact of capitalized interest. Specifically, an analyst should make the following adjustments:

- Interest that was capitalized during the year should be added to interest expense. The amount of interest capitalized is disclosed in the financial statement footnotes.
- The amortization of interest capitalized in previous years should be deducted from depreciation expense. However, capitalized interest from previous years might not be disclosed in the financial statements. If this amount is small, the analyst can ignore it. If it is large, the analyst must estimate the adjustment by using the historical ratio of capitalized interest to total capital expenditures.
- The interest that was capitalized during the year should be added back to cash flow from investment and subtracted from cash flow from operations.
- Ratios such as interest coverage and profitability ratios should be recalculated with the restated figures. Interest coverage ratios and net profit margins are likely lower without capitalization.

Capitalization of Interest and Interest Coverage Ratios

The interest coverage ratio, often called times interest earned, is EBIT (operating earnings) divided by interest expense. This ratio gives an indication of the margin of safety the company has in regard to making interest payments on debt. When interest is capitalized, current period interest costs are decreased and the interest coverage ratio is increased. There is an effect of capitalizing interest on EBIT since capitalizing interest incurred during construction increases the asset value, and thereby increases depreciation expense. In the period of capitalization, the decrease in interest expense will be larger than any decrease in EBIT from increased depreciation, so that the interest coverage ratio is unambiguously increased by capitalization. Since capitalization of interest in a prior period has no effect on interest expense in subsequent periods, any decrease in subsequent period EBIT from greater depreciation will decrease the interest coverage ratio for that period. If interest is capitalized over a number of accounting periods, interest coverage ratios may be higher than without capitalization in each period.

LOS 42.b: Explain the circumstances in which intangible assets, including software development costs and research and development costs are capitalized.

An **intangible asset** is an asset that has no physical existence and there is a high degree of uncertainty regarding future benefits.

When acquired in an arm's-length transaction, identifiable intangible assets (e.g., patents, trademarks, franchises) are recorded at acquisition cost. The expense of their use is recognized by amortization of cost over the shorter of estimated useful or legal lives.

The capitalize-versus-expense issue is relevant to intangible assets and resources such as patents, copyrights, licenses, brand names, goodwill, etc. The particular troubles with accounting for internally generated intangible assets are that the costs may not be easily separable, potential benefits may be difficult to measure (e.g., advertising), and economic life may be nearly impossible to establish (e.g., brand names).

Types of intangible assets include:

- *Research and development* (R&D): Although risky, R&D expenditures are clearly economic assets. (Empirical research suggests the average life is seven to ten years, depending on the assets and the industry). However, under Generally Accepted Accounting Principles (GAAP), specifically SFAS 2, it is required that *research and development expenditures be expensed* when incurred. Outside the U.S., R&D expenditures may be capitalized if various conditions are met (e.g., International Accounting Standard 9 requires expensing research costs but capitalizing development costs).
- *Patents and copyrights* costs (except legal fees of registering, which are capitalized) incurred in developing patents and copyrights are expensed. However, if the patent or copyright is purchased, then the cost is capitalized.
- *Franchise and license* costs are typically capitalized by the purchasing firm.
- *Brands and trademarks:* If *acquired* in arm's-length transactions, the cost is capitalized.
- *Advertising costs,* like R&D expenditures, are expensed when incurred. However, direct-response [direct relation between marketing and sales (e.g., orders taken in response to a call)] advertising costs are capitalized.
- *Goodwill* is an intangible asset representing the difference between the amount paid for an acquired firm and the fair market value of its net assets. Goodwill may be recognized and capitalized only in purchase transactions. Please note that under U.S. GAAP, capitalized goodwill is not expensed (amortized) on a regularly scheduled basis. Instead, an impairment exercise is performed each year to determine if purchased goodwill has been impaired relative to its balance sheet value. If an impairment has occurred, this impairment write off hits the income statement as an expense.
- *Computer software development costs:* SFAS 86 requires that all costs incurred to *establish* the technological or economic feasibility of software intended to be sold to others be expensed (e.g., R&D). Subsequent costs may be capitalized as part of inventory. Disparate accounting for software development costs (e.g., Microsoft expenses all software costs) requires the analyst to *evaluate and eliminate the impact of capitalization* to facilitate company comparisons. SOP 98-1 *requires* expensing of development costs prior to establishing feasibility for software intended for internal use, and requires capitalization of development costs for internal-use software after technological feasibility has been established. Net income computed after "undoing" the effects of capitalizing software development cost will typically be lower. Reclassifying these costs as operating rather than investing cash flows can have a significant impact on cash flow classification, reducing CFO and increasing CFI.

The financial statement effects of intangibles. Consistent with the effects of expensing versus capitalizing, capitalizing development costs will increase current net income. If expenditures are increasing, future net incomes will be greater for the capitalizing firm. Thus, return on assets will be greater and debt-to-equity ratio lower (more income, more equity) for the capitalizing firm. If development expenditures are decreasing, then the amortization of the capitalized expenditures will result in lower future net incomes (and lower ROA) for the capitalizing firm.

Although total cash flows are unaffected, capitalizing development costs will result in lower cash flow from investing and greater cash flow from operations. This is summarized in Figure 4:

Figure 4: Impact of Capitalizing vs. Expensing Development Cost

Effect on ...	If capitalized ...	If expensed ...
Current net income	Greater	Smaller
Future income (increasing capitalized expenditures)	Greater	Smaller
Future income (decreasing capitalized expenditures)	Smaller	Greater
Debt-equity ratio	Smaller	Greater
Return on assets (initial)	Greater	Smaller
Return on assets (future)	Smaller	Greater
Total cash flow	Same	Same
Cash flow from operations	Greater	Smaller
Cash flow from investing	Smaller	Greater

The effect of capitalizing expenditures of various types on ROE and ROA is sometimes confusing to students because the numerator (net income) as well as the denominators (equity and assets) both go up with capitalization. The key to the overall effect on the ratios is that we can safely assume in almost all cases that both equity and assets are significantly larger than net income. For a simple example, consider a non-capitalizing company with NI of 10, equity of 100, and assets of 200. ROE = 10% and ROA = 5%. If expenditures of 2 are capitalized rather than expensed, $ROE = \frac{12}{102} = 11.8\%$ and $ROA = \frac{12}{202} = 5.9\%$ in the year of capitalization.

LOS 42.c: Calculate and describe both the initial and long-term effects of asset revaluations on financial ratios.

Revaluation of assets with values that have decreased below their balance sheet values is permitted under both U.S. GAAP and IAS GAAP and reduction in asset carrying values (impairments) are covered separately. Revaluations to recognize increases in fixed asset values are not permitted under U.S. GAAP, but are permitted under IAS GAAP under IAS 16. Non-depreciable assets such as land typically appreciate over time to levels significantly above the book (historical) values recorded on the balance sheet and are therefore subject to upward revaluations.

A positive asset revaluation will result in an increase in the values of both equity and assets. In general, this will decrease debt ratios (D/E and D/A), decrease profitability ratios (ROE and ROA), and decrease asset turnover (sales/assets). For an upward revaluation of *depreciable* assets, EBIT and net income will be reduced, due to the increase in periodic depreciation, as will interest coverage ratios. The decrease in net income will further decrease profitability ratios and will, over time, decrease book value per share as well.

Example: Effects of Revaluation

Coser Inc. has assets with a book value of $8 million, debt with a book value of $5 million, and equity with a book value of $3 million. It has land (a non-depreciable asset) with a book value of $2 million and under IAS 16, Coser will revalue the land to its current market value of $4 million. Before the revaluation, net income for the year is expected to be $0.5 million. Calculate the effects on ROE, ROA, and the D/E ratio.

Answer:

The revaluation will increase the value of the land by $2 million from $2 million to $4 million, resulting in an increase in the value of assets from $8 million to $10 million and an increase in the book value of equity from $3 million to $5 million. There will be no effect on the income statement since it is a positive revaluation and the land is not depreciated.

The return on equity (ROE) will decrease from $0.5 million/$3 million = 16.67% to $0.5 million/$5 million = 10%.

The return on assets (ROA) will decrease from $0.5 million/$8 million = 6.25% to $0.5 million/$10 million = 5%.

The debt to equity ratio will decrease from $5 million/$3 million = 1.67 to $5 million/$5 million = 1.00.

KEY CONCEPTS

1. Capitalization of outlays, compared to expensing, causes lower variability of net income, higher net income, higher operating cash flow, and lower leverage ratios. Capitalization causes return on assets (ROA) and return on equity (ROE) to be higher in the year of capitalization and lower in later years unless capitalized expenditures are increasing.
2. Capitalization of interest causes interest expense to be lower, depreciation to be slightly higher, cash flow from operations to be higher, and the interest coverage ratio to be higher. Analysts often adjust financial statements to remove the effects of capitalized interest.
3. In general, intangible asset costs are capitalized when the assets are acquired from an outside entity. In most countries, R&D costs cannot be capitalized; only the legal fees to obtain a patent or trademark internally can be capitalized, and development costs for software for external sale may be capitalized after technical and economic feasibility have been established.
4. Upward asset revaluations (allowed under IASB GAAP) will increase asset and equity values, decreasing ROA, ROE, D/E, D/A, and asset turnover; and will decrease EBIT and NI when depreciable asset values are increased.

CONCEPT CHECKERS: ANALYSIS OF LONG-LIVED ASSETS, PART I: THE CAPITALIZATION DECISION

1. Which of the following statements is **TRUE**?
   A. The choice between capitalization and expensing makes no operational difference.
   B. Firms that capitalize costs will show more variability in reported income.
   C. Firms that capitalize costs will have lower assets and equity.
   D. Cash flow from operations is not affected by the capitalization or expensing choice.

2. For purposes of analysis, capitalized interest should be:
   A. added to fixed assets.
   B. added back to the cash flows for investment.
   C. added to interest expense and results in higher net income.
   D. subtracted from interest expense and results in higher net income.

3. With the exception of legal costs, generally accepted accounting principles (GAAP) require that costs incurred in:

	Developing Patents Are:	Purchased Patents Are:
A.	expensed	expensed
B.	expensed	capitalized
C.	capitalized	expensed
D.	capitalized	capitalized

4. Which of the following statements is **FALSE**? All other things being equal, firms that capitalize costs will:
   A. show smoother reported income than expensing firms.
   B. have higher operating cash flow and lower investment cash flow than expensing firms.
   C. have lower leverage ratios than expensing firms.
   D. have lower profitability ratios in the early years than expensing firms.

5. With the exception of legal costs, generally accepted accounting principles (GAAP) require that costs incurred in establishing the technological feasibility of software be:
   A. expensed, and interest expenses relative to the construction of a building must be expensed.
   B. expensed, and interest expenses relative to the construction of a building must be capitalized.
   C. capitalized, and interest expenses relative to the construction of a building must be expensed.
   D. capitalized, and interest expenses relative to the construction of a building must be capitalized.

6. Which of the following statements is *most* correct? Accounting choices:
   A. never affect cash flows.
   B. always affect cash flows.
   C. may affect the classification of cash flow components without affecting total cash flow.
   D. never affect the classification of cash flow components without affecting total cash flow.

7. Firm A expenses costs while Firm B capitalizes them. All other things being equal, which of the following choices *best* describes the relationship between the debt ratios of Firm A and Firm B?
   A. They will be equal.
   B. Firm A's will be lower.
   C. Firm A's will be higher.
   D. Cannot be determined without more information.

8.   Capitalizing construction interest costs leads to:
     A. a lower debt ratio.
     B. higher future depreciation expense.
     C. lower reported income after the first year.
     D. all of the above.

Use the following data to answer Questions 9 and 10.

Smokee Enterprises capitalizes most costs and Eb One Manufacturing expenses most costs.

9.   Which of the following choices **CORRECTLY** describes Smokee's financial results for current income, debt-to-equity ratio, and cash flow from operations as compared to Eb One's results?

	Current Net Income	Debt-to-Equity Ratio	Cash Flows From Operations
A.	Greater	Smaller	Smaller
B.	Greater	Smaller	Greater
C.	Smaller	Greater	Smaller
D.	Smaller	Smaller	Greater

10. Which of the following choices **CORRECTLY** describes Eb One's financial results for initial return on assets, total cash flow, and cash flow from investing as compared to Smokee's results?

	Initial Return on Assets	Total Cash Flow	Cash Flows From Investing
A.	Smaller	Larger	Equivalent
B.	Larger	Equivalent	Smaller
C.	Smaller	Equivalent	Larger
D.	Equivalent	Larger	Smaller

11. Which of the following statements about the treatment of intangible assets is **FALSE**?
     A. Advertising costs are expensed when incurred.
     B. All software development costs may be capitalized.
     C. Internally developed patent and copyright costs are expensed when incurred.
     D. In the U.S., research and development costs are expensed when incurred.

12. The interest costs during construction are:
     A. expensed as incurred.
     B. expensed at the completion of the construction project.
     C. capitalized and then, once construction is completed, amortized over the life of the loan.
     D. capitalized and then, once construction is completed, amortized over the life of the constructed asset.

13. Which of the following statements is **TRUE**?
     A. Research and development is capitalized according to U.S. GAAP.
     B. The costs associated with the creation of a brand name within a company are capitalized.
     C. In the case of a patent, the costs of developing the patent are expensed but legal costs can be capitalized.
     D. The difference between the purchase price and the fair value of identifiable net assets acquired in a purchase transaction is expensed in the period in which the acquisition is made.

14.   Wildwood Builders has assets of €315 million and liabilities of €112 million. The book value of its land holdings (a non-depreciable asset) is currently €30 million but its market value has increased since purchase to €45 million. If Wildwood revalues its land on the balance sheet to reflect this increase in value, the effect on ROE and net income in the period of the revaluation will be:

	ROE	Net Income
A.	decrease	decrease
B.	unchanged	increase
C.	decrease	unchanged
D.	increase	unchanged

ANSWERS – CONCEPT CHECKERS: ANALYSIS OF LONG-LIVED ASSETS, PART I: THE CAPITALIZATION DECISION

1. **A**   There is no operational difference.

2. **B**   For analysis purposes, interest expense should be added to cash flows for investment.

3. **B**   If a firm develops the patent as part of its own operations, the cost is expensed. Only costs for purchasing a patent are capitalized.

4. **D**   Firms that capitalize costs will show higher profitability ratios in early years due to the costs being spread out.

5. **B**   Establishing technological feasibility of software is an operational activity and costs must be expensed. Interest related to construction must be capitalized.

6. **C**   Overall cash flow may be the same even when accounting choices affect the classification of cash flow components. Accounting choices will affect cash flows if they affect taxes.

7. **C**   Firm A will have a lower level of assets, making the expensing firm's debt ratio appear higher.

8. **D**   All statements are true. The company will have a lower debt ratio because total equity (the denominator) will increase while the numerator is unchanged. The higher future depreciation expense results from the amortization of the capitalized interest, which an expensing firm would not have. This also results in lower reported income.

9. **B**   Capitalizing firms will have greater net incomes, smaller debt-to-equity ratios due to the larger amount of equity, and greater cash flow from operations due to the classification of expenditures as investment cash flows.

10. **C**   Firms that expense costs will have a smaller initial return on assets due to the effect of lower net income, the same total cash flows (only classification is different), and larger CFI due to expenses being considered CFO.

11. **B**   Software development costs are operational in nature and must be expensed.

12. **D**   Interest costs from construction are capitalized and amortized over the life of the asset.

13. **C**   R&D costs are expensed, only acquired brand names are capitalized, and goodwill is capitalized. Legal costs of securing a patent can be capitalized.

14. **C**   Equity value will be increased with no effect on net income.

The following is a review of the Financial Statement Analysis principles designed to address the learning outcome statements set forth by CFA Institute®. This topic is also covered in:

ANALYSIS OF LONG-LIVED ASSETS: PART II – ANALYSIS OF DEPRECIATION AND IMPAIRMENT

EXAM FOCUS

Depreciation is allocating the cost of an asset to expense over time. In reality, depreciation is an allocation of past cash flows; depreciation expense appears on the income statement but has no impact on the statement of cash flows. There are multiple acceptable methods of calculating depreciation, and the method the firm chooses is its own decision. A firm using a slower method of depreciation will show higher net income. A firm may choose to use an accelerated method on its tax return to show lower taxable income and thus pay less in taxes. On the Level 1 exam, be prepared to calculate depreciation using all of the methods discussed in this topic review. Also know the effects of accelerated versus straight-line depreciation, as well as the effects on financial statements and ratios of taking a write-down on an impaired asset.

LOS 43.a: Identify the different depreciation methods and discuss how the choice of depreciation method affects a company's financial statements, ratios, and taxes.

The underlying *principle of depreciation* is that cash flows generated by an asset over its life cannot be considered income until provision is made for the asset's replacement. This means that the *definition of income* requires a subtraction for asset replacement.

The accounting problem is how to allocate the cost of the asset over time. Depreciation is the systematic allocation of the asset's cost over time.

Two important terms are:

- *Book value.* The net value of an asset or liability as it is listed on the balance sheet. For property, plant, and equipment, book value equals historical cost minus accumulated depreciation.
- *Historical cost.* The original purchase price of the asset including installation and transportation costs. The gross investment in the asset is the same as its historical cost.

Depreciation is a real and significant operating expense. Even though depreciation doesn't require current cash expenditures (the cash outflow was made in the past when the company invested in the depreciable assets), it is an expense that is just as important as labor or material expense. Therefore, analysis should *not* exclude depreciation expense. For financial statements, the analyst must decide whether the depreciation expense the firm reports is significantly more or less than the true decline in the value of the asset over the period, its *economic depreciation*. One chain of video rental stores was found to be overstating income by depreciating its stock of movies by equal amounts each year. In fact, a greater portion of the decrease in the value of newly released movies was realized in the first year. Depreciating this asset by a greater amount during the first year would have better approximated economic depreciation than depreciating it by equal amounts over three years.

Four methods of calculating depreciation are described here.

Straight-line (SL) depreciation is the dominant method of computing depreciation. It applies an equal amount of depreciation to each year over the asset's estimated depreciable life:

$$\text{depreciation expense} = \frac{\text{original cost} - \text{salvage value}}{\text{depreciable life}}$$

Example: Calculating straight-line depreciation expense

Melfi Co. has purchased a machine with a 4-year useful life. The machine cost $4,000 and has an estimated salvage value of $1,000. Using the SL method, calculate depreciation expense in year 1 and year 4. Note: This same example will be used throughout this discussion.

Answer:

The constant depreciation expense over all years will be:

$$\frac{\text{original cost} - \text{salvage value}}{\text{depreciable life}} = \frac{(\$4,000 - \$1,000)}{4} = \$750$$

There are some flaws with using straight-line depreciation.

- Straight-line depreciation is constant through time, while repair and maintenance expense will typically increase over the life of the asset. This will cause a decrease in reported income over time.
- This method yields an increasing rate of return over the life of the asset.

For example, assume the asset discussed above generates an annual income of $1,200 before the $750 depreciation charge. Net income will be $450 a year for each of the asset's four years of useful life. The book value (cost less accumulated depreciation) of the asset begins at cost, then decreases with the added depreciation expense each year. This decreasing book value and constant income results in an increasing rate of return on the asset, as shown in Figure 1.

Figure 1: ROA Calculation

Year	Beginning Carrying Value	Straight-Line Depreciation	Net Income	Rate of Return on Assets
1	$4,000	$750	$450	11.25%
2	$3,250	$750	$450	13.85%
3	$2,500	$750	$450	18.00%
4	$1,750	$750	$450	25.71%

The increase in maintenance generally does not negate the increase in return on assets (ROA) caused by the constant depreciation expense.

There are two **accelerated depreciation methods**, sum-of-year's digits (SYD) and double-declining balance (DDB), which recognize greater depreciation expense in the early part of an asset's life and less expense in the latter portion of its life.

The economic justifications of accelerated depreciation methods include increasing repair and maintenance costs, decreasing revenues and operating efficiency, and greater uncertainty about revenues due to obsolescence in the later years of the asset's life.

Accelerated depreciation methods are usually used on tax returns (when allowed) because greater depreciation expense in the early portion of the asset's life results in less taxable income and a smaller tax payment. A firm may use straight-line depreciation for its financial statements and an accelerated method on its tax returns. This initial saving on taxes is a deferral because a greater tax payment will be required in the latter part of the asset's life. Note that total depreciation is initial cost minus salvage value over the asset's life in either case; an accelerated method just moves some depreciation to earlier periods.

The **sum of the years' digits** (SYD) method applies more depreciation in the early years of an asset's life than the later years. The formula to calculate SYD depreciation is:

$$\text{depreciation in year x} = \frac{\left(\text{original cost} - \text{salvage value}\right) \times \left(n - x + 1\right)}{SYD}$$

where:
n = depreciable life
$SYD = (1 + 2 + \ldots + (n - 1) + n)$

A quick way to calculate the sum is to use the following formula: sum = [n (n+1)]/2. Therefore, the sum for a 5-year useful life is [(5)(6)] / 2 = 15 and for a 10-year useful life is [(10)(11)] / 2 = 55.

Example: Calculating sum of the year's digits depreciation expense

Melfi Co. has purchased a machine with a 4-year useful life that cost $4,000 and has an estimated salvage value of $1,000. Using the sum of the years' digits method, calculate depreciation expense in year 1 and year 4.

Answer:

$SYD = 1 + 2 + 3 + 4 = 10$, or $SYD = [(4)(5)]/2 = 20/2 = 10$

$$\text{depreciation in year x} = \frac{\left(\text{original cost} - \text{salvage value}\right) \times \left(n - x + 1\right)}{SYD}$$

$$\text{depreciation in year 1} = \frac{\left(\$4{,}000 - \$1{,}000\right) \times \left(4 - 1 + 1\right)}{10} = \$1{,}200$$

$$\text{depreciation in year 4} = \frac{\left(\$4{,}000 - \$1{,}000\right) \times \left(4 - 4 + 1\right)}{10} = \$300$$

Note that the factors are simply 4/10, 3/10, 2/10, and 1/10 for the four years. Observe that the *total* depreciation expense calculated with the sum-of-years'-digits (SYD) method over the useful life of the asset is the same as that given by the straight-line method. That is, cost less salvage, which is $3,000.

The **double-declining balance** (DDB) method is a second accelerated method. The formula to calculate DDB depreciation is:

$$\text{depreciation in year } x = \frac{2}{\text{depreciable life}} \times \text{book value at beginning of year } x$$

The salvage value is not used in the formula. The remaining book value is not allowed to go below the salvage value. If the amount of depreciation in year x would take the book value below the salvage value, the depreciation in year x is equal to the difference between book value at the beginning of the year and the salvage value.

- The use of the *declining balance method* results in a constant percentage of an asset's carrying value (book value) being depreciated each period.

- The constant percentage can be any rate, but the most common are 200 DB (a.k.a. double declining balance or DDB) and 150 DB. The rate is stated as a percentage of the straight-line rate. If the asset has a 10-year life, the straight-line rate is 10% per year and the 200DB rate is 20%; if the asset has a 20-year life, the straight-line rate is 5% and the 150DB rate is 150% of 5% or 7.5%.

Example: Calculating double declining balance depreciation expense

Melfi Co. has purchased a machine with a 4-year useful life that cost $4,000 and has an estimated salvage value of $1,000. Using the double-declining balance method, calculate depreciation expense in year 1 and year 4.

Answer:

$$\text{depreciation in year x} = \frac{2}{\text{depreciable life}} \times \text{book value at beginning of year x}$$

$$\text{depreciation in year 1} = \frac{2}{4} \times \$4,000 = \$2,000$$

$$\text{book value at the beginning of year 2} = \$4,000 - \$2,000 = \$2,000$$

$$\text{depreciation in year 2} = \frac{2}{4} \times \$2,000 = \$1,000$$

Book value at the end of year 2 is $2,000 – $1,000 = $1,000. Because book value at the end of year 2 is equal to salvage value, depreciation in years 3 and 4 will be zero.

The **units-of-production** and **service hours** methods apply depreciation at the rate at which an asset is being used. Either the production capacity or the service life of the asset is estimated when the asset is put into service. The cost of the asset minus the salvage value is divided by either the production capacity or service life to achieve either a rate per unit or a rate per hour. Depreciation is then charged based on the year's production or usage. Depreciation is never charged once the asset's book value reaches its estimated salvage value.

Example: Calculating units-of-production and service hours depreciation expense

Melfi Co. has purchased a machine with a 4-year useful life. The machine cost $4,000 and has an estimated salvage value of $1,000. The depreciable life is four years, and the machine is estimated to last 6,000 hours and produce 30,000 units. The machine is operated 1,200; 2,000; 2,000; and 1,500 hours in years 1 through 4; and the machine produces 12,000; 11,000; 10,000; and 9,000 units in years 1 through 4. Calculate depreciation expense in year 1 and year 4 using the units-of-production and service hours methods.

Answer:

Units of production:

$$\text{rate per unit} = \frac{\$4,000 - \$1,000}{30,000 \text{ units}} = \$0.10$$

depreciation in year 1 = $0.10 × 12,000 = $1,200
depreciation in year 2 = $0.10 × 11,000 = $1,100
depreciation in year 3 = $0.10 × 10,000 = $1,000

However, book value at the beginning of year 3 was $1,700 (= $4,000 – $1,200 – $1,100), so only $700 would be charged to depreciation in year 3 to make the book value equal to the salvage value of $1,000, and no depreciation would be charged in year 4.

Service hours:

$$\text{rate per hour} = \frac{\$4,000 - \$1,000}{6,000 \text{ hours}} = \$0.50$$

depreciation in year 1 = $0.50 × 1,200 = $600
depreciation in year 2 = $0.50 × 2,000 = $1,000
depreciation in year 3 = $0.50 × 2,000 = $1,000
depreciation in year 4 = $0.50 × 1,500 = $750

However, book value at the beginning of year 4 was $1,400 ($4,000 – $600 – $1,000 – $1,000), so only $400 would be charged to depreciation in year 4 to make book value equal to the salvage value of $1,000.

Sinking fund depreciation, sometimes called the annuity method, is seldom used and is prohibited in the U.S. and other countries. Depreciation expense actually *increases* each year so that the asset earns the same rate of return each year.

You can think about the rate of return on an asset or its return on investment as the net income generated from using the assets divided by its book value. If net income is changing over an asset's life only because depreciation is changing, both SL and accelerated depreciation methods lead to an increasing return on investment over time. With straight-line depreciation, the net income is the same each year, but the book value is decreasing, which produces an increasing return on investment. With accelerated methods, net income (net of depreciation) is increasing each year as well, and the return on investment increases even more in later years. With sinking fund depreciation, depreciation increases each year so that net income decreases in proportion to the decrease in book value and keeps return on investment constant over the asset's life.

Effects of the Choice of Depreciation Method on Financial Statements, Ratios, and Taxes

Depreciation is an allocation of past investment cash flows, and the choice of depreciation method on the firm's financial statements has no impact on the statement of cash flows. It is important for the analyst to consider the capital expenditures to better understand the impact of the choice of depreciation methods.

In the early years of an asset's life, accelerated methods tend to depress net income and retained earnings and result in lower return measures [return on equity (ROE) and return on assets (ROA)]. At the end of the asset's life, the effect reverses. For firms with stable or rising capital expenditures, the early year effect will dominate, and depreciation expense on the total firm basis will be higher using accelerated methods.

A firm that chooses an accelerated depreciation method (e.g., DDB) instead of using straight-line, will tend to have greater depreciation expense and lower net income. This will persist if the firm is investing in new assets such that the lower depreciation on old assets is more than compensated for by the higher depreciation on new assets. (If the firm is not investing in new assets, then the higher depreciation expense and lower net income are reversed in the later part of the asset's life.)

Although accelerated depreciation methods produce lower net assets and equity than straight-line, the lower net income causes a lower return on equity and return on assets. Regarding turnover ratios (e.g., sales over total assets), the lower asset levels for accelerated methods imply a higher ratio. There is no effect on cash directly caused by choice of depreciation methods, although the use of accelerated depreciation on tax returns reduces the cash paid for income taxes early in the asset's life and increases taxes paid in the later years of the asset's life. These relationships are summarized in Figure 2, assuming the firm is investing in a new asset.

Figure 2: Financial Statement Impact of Depreciation Methods*

	Straight Line	Accelerated (DDB & SYD)
Depreciation expense	Lower	Higher
Net income	Higher	Lower
Assets	Higher	Lower
Equity	Higher	Lower
Return on assets	Higher	Lower
Return on equity	Higher	Lower
Turnover ratios	Lower	Higher
Cash flow**	Same	Same

*   The relationships indicated in the table are for the early years of an
    asset's life and are reversed in the latter years of the asset's life if the
    firm's capital expenditures decline.
** Assuming the depreciation method used for tax purposes is unchanged.

LOS 43.b: Explain the role of depreciable lives and salvage values in the computation of depreciation expenses, and compute and describe how changing depreciation methods or changing the estimated useful life or salvage value of an asset affects financial statements and ratios.

Depreciable Lives and Salvage Values

In general, a longer useful life estimate decreases annual depreciation and increases reported net income, while a shorter estimate of the asset's useful life will have the opposite effect. A higher estimate of the residual (salvage) value will also decrease depreciation and increase net income, while a lower estimate of the salvage value will increase depreciation and decrease net income.

The choice of estimated lives and residual values gives companies some ability to manage earnings, and an analyst should be alert to instances of excessively long depreciable life assumptions or excessively high residual (salvage) values, both of which will lead to an overstatement of net income. Although companies are required to disclose information on depreciable lives, such disclosures are often given as ranges and cover groups of assets rather than specific assets.

- Management could estimate a useful life longer than that warranted (thus reducing depreciation expense and increasing income) and then write down the overstated assets in a restructuring process.
- Management might also write down assets, taking an immediate charge against income, and then record less future depreciation expense based on the written-down assets. This results in higher future net income in exchange for a one-time charge to current income.
- Although not as significant as misspecifying the life of a depreciable asset, the residual value could be significantly overstated, thus understating depreciation expense during the life of the asset and overstating the loss when the asset is retired.

Changing Depreciation Methods or Changing the Estimated Useful Life or Salvage Value of an Asset

There are three ways that a company can change the way depreciation is applied.

Change in method for new assets. A company can change its method of depreciation for new assets but keep depreciating existing assets the same way it has done in the past. This will cause estimates of future income to be revised. The effect of this type of change on income will be gradual.

Change in method for existing assets. If the company changes its method of depreciation for all assets, several changes will occur:

- The firm must show the effect the change would have had on prior-period results.
- Existing depreciation expense will change.
- Because this change represents a change in an accounting principle, the cumulative effect of the change on past income will be shown net of tax on the income statement.
- Estimates of future income will be revised. These changes may be significant.

Changes in depreciable lives or salvage values. Changes in depreciable lives or salvage values are considered changes in accounting estimates and not a change in an accounting principle. Past income does not need to be restated. However, current income will change and estimates of future income will be revised, so the analyst should be alert to the possibility of earnings manipulation from such a change. Although no cumulative effect exists when estimated life is increased (change in estimate), a more liberal estimate of an asset's economic life will decrease depreciation and increase net income, ROA, and ROE. The opposite will occur if the firm reduces estimated asset life or changes to an accelerated depreciation method.

Effect of changes on financial statements. Switching from accelerated methods to straight-line will cause expenses to be lower and income to be higher. If a firm changes from an accelerated to straight-line depreciation method, the effect on financial statements is summarized in Figure 3.

Figure 3: Effect of Changing Depreciation Methods

Cumulative effect if applied to all assets	Increases net income—no change in income from continuing operations
Cumulative effect if applied only to newly acquired assets	No cumulative effect exists
Depreciation expense	Decreases
Net income from continuing operations	Increases
ROA and ROE	Although assets and equity increase, the larger net income will increase these ratios

LOS 43.c: Discuss the use of fixed asset disclosures to compare companies' average age of depreciable assets, and calculate, using such disclosures, the average age and average depreciable life of fixed assets.

The footnotes to the financial statements typically provide the analyst with a wealth of information regarding the structure of the company's fixed asset base. An analyst can use this data and other financial statement data to compute average age estimates. Average age data is useful for two reasons:

- It helps identify portfolios of older, less-efficient assets, which may make the firm less competitive.
- An analyst can estimate when major capital expenditures will be required, which will help the analyst forecast when the firm will face significant financing requirements.

In addition:

- If a firm's average depreciable life is significantly greater than that of a similar firm, then one would expect it to have a lower depreciation expense and higher net income because it has used the longer useful life expectation.
- If the average age of assets is large and the cost of new PP&E has risen over time, then the firm's profit margins will be higher because depreciation expense is based on less costly, but potentially less efficient, PP&E.

There are three calculations that are useful concerning the quality of fixed assets on the balance sheet.

- **Average age** (in years) is approximated by:

$$\frac{\text{accumulated depreciation}}{\text{depreciation expense}}$$

This is only a rough estimate and can be significantly affected by changes in the asset mix.

- **Relative age,** or average age as a percentage of depreciable life, is:

$$\frac{\text{accumulated depreciation}}{\text{ending gross investment}}$$

This calculation is more accurate when straight-line depreciation is being used and provides a better indication of whether the firm's assets are old or new.

- **Average depreciable life** is approximated by:

$$\frac{\text{ending gross investment}}{\text{depreciation expense}}$$

As is true for average age (in years), this is only an approximation and is affected by changes in the asset mix.

Example: Calculating average age and depreciable life

At the end of 2003, a company has gross fixed assets of $3 million and accumulated depreciation of $1 million. During the year, depreciation expense was $500,000.

What is the average age in years and in percentage of the fixed assets, and what is the average depreciable life?

Answer:

$$\text{average age in years} = \frac{\text{accumulated depreciation}}{\text{depreciation expense}} = \frac{\$1,000,000}{\$500,000} = 2 \text{ years}$$

$$\text{average age as a percentage} = \frac{\text{accumulated depreciation}}{\text{ending gross investment}} = \frac{\$1,000,000}{\$3,000,000} = 33\%$$

$$\text{average depreciable life} = \frac{\text{ending gross investment}}{\text{depreciation expense}} = \frac{\$3,000,000}{\$500,000} = 6 \text{ years}$$

If a firm's relative age of plant and equipment is high, then the firm has not been adding to its capital stock. The firm is probably a less efficient and less competitive producer and will have to invest in PP&E in the future. However, the measure is sensitive to the estimated life and salvage value used—the shorter the estimated life, the greater the depreciation and the higher the average age percentage.

LOS 43.d: Define impairment of long-lived assets and explain what effect such impairment has on a company's financial statements and ratios.

Financial reporting of impaired assets. Generally accepted accounting principles (GAAP) *require* that assets be carried at acquisition cost less accumulated depreciation. There is also a requirement that carrying amounts be reduced to market value when there is no longer an expectation that net balance sheet values can be recovered from future operations.

Assets carried at more than the recoverable amounts are considered *impaired*. For impaired assets retained by the firm, the issue is how to report the firm's inability to fully recover its carrying amount. Since management largely controls the timing and amount of impairment recognition, it is a potential tool for income manipulation. It is difficult to compare the impact of impairment and the resulting ratios over time and across companies.

Professor's Note: Impairments are reported on the income statement pretax (above the line) as a component of income from continuing operations.

Impairment losses are sometimes reported as a component of restructuring, which also includes elements that affect cash flows (e.g., severance pay). It is, therefore, important to separate writedowns of assets that do not affect cash flow from those components of restructuring that do affect cash flow.

Loss from the impairment of assets must be recognized when there is evidence of a lack of recoverability of the carrying amount. Lack of recoverability may be signaled by:

- Changes in business environment or laws and regulations.
- A decline in the usage rate or market value of an asset.
- A forecast for a significant decline in profitability related to the asset.
- Significantly higher costs than expected.

The impairment of an asset cannot be restored under U.S. GAAP. However, some foreign countries and the IASB allow firms to recognize increases in value.

If an asset is held for disposition, it is carried on the balance sheet at the lower of cost or net realizable value.

Recoverability test. An asset is considered impaired if the carrying value (asset cost less accumulated depreciation) is more than the undiscounted cash flow from the asset's use and disposal.

$$\text{Impaired if:} \quad \frac{\text{carrying value}}{\text{of assets}} > \frac{\text{undiscounted expected}}{\text{future cash flows}}$$

Loss measurement. If a long-lived asset becomes permanently impaired, the relevant portion of its book value should be immediately recognized as a loss on the income statement. The loss is the excess of carrying value over the asset's fair market value (if known) or an estimate of present value of future cash flows if market value is unknown.

Professor's Note: The difference between the way cash flows are treated in testing for and measuring impairment can be confusing. In testing for impairment, undiscounted future cash flows are used. Once impairment has been detected, it should be estimated using discounted future cash flows.

Impact of Impairment on Financial Statements

- A writedown of assets affects the balance sheet categories of assets (PP&E), deferred tax liabilities, and stockholders' equity (retained earnings). Deferred tax liabilities result because financial statement depreciation is less than tax return depreciation. An impairment charge on the financial statements moves depreciation closer to tax return depreciation and reduces the future tax liability expected as these amounts come together. Deferred tax liabilities are fully described in the next study session.
- During the year of writedown, the loss from impairment decreases income from continuing operations. This decreases retained earnings. The assets and associated deferred taxes are reduced.
- Fixed asset turnover and total asset turnover both increase because asset values are lower.
- Writedowns increase a firm's debt-to-equity ratio as a result of the decrease in retained earnings and equity.
- Cash flow is not affected. Recognition of the impairment leads to a reduction in a deferred tax liability, not a current refund.
- In future years, less depreciation expense is recognized on the written-down asset, resulting in higher net income. Figure 4 relates the effects of impairments.

Figure 4: Impairment—Effects on Financial Statements

Impairment Effects	
Cash flow	No effect
Assets (PP&E)	Decrease
Deferred tax liabilities	Decrease
Stockholders' equity	Decrease
Current net income, ROA, ROE	Decrease
Future net income, ROA, ROE	Increase
Future depreciation expense	Decrease
Asset turnover ratio	Increase
Debt-to-equity ratio*	Increase

*Current D/E increases as equity goes down with the impairment charge and then decreases over time because lower depreciation going forward increases net income, retained earnings, and equity.

Analysis of Impairments

- Impairments may compensate for past underdepreciation or changes in market conditions and are quite difficult to forecast.
- Cash flow resulting from tax effects is difficult to determine, although generally there is none because impairments are not deductible for taxes.
- Impairments have resulted in diverse accounting practices, undermining comparability across firms and through time.

LOS 43.e: Discuss the liability for closure, removal, and environmental effects of long-lived operating assets, and discuss the financial statement impact and ratio effects of that liability.

Companies often own and operate assets that cause environmental damage, including strip mines, nuclear power plants, offshore oil platforms, and production plants that produce toxic waste as a by-product. Governments often require the company to clean up the site after the company ceases using the asset, and restore the asset or land to its original condition. Prior to the issuance of SFAS 143, companies took different approaches to the accounting for this **asset retirement obligation** (ARO).

SFAS 143 requires a consistent treatment of the ARO resulting from obligations related to remedying environmental damage caused by a company. The following rules apply:

- SFAS 143 applies to all companies and all legal and contractual obligations, including leased assets and legally enforceable contracts.
- The fair value of the ARO (liability) must be recognized. Fair value is either the liability's market value or, if market value is not available, the present value of the expected cash flows necessary to retire the liability (return the asset to the condition required). An equal amount must be added to the carrying value of the asset.
- The company must recognize accretion of the liability on the income statement as part of interest expense. The liability on the balance sheet increases each year.
- Prior-period amounts are not adjusted for changes in the estimated amount of the liability.

The company is required to disclose the following information:

- A description of the ARO and the asset.
- A reconciliation of the ARO liability, including specific information on new liabilities incurred, old liabilities extinguished, accretion expense, and revisions to the ARO estimate.
- The fair value of funds set aside to retire the ARO obligation.

Most companies will experience the following financial statement effects from the implementation of SFAS 143:

- Fixed assets and liabilities reported on the balance sheet will increase.
- Net income will be lower because of the additional depreciation of the asset and the accretion of the liability. The accretion will increase each year.

In general, the implementation of SFAS 143 will make the financial statements of a firm with an ARO look worse. Figure 5 shows the ratio effects of implementation of SFAS 143.

Figure 5: Ratio Effects of SFAS 143

Ratio	Numerator	Denominator	Effect on Ratio
Asset turnover	Sales will not change.	Assets will increase because of higher fixed assets.	Decrease
Liabilities-to-equity	Liabilities will increase because of ARO liability.	Equity will decrease because of lower net income.	Increase
Return on assets	Net income will decrease.	Assets will increase.	Decrease
Interest coverage	EBIT will decrease because of higher depreciation.	Interest expense will increase because of accretion of ARO liability.	Decrease

KEY CONCEPTS

1. Depreciation methods include straight-line and accelerated methods, units of production and service hours methods, and the sinking fund method.
2. Compared to straight-line methods, accelerated methods decrease operating earnings and net income in the early years of an asset's life and increase them in the later years.
3. The choice of depreciation method on the firm's financial statements does not affect the firm's cash flow, but the use of accelerated depreciation methods for tax reporting lowers taxable income and taxes due, increasing the firm's cash flow by the reduction in taxes.
4. A change in accounting method requires a restatement of prior income and an adjustment on the income statement for the cumulative after-tax effect of the change.
5. Longer estimates of useful lives and higher estimates of residual asset values both reduce depreciation expense and increase reported earnings.
6. Using balance sheet items, an analyst can estimate average age and average depreciable asset lives (both are approximate and affected by asset mix) and can estimate the relative age of the assets when straight-line depreciation is used.
7. Impairment must be recognized when the carrying value of an asset is higher than the sum of the future cash flows (undiscounted) from their use and disposal. Impairments will cause income, asset value, deferred taxes, equity, and future depreciation to decline, resulting in an increase in future net income.
8. SFAS 143 requires capitalization of environmental remediation expenses and for most firms will lead to higher assets, liabilities, depreciation expense, and interest expense, which will tend to decrease net income. ROA, asset turnover, and interest coverage ratios will all decrease, and liabilities-to-equity will increase.

CONCEPT CHECKERS: ANALYSIS OF LONG-LIVED ASSETS, PART II–ANALYSIS OF DEPRECIATION AND IMPAIRMENT

1. Which of the following accounts is *least likely* to be affected by an asset impairment?
    A. Inventory.
    B. Fixed assets.
    C. Deferred taxes.
    D. Stockholders' equity.

2. Which of the following will **NOT** enable a firm to report higher income in the future?
    A. Changing from sum of the years' digits to straight-line while capital expenditures are increasing.
    B. Declaring an asset impairment.
    C. Resetting the salvage values of all of its assets to zero.
    D. Increasing the depreciable life of all of its assets.

Use the following data to answer Questions 3 through 6.

Acquisition cost of asset	$25,000
Salvage value	$3,000
Useful life	4 years
Cash flow per year	$8,000
Expected output of machine	25,000 units

3. Based on the straight-line (SL) method, the first year's depreciation will be:
    A. $4,460.
    B. $5,500.
    C. $6,250.
    D. $8,800.

4. Based on the sum of the years' digits (SYD) method, the first year's depreciation will be:
    A. $4,460.
    B. $5,500.
    C. $6,250.
    D. $8,800.

5. Based on the double-declining balance (DDB) method, the first year's depreciation will be:
    A. $4,400.
    B. $5,500.
    C. $8,800.
    D. $12,500.

6. If the actual usage of the asset in the first year is 7,200 units, then depreciation under the units-of-production method will be:
    A. $4,400.
    B. $5,500.
    C. $6,336.
    D. $7,200.

7. Compared to firms using the sum of the years' digits (SYD) method, a firm using straight-line (SL) depreciation will initially report earnings that are:
   A. lower.
   B. equal.
   C. greater.
   D. dependent on usage.

Use the following data to answer Questions 8 through 10.

Tofu Products, Inc., has purchased a new soybean processor for $300,000 (shipping and installation included).

- The processor has a useful life of 15 years.
- The expected salvage value is $10,000.
- Their corporate tax rate is 39%.
- They expect to earn $500,000 before depreciation and taxes.

8. What is the depreciation expense for year 3 if the sum of the years' digits (SYD) depreciation method is used?
   A. $19,333.
   B. $29,604.
   C. $31,417.
   D. $36,250.

9. What is the depreciation expense for year 2 if the double-declining balance (DDB) method is used?
   A. $19,333.
   B. $24,242.
   C. $34,667.
   D. $40,000.

10. Which of the three methods—SL, SYD, or DDB—will produce the *most* year-1 net income?
   A. Straight-line.
   B. Sum of the years' digits.
   C. Double-declining balance.
   D. They all will produce the same level of net income.

Use the following data to answer Questions 11 through 13.

Gross plant and equipment $1,500,000
Depreciation expense $225,000
Accumulated depreciation $675,000
The firm uses SL depreciation.

11. The average depreciable life of plant and equipment is:
   A. 3.00 years.
   B. 3.67 years.
   C. 6.67 years.
   D. 10.33 years.

12. The average age, given as percent, of the plant and equipment is:
   A. 40%.
   B. 45%.
   C. 50%.
   D. 55%.

13.   The average age in years of plant and equipment is:
      A. 2.67 years.
      B. 3.00 years.
      C. 3.67 years.
      D. 6.67 years.

14.   Which of the following statements about depreciation methods is FALSE?
      A. Sinking fund depreciation is a common depreciation method in the U.S.
      B. The cost of plant and equipment includes all necessary expenditures made prior to placing the asset into service.
      C. When using the DDB method, depreciation is ended when book value is reduced to salvage value.
      D. Accelerating deductions by using SYD for tax purposes and SL for financial reporting will result in the creation of a deferred tax liability.

15.   Which of the following statements is *most likely* FALSE? Assuming the firm continues to invest in new assets, firms that choose accelerated depreciation over straight-line (SL) depreciation will tend to have lower:
      A. equity.
      B. net income.
      C. return on assets.
      D. depreciation expense.

16.   Which of the following statements is TRUE? When a company changes the salvage values of an asset:
      A. past earnings must be restated.
      B. the company must report a change in accounting principles.
      C. current and future income will be slightly affected.
      D. an impairment is declared.

17.   Which of the following statements about how inflation affects the measurement of economic depreciation is FALSE? In an inflationary period:
      A. reported ROAs and ROEs will be too low.
      B. reported income will be too high.
      C. depreciation based on historical costs will not be sufficient to replace the asset.
      D. depreciation based on the current cost of the asset (rather than historical costs) will create superior future cash flow estimates.

18.   A change in depreciation method is:
      A. not allowed under GAAP.
      B. considered a change in accounting estimates.
      C. considered a change in accounting principles.
      D. required when an asset is judged to be impaired.

19.   An asset is impaired when:
      A. accumulated depreciation exceeds acquisition costs.
      B. the firm can no longer fully recover the carrying amount of the asset through operations.
      C. accumulated depreciation plus salvage value exceeds acquisition costs.
      D. the present value of future cash flows exceeds the carrying amount of the asset.

20. Which of the following statements is FALSE? During the year of a writedown, the loss from impairment will decrease:
    A. cash flows.
    B. asset values.
    C. retained earnings.
    D. income from continuous operations.

21. Which of the following choices describes a *benefit* of calculating average age of assets?
    A. Firms with low average age of assets typically are inefficient.
    B. An analyst can use the data to help forecast future capital expenditures.
    C. Average age multiplied by asset turnover will be equal to the DuPont ROE.
    D. Risk arbitrage analysts view companies with low average age as takeover candidates.

22. To determine whether an asset is impaired, an analyst should use:
    A. discounted cash flows and should use discounted cash flows to calculate the amount of the impairment.
    B. discounted cash flows and should use undiscounted cash flows to calculate the amount of the impairment.
    C. undiscounted cash flows and should use discounted cash flows to calculate the amount of the impairment.
    D. undiscounted cash flows and should use undiscounted cash flows to calculate the amount of the impairment.

23. Which of the following statements about SFAS 143 on environmental remediation is FALSE?
    A. Implementation of SFAS 143 inflates depreciation expense.
    B. Ratio impacts include lower asset turnover and higher debt-to-equity ratios.
    C. The periodic interest accretion increases expenses and decreases cash flow from operations.
    D. The asset and liability are recorded at the time of asset acquisition and include the costs to return the land to the condition required.

24. Which depreciation method will NOT lead to an increasing return on investment when net asset cash flows are level over the asset's life?
    A. Sum-of-the-year's-digits.
    B. Straight line.
    C. Double declining balance.
    D. Sinking fund.

ANSWERS – CONCEPT CHECKERS: ANALYSIS OF LONG-LIVED ASSETS, PART II–ANALYSIS OF DEPRECIATION AND IMPAIRMENT

1. **A**   Inventory will not be affected.

2. **C**   Decreasing salvage values to zero would result in higher depreciation expense and, thus, decreased income. To increase income, the company would need to increase salvage values. The other choices would result in less depreciation expense and, thus, higher income.

3. **B**   Straight-line (SL) depreciation is equal for all years.

$$\text{year 1 SL depreciation} = \frac{\text{original cost} - \text{salvage value}}{\text{depreciable life}}$$

$$\frac{\$25,000 - \$3,000}{4} = \$5,500$$

4. **D**   Sum of years' digits (SYD) depreciation for year 1 $= (\text{original cost} - \text{salvage value}) \times \dfrac{(\text{useful life} - \text{year of interest} + 1)}{\text{sum of the useful life's digits}}$

$$= \frac{(\$25,000 - \$3,000)(4 - 1 + 1)}{(4 + 3 + 2 + 1)} = \$8,800$$

5. **D**   Using the double-declining balance method:

$$\text{year 1 depreciation} = \frac{2}{\text{useful life}} \times \text{original cost} = \frac{2}{4} \times \$25,000 = \$12,500$$

6. **C**   Using the units of production method, the year 1 depreciation = rate per unit × number of units.
Rate per unit = (original cost − salvage value) / expected output = (25,000 - 3,000 / 25,000) = 0.88
Thus, year 1 depreciation = 0.88 × (7,200) = \$6,336.

7. **C**   The sum of years' digits (SYD) method will report greater depreciation early on, thus reporting lower earnings. A firm using straight-line (SL) depreciation will report greater earnings. Neither method considers usage.

8. **C**   SYD depreciation for year 3 $= (\text{original cost} - \text{salvage value}) \times \dfrac{\text{useful life} - \text{year of interest} + 1}{\text{sum of the useful life's digits}}$

$$\text{SYD} = 1 + 2 + \ldots + 15 = 120$$

$$\text{depreciation} = \frac{(15 - 3 + 1)}{120} \times 290,000 = \$31,417$$

9. **C**   Depreciation in year 1: $\dfrac{2}{15} \times 300,000 = \$40,000.$

Book value in the beginning of the second year = 300,000 − 40,000 = \$260,000.

Depreciation in year 2: $\dfrac{2}{15} \times 260,000 = \$34,667.$

10. **A**   Because straight-line (SL) depreciation reports the lowest expense, it will report the highest year-1 income. The other two methods accelerate depreciation expense.

11. **C**   Average depreciable life $= \dfrac{\text{ending gross investment}}{\text{depreciation expense}} = \dfrac{1,500,000}{225,000} = 6.67 \text{ years.}$

12. **B** Average age as a percentage of plant and equipment $= \dfrac{\text{accumulated depreciation}}{\text{ending gross investment}} = \dfrac{675,000}{1,500,000} = 45\%$

13. **B** Average age $= \dfrac{\text{accumulated depreciation}}{\text{depreciation expense}} = \dfrac{675,000}{225,000} = 3.00$ years

14. **A** Sinking fund depreciation is prohibited in the U.S.

15. **D** A firm that continues to invest in new assets will have higher depreciation expense due to the use of accelerated methods.

16. **C** Changing the salvage value of an asset is considered a change in accounting estimate; past income does not need to be restated.

17. **A** Inflation causes ROA and ROE to be too high because the true cost of replacing the asset is not reflected by depreciation.

18. **C** A change in depreciation method is a change in the method of accounting. The cumulative effect on past income should be noted.

19. **B** This statement correctly describes an impaired asset.

20. **A** The loss from impairment does not affect cash flow.

21. **B** Average age calculations can be useful because they allow an analyst to assess the quality of a company's assets and help the analyst forecast when major capital expenditures will be required.

22. **C** Don't let this confuse you. In testing for impairment, undiscounted cash flows are used. Once impairment has been detected, it should be measured using discounted cash flows.

23. **C** Cash flow is not decreased by SFAS 143 since the annual accretion is not a cash charge. The other statements are true. The debt-equity ratio is higher because debt will be higher and equity will be lower. Asset turnover ratios are lower because assets are higher. The present value of the liability added to the asset's balance at the time of purchase is depreciated over the asset's useful life, thus increasing depreciation expense.

24. **D** Sinking fund depreciation is calculated to produce a constant return on investment.

ANALYSIS OF INCOME TAXES

EXAM FOCUS

Legally, companies are permitted to keep two sets of financial records in the U.S.—one for financial reporting and one for tax reporting. Candidates should be aware of the terminology that relates to each set of records, notably taxes payable, which are the taxes actually due to the government; and income tax expense, which is reported on the income statement and reflects taxes payable plus any deferred income tax expense. Because tax reporting uses a modified cash basis and financial reporting uses accrual accounting according to Generally Accepted Accounting Principles, differences in income can result. This leads to the creation of deferred tax liabilities, which the company may have to pay in the future, or deferred tax assets, which may provide benefits in the future. For the exam, you should know that some differences between taxable and pretax income are temporary, while some are permanent and will never reverse. Be prepared to calculate taxes payable, tax expense, deferred tax liabilities and assets, and be able to adjust financial statements for permanent income differences.

LOS 44.a: Discuss the key terms (e.g., deferred tax asset, valuation allowance, deferred tax liability, taxes payable, income tax expense, temporary difference, permanent difference, etc.) used in income tax accounting, explain why and how deferred tax liabilities and assets are created, and describe the liability method of accounting for deferred taxes.

Professor's Note: Accounting definitions are not usually included directly in an LOS. You should expect to see questions involving tax terminology and definitions on the exam. To understand the material, pay particular attention to the difference between the definitions of taxable income (on the tax return) and pretax income (on the income statement) and the difference between the definitions of taxes payable (on the tax return) and income tax expense (on the income statement).

Tax Return Terminology

- **Taxable income.** Income subject to tax based on the tax return.
- **Taxes payable.** The tax liability on the balance sheet caused by taxable income. This is also known as current tax expense, but do not confuse this with income tax expense (see below).
- **Income tax paid.** Actual cash flow for income taxes, including payments or refunds for other years.
- **Tax loss carryforward.** The current net taxable loss that is used to reduce taxable income (thus, taxes payable) in future years and can generate a deferred tax asset.

Financial Reporting Terminology

- **Pretax income.** Income before income tax expense.
- **Income tax expense.** The expense recognized on the income statement that includes taxes payable and deferred income tax expense. It is extremely important to note that income tax expense is composed of taxes payable plus noncash items such as changes in deferred tax assets and liabilities (DTA and DTL).

    Income tax expense = taxes payable + ΔDTL – ΔDTA
- **Deferred tax expense.** The difference between taxes payable and income tax expense. This results from changes in deferred tax assets and liabilities.

- **Deferred tax asset.** Balance sheet amounts that result from an excess of taxes payable over income tax expense that are expected to be recovered from future operations.
- **Deferred tax liability.** Balance sheet amounts that result from an excess of income tax expense over taxes payable that are expected to result in future cash outflows. Deferred tax liabilities are created when more expense is applied to the tax return relative to the income statement (e.g., more depreciation). This results in lower taxable income and lower taxes payable on the tax return relative to the pretax income and tax expense that are shown on the income statement.
- **Valuation allowance.** Reserve against deferred tax assets based on the likelihood that those assets will not be realized.
- **Timing difference.** The difference between the treatment of expenditures on the tax return and for financial reporting.
- **Temporary difference.** The differences between tax and financial reporting that will reverse in the future and will affect taxable income when they reverse, including the differences in the carrying cost of depreciable assets on tax and accounting records.
- **Permanent difference.** The differences between tax and financial reporting that are not expected to reverse in the future.

Why and How Deferred Tax Liabilities and Assets are Created

A *deferred tax liability* is created when an income or expense item is treated differently on financial statements than it is on the company's tax returns, and that difference results in greater tax expense on the financial statements than taxes payable on the tax return.

Deferred tax liabilities are accounted for because the differences arising from unique accounting treatments for tax and financial reporting purposes are expected to reverse themselves (i.e., they are temporary differences) and they result in future cash outflows related to the payment of taxes.

The most common way that deferred taxes are created is when different depreciation methods are used on the tax return and income statement.

Let's look at how a DTL is created.

Situation: Asset cost $600,000, 3-year life, zero salvage value

Tax return depreciation is sum of years' digits (SYD), Year 1 $300,000, Year 2 $200,000, Year 3 $100,000.

Income statement depreciation is straight line (SL), $200,000 each year.

EBITDA is $500,000 each year.

Figure 1: Tax Return (40% Rate, SYD Depreciation)

	Year 1	Year 2	Year 3	Total 1-3
EBITDA	$500,000	$500,000	$500,000	1,500,000
Dep	−300,000	−200,000	−100,000	600,000
Taxable income	$200,000	$300,000	$400,000	$900,000
Tax Rate	× 0.40	× 0.40	× 0.40	× 0.40
Tax Payable	$80,000	$120,000	$160,000	$360,000

©2007 Schweser

Figure 2: Income Statement (40% Tax Rate, SL Depreciation)

	Year 1	Year 2	Year 3	Total 1-3
EBITDA	$500,000	$500,000	$500,000	1,500,000
Depreciation	–200,000	–200,000	–200,000	600,000
Pre-Tax Income	$300,000	$300,000	$300,000	$900,000
Tax Rate	× 0.40	× 0.40	× 0.40	× 0.40
Income Tax Expense	$120,000	$120,000	$120,000	$360,000

In year 1, taxes payable = $80,000 and income tax expense is $120,000, so $40,000 of the tax expense is deferred to a future period by using an accelerated depreciation method for tax purposes. We note this on the balance sheet by creating a deferred tax liability of $40,000, and income tax expense = taxes payable + change in DTL ($120,000 = $80,000 + $40,000).

In year 2, depreciation is equal for tax and income statements, taxable income equals pretax income, and there is no change in the deferred tax liability. DTL remains at $40,000.

In year 3, depreciation for tax purposes ($100,000) is less than depreciation on the income statement ($200,000); taxable income is greater than pretax income; and the DTL is reduced from $40,000 to zero. Income tax expense = taxes payable + change in DTL [$120,000 = $160,000 + (–$40,000)].

Note that over the useful life of the asset, total depreciation, total taxable (and pre-tax) income, and total taxes payable (income tax expense) are all equal. By using accelerated depreciation for tax purposes we *deferred* $40,000 of taxes from year 1 to year 3.

A *deferred tax asset* is created when an income or expense item is treated differently on financial statements than it is on the company's tax returns, and that difference results in lower taxes payable on the financial statements than on the tax return.

Similar to deferred tax liabilities, deferred tax assets are expected to reverse themselves through future operations and provide tax savings and, therefore, are accounted for on the balance sheet.

Warranty expenses and *tax-loss carry forwards* are typical causes of deferred tax assets.

The Liability Method of Accounting for Deferred Taxes

The liability method of accounting for deferred taxes starts from the premise that differences between taxes calculated on the income statement [Generally Accepted Accounting Principles (GAAP) accounting] and taxes from the income tax return (determined by the Internal Revenue Code) will be reversed at some future date. When income tax expense based on GAAP is greater than taxes payable on the income tax return, a deferred tax liability in the amount of the difference is entered on the balance sheet. Activities in the current period have caused the company to incur a tax liability that must be paid in a future period.

If a company has an expense item (e.g., estimated warranty expense) on its financial statements that is not deductible for tax purposes currently, a deferred tax asset will be created. This represents the future tax savings that will result when the deduction is taken (e.g., when warranty expense is actually paid).

Both deferred tax assets and liabilities are adjusted for changes in the tax rate expected for the period(s) in which the deferred tax asset/liability is expected to be reversed (usually the current tax rate). Additionally, deferred tax assets are adjusted for the probability that they will actually be realized in future periods. This adjustment is made by creating or adjusting a "valuation allowance" on the balance sheet. This item serves to reduce the DTA to reflect the probability that the DTA will not actually be realized in future periods.

LOS 44.b: Discuss the implications of a valuation allowance for deferred tax assets (i.e., when it is required, what impact it has on the financial statements, and how it might affect an analyst's view of a company).

Deferred tax assets can have a **valuation allowance**, which is a contra account (offset) against deferred tax assets based on the likelihood that these assets will not be realized.

For deferred tax assets to be beneficial, the firm must have future taxable income. If it is more likely than not (> 50% probability) that a portion of deferred tax assets will not be realized (insufficient future taxable income to take advantage of the tax asset), then the deferred tax asset must be reduced by a valuation allowance.

It is up to management to defend the recognition of all deferred tax assets. If a company has order backlogs or existing contracts which are expected to generate future taxable income, a valuation allowance would not be necessary. However, if a company has cumulative losses over the past few years or a history of an inability to use tax credit carryforwards, then the company would need to use a valuation allowance to reflect the likelihood that the deferred tax asset would never be realized.

A valuation allowance reduces income from continuing operations. Because an increase (decrease) in the valuation allowance will serve to decrease (increase) operating income, changes in the valuation allowance are a common means of managing or manipulating earnings.

Whenever a company reports substantial deferred tax assets, an analyst should review the company's financial performance to determine the likelihood that those assets will be realized. Analysts should also scrutinize changes in the valuation allowance to determine whether those changes are economically justified.

Professor's Note: The valuation allowance applies exclusively to deferred tax assets.

LOS 44.c: Explain the factors that determine whether a company's deferred tax liabilities should be treated as a liability or as equity for purposes of financial analysis.

If deferred tax liabilities are expected to reverse in the future, then they are best classified as liabilities. If, however, they are not expected to reverse in the future, they are best classified as equity. The key question is, "when or will the total deferred tax liability be reversed in the future?" In practice, the treatment of deferred taxes for analytical purposes varies. An analyst must decide on the appropriate treatment on a *case-by-case basis*. Some guidelines follow:

- In many cases, it may be unlikely that deferred tax liabilities will be paid. For example, if a company has deferred tax liabilities occurring solely because of the use of accelerated depreciation for tax purposes and the company's capital expenditures are expected to continue to grow in the foreseeable future, the deferred tax liability will not reverse and should be considered as equity. However, if growth is expected to stop or slow considerably, the liability will reverse and it should be considered as a true liability.
- If it is determined that deferred taxes are not a liability (i.e., non-reversal is certain), then the analyst should reduce the deferred tax liability and increase stockholders' equity by the same amount. This decreases the debt-to-equity ratio, sometimes significantly.
- Sometimes, instead of reclassifying deferred liabilities as stockholders' equity, the analyst might just ignore deferred taxes altogether. This is done if non-reversal is uncertain or financial statement depreciation is deemed inadequate and it is therefore difficult to justify an increase in stockholders' equity. Some creditors, notably banks, simply ignore deferred taxes.

Let's work through an example of the impact of growth on deferred tax liabilities using the following assumptions:

- A firm purchases an asset each year for three years: Asset 1 in the first year, Asset 2 in the second year, and Asset 3 in the third year.
- The cost of each of these assets is $3,000 with no salvage value and a 3-year life.
- Double-declining balance (DDB) method is used on tax returns and SL for financial statements.
- The tax rate is 30%.

Figures 3 through 5 reveal total tax deduction and total depreciation expense for these assets purchased in each of the first three years.

Figure 3: Tax Return Calculations—Double-Declining Balance (tax deduction)

	Year 1	Year 2	Year 3
Asset 1	$2,000	$667	$333
Asset 2	0	2,000	667
Asset 3	0	0	2,000
Total DDB depreciation	$2,000	$2,667	$3,000

Figure 4: Financial Statement Calculations—Straight line (financial statements)

	Year 1	Year 2	Year 3
Asset 1	$1,000	$1,000	$1,000
Asset 2	0	1,000	1,000
Asset 3	0	0	1,000
SL depreciation	$1,000	$2,000	$3,000

Figure 5: Cumulative Deferred Tax Liability

	Year 1	Year 2	Year 3
Deferred liability	$300	$500	$500

In year 1, the change in deferred tax liability is $(2,000 - 1,000)(0.30) = +\$300$. In year 2, the change is $(2,667 - 2,000)(0.30) = +\$200$.

Note: There is no reversal of the deferred liability. The cumulative deferred liability will continue to increase as long as the firm continues to grow.

LOS 44.d: Distinguish between temporary and permanent items in pretax financial income and taxable income.

Temporary differences are differences in taxable and pretax incomes that will reverse in future years. That is, current lower (higher) taxes payable will mean future higher (lower) taxes payable. These differences result in deferred tax assets or liabilities. Various examples and how they are classified on the financial statements are as follows:

- *Current liabilities.* The temporary difference that results from using the installment sales method for taxes and the sales method for pretax income. Recall that the installment sales and sales basis methods are used in revenue recognition.
- *Long-term liabilities.* The long-term tax liability that results from using the declining balance depreciation for the tax returns and SL depreciation for the financial statements.
- *Current assets.* The deferred tax assets created when warranty expenses are accrued on the financial statements but are not deductible on the tax returns until the warranty claims are paid.
- *Long-term assets.* The deferred tax asset created when post-retirement benefits expense in pretax income exceeds that allowed for a deduction on tax returns.
- *Stockholders' equity.* The gains or losses from carrying marketable securities at market value are deferred tax adjustments to stockholders' equity.

Permanent differences are differences in taxable and pretax incomes that will not reverse.

- Tax-exempt interest income and the proceeds from life insurance on key employees are not taxable but are recognized as *revenue* on the financial statements.
- Tax-exempt interest expense, premiums paid on life insurance of key employees, and goodwill amortization (under International Accounting Standards, or IAS) are examples of *expenses* on the financial statements, but they are not deductions on the tax returns. Remember that goodwill amortization is no longer permitted under U.S. GAAP.
- Tax credits for some expenditures directly reduce taxes and, unlike accelerated recognition of expenses for tax purposes, will not reverse in the future.

Permanent differences do not result in deferred tax liabilities or assets. Permanent differences between taxable income and pretax income are reflected in a difference between a firm's effective tax rate and its statutory tax rate.

A firm's *reported* effective tax rate is simply $\dfrac{\text{income tax expense}}{\text{pretax income}}$.

The statutory tax rate is the marginal tax rate in the jurisdiction in which the firm operates. Income recognized on the financial statements (e.g., tax-exempt interest income) that is not included in taxable income, will result in an effective tax rate lower than the statutory rate. Expenses recognized on the income statement that are not deductible for tax purposes (e.g., premiums paid on key employee life insurance) will tend to increase the effective tax rate relative to the statutory tax rate. Differences between the statutory rate and the effective rate can also arise when a firm's operations are in different geographic locations and subject to different tax laws. Sometimes the income of a foreign subsidiary is reinvested in the subsidiary and not remitted to the parent company, postponing taxation at the statutory rate. Remitting accumulated subsidiary income from prior periods would, of course, have an opposite effect on the difference between statutory and effective rates.

Indefinite reversals. There is uncertainty about whether some differences will reverse in the future. The most common of these differences is the undistributed earnings of unconsolidated subsidiaries or joint ventures. If income is earned but not distributed back to the parent company in the form of dividends, the income will be reflected on the income statement as pretax income but will not appear on the tax return. The parent may consider this income to be permanently reinvested in the subsidiary. In that case, the difference will never be reversed. The company can treat this difference as permanent if the parent controls the subsidiary or joint venture.

LOS 44.e: Determine income tax expense, income taxes payable, deferred tax assets, and deferred tax liabilities, and calculate and interpret the adjustment to the financial statements related to a change in the tax rate.

Calculations of deferred taxes require going through the tax returns and the income statement and noting the differences between taxable income on the tax return and pretax income on the income statement.

Example: Deferred tax liabilities

An asset costs $200,000, has a depreciable life of four years, and has zero salvage value. It is expected to produce $150,000 in annual revenue. It is depreciated by the DDB method for tax purposes and by SL for financial reporting purposes. The firm has a tax rate of 40%. Calculate the deferred tax liability stemming from the asset at the end of each of the next four years.

Answer:

Using the DDB method, depreciation will be $100,000, $50,000, $25,000, and $25,000 in each of the next four years. Year 1 = $100,000 = ($200,000 – 0)(2/4); Year 2 = $50,000 = ($200,000 – $100,000)(2/4); Year 3 = $25,000 = ($200,000 – $150,000) (2/4); Year 4 depreciation is the remaining $25,000 of book value.

The firm will report the following *for tax reporting*:

Figure 6: Tax Reporting—Deferred Tax Liability

	Year 1	*Year 2*	*Year 3*	*Year 4*	*Total*
Revenue	$150,000	$150,000	$150,000	$150,000	$600,000
Depreciation	$100,000	$50,000	$25,000	$25,000	$200,000
Taxable income	$50,000	$100,000	$125,000	$125,000	$400,000
Taxes payable	$20,000	$40,000	$50,000	$50,000	$160,000
Net income	$30,000	$60,000	$75,000	$75,000	$240,000

Depreciation using SL will be $50,000 per year.

The tax expense is calculated as the tax rate times pretax income, so for *financial reporting*:

Figure 7: Financial Reporting—Deferred Tax Liability

	Year 1	*Year 2*	*Year 3*	*Year 4*	*Total*
Revenue	$150,000	$150,000	$150,000	$150,000	$600,000
Depreciation	$50,000	$50,000	$50,000	$50,000	$200,000
Pretax income	$100,000	$100,000	$100,000	$100,000	$400,000
Tax expense	$40,000	$40,000	$40,000	$40,000	$160,000
Net income	$60,000	$60,000	$60,000	$60,000	$240,000

Total tax ($160,000) and total net income ($240,000) are the same for tax and financial reporting.

This approach to reporting taxes is based on an **income statement approach**. Income taxes are treated as a cost of operations and the matching principle implies tax expenses should be based on pretax income. The accelerated depreciation allowed for tax purposes results in lower taxes in the early years that are then reversed (or paid off) in later years.

The difference between pretax income on the financial statements and taxable income on the tax return is attributable to the different accounting treatments. For example, in year 1 the difference between tax expense and taxes payable is $40,000 – $20,000 = $20,000. Because the differences are expected to reverse, a *balance sheet perspective* recognizes a *liability* in the early years equal to the amount of tax that must eventually be paid back in later years. Note that the differences accrue over the life of the asset.

The firm will report the following deferred tax liabilities (represented as the cumulative figure) on the balance sheet shown in Figure 8.

Figure 8: Deferred Tax Calculation—Deferred Tax Liability

	Year 1	Year 2	Year 3	Year 4
Tax expense	$40,000	$40,000	$40,000	$40,000
Taxes payable	$20,000	$40,000	$50,000	$50,000
Annual deferred taxes	$20,000	$0	–$10,000	–$10,000
Deferred taxes (cumulative)	$20,000	$20,000	$10,000	$0

Example: Deferred tax assets

Consider warranty guarantees and associated expenses. Pretax income (financial reporting) includes an accrual for warranty expense, but warranty cost is not deductible for taxable income until the firm has made actual expenditures to meet warranty claims. Suppose:

- A firm has sales of $5,000 for each of two years.
- The firm estimates that warranty expense will be 2% of annual sales ($100).
- The actual expenditure of $200 to meet all warranty claims was not made until the second year.
- Assume a tax rate of 40%.

For tax reporting, taxable income and taxes payable for two years are:

Figure 9: Tax Reporting—Deferred Tax Asset

	Year 1	Year 2
Revenue	$5,000	$5,000
Warranty expense	0	200
Taxable income	$5,000	$4,800
Taxes payable	2,000	1,920
Net income	$3,000	$2,880

For financial reporting, pretax income and tax expense are:

Figure 10: Financial Reporting—Deferred Tax Asset

	Year 1	Year 2
Revenue	$5,000	$5,000
Warranty expense	100	100
Pretax Income	$4,900	$4,900
Tax expense	1,960	1,960
Net Income	$2,940	$2,940

In this example, year 1 and year 2 tax expense (on financial statements) is $1,960. Year 1 and year 2 taxes payable are $2,000 and $1,920. The year 1 difference of $40 (taxes paid greater than tax expense) is a deferred tax asset. In the second year, the temporary difference associated with warranties is reversed when tax expense of $1,960 is $40 more than taxes payable of $1,920.

Professor's Note: To summarize deferred tax asset and liability creation, if taxable income (on the tax return) is less than pretax income (on the income statement) and the cause of this difference is expected to reverse in future years, then a deferred tax liability is created; and if taxable income is more than pretax income and the difference is expected to reverse in future years, then a deferred tax asset results.

Adjustment to the Financial Statements Related to a Change in the Tax Rate

Besides the impact on current period taxes payable and income tax expense, under the liability method, *all balance sheet deferred tax assets and liabilities are revalued* when the tax rate the firm will face in the future changes. An increase (decrease) in the tax rate increases (decreases) both deferred tax assets and liabilities.

If the *tax rate increases*, the increase in deferred tax liabilities increases the income tax expense, and the increase in deferred tax assets decreases the income tax expense. As long as deferred tax liabilities exceed deferred tax assets (the most common occurrence), the net impact of the increase in the tax rate will be to increase tax expense, which will cause net income and stockholders' equity to decline.

If the *tax rate decreases*, the decrease in deferred tax liabilities decreases income tax expense, and the decrease in deferred tax assets increases income tax expense. As long as deferred tax liabilities exceed deferred tax assets (the most common occurrence), the net impact of the decrease in the tax rate will be to decrease the tax expense, which will cause net income and stockholders' equity to rise. The basic equation is:

$$\text{income tax expense} = \text{taxes payable} + \Delta DTL - \Delta DTA$$

Let's work through an example of financial statements and a change in tax rates:

Consider a firm that has a DTL of $16,000 and a DTA of $4,000 on the balance sheet at year-end, based on a tax rate of 40%. For the current year, accelerated depreciation used on the tax return is $20,000 more than straight line (income statement) depreciation, *and* warranty expense on the tax return is $5,000 less than warranty expense shown on the income statement. During the year the firm's tax rate is reduced from 40% to 30%.

Initially ignoring the balance sheet amounts, the current year calculations are:

	Tax Return	Income Statement	
Taxable income before dep. & warranty expense	$100,000	$100,000	
–Depreciation	–30,000	–10,000	adds 0.3 × 20,000 = +6,000 to DTL
–Warranty expense	–5,000	–10,000	adds 0.3 × 5,000 = +1,500 to DTA
	Taxable inc 65,000	Pretax inc 80,000	
	× 0.3	× 0.3	
	Tax payable 19,500	Tax expense 24,000	ΔDTL – ΔDTA = $4,500

Income tax expense = tax payable + ΔDTL – ΔDTA

$24,000 = $19,500 + $6,000 – $1,500

There are additional effects, however, from the adjustments to the DTL and DTA already on the balance sheet at the beginning of the year. The existing DTL of $16,000 must be reduced to $12,000 because the tax rate has

decreased by 25%, from 40% to 30% $\left(\dfrac{0.30}{0.40} \times \$16,000 = \$12,000\right)$. The existing DTA is reduced to

$\dfrac{0.30}{0.40} \times \$4,000 = \$3,000$. So the change in tax rate requires changes to existing balance sheet amounts:

ΔDTL = –$4,000 and ΔDTA = –$1,000

The calculation of income tax expense for the year will take all these effects into account.

For the current year we had income tax expense = taxes payable + ΔDTL – ΔDTA which was $24,000. When we also adjust income tax expense for the changes in existing balance sheet DTL and DTA amounts as computed above, we have:

$24,000 – $4,000 – (–$1,000) = $21,000

The net effect of the change in balance sheet deferred taxes on income tax expense is –($4,000 – $1,000) = –$3,000. Since the DTL was greater than the DTA, the decrease in the tax rate reduced the liability by more than it reduced the asset, resulting in a decrease in the current year income tax expense.

LOS 44.f: Analyze disclosures relating to deferred tax items and the effective tax rate reconciliation and discuss how information included in these disclosures affects a company's financial statements and financial ratios.

LOS 44.g: Compare and contrast a company's deferred tax items and effective tax rate reconciliation between reporting periods and/or to other companies.

The disclosure requirements of SFAS 109 include separate disclosure of the following information:

- Deferred tax liabilities, deferred tax assets, any valuation allowance, and the net change in the valuation allowance over the period.
- Any unrecognized deferred tax liability for undistributed earnings of subsidiaries and joint ventures.

- Current-year tax effect of each type of temporary difference.
- Components of income tax expense.
- Reconciliation of reported income tax expense and the tax expense based on the statutory rate.
- Tax loss carryforwards and credits.

Analyzing Effective Tax Rates

The firm's effective tax rate is an important input to valuation models because the forecast of future after-tax cash flows depends on the tax rate applied to those cash flows. The reported effective tax rate uses income tax expense and pretax income from the firm's financial statements (f/s):

$$\text{reported effective tax rate} = \frac{\text{income tax expense}\,(\text{from the f/s})}{\text{pretax income}\,(\text{from the f/s})}$$

There are two alternatives to this measure, however, which use items in the numerator derived from the firm's tax returns: taxes payable or income tax paid. Taxes payable is the tax liability on the balance sheet caused by taxable income. Income tax paid is the actual cash flow for income taxes, including payments or refunds from other years. These measures may be more useful for analysis because they are less affected by management's choice of accounting methods.

$$\text{effective tax rate measure \#1} = \frac{\text{taxes payable}\,(\text{from the tax return})}{\text{pretax income}\,(\text{from the f/s})}$$

$$\text{effective tax rate measure \#2} = \frac{\text{income tax paid}\,(\text{from the tax return})}{\text{pretax income}\,(\text{from the f/s})}$$

Low effective tax rates according to either of these measures (relative to effective tax rates of comparable companies) are a potential red flag indicating possible earnings manipulation.

When analyzing the firm's income tax disclosures, watch for these other warning signals:

- Companies that generate significant pretax income on their financial statements while reporting low taxes payable (i.e., low effective tax rates as measured with the alternative definitions previously discussed) are likely to be employing aggressive accounting methods and have low-quality earnings.
- A decrease in capital spending may signal a reversal of past temporary differences related to depreciation methods, resulting in higher taxes payable.
- Restructuring charges typically have no tax cash flow effects in the year they are recorded but may have significant effects in future years as the restructured operations and impaired assets are sold.
- Temporary differences may reverse because of changes in tax law, causing higher taxes payable.

Analyzing the Effective Rate Reconciliation

Some firms' reported income tax expense differs from the amount based on the statutory income tax rate. This is referred to as the difference between the effective tax rate and the statutory rate. The differences are generally the result of:

- Different tax rates in different tax jurisdictions (countries).
- Permanent tax differences: tax credits, tax-exempt income, nondeductible expenses, and tax differences between capital gains and operating income.
- Changes in tax rates and legislation.
- Deferred taxes provided on the reinvested earnings of foreign and unconsolidated domestic affiliates.

- Tax holidays in some countries (watch for special conditions such as termination dates for the holiday or a requirement to pay the accumulated taxes at some point in the future).

Accounting standards require a disclosure reconciling the difference between reported income tax expense and the amount based on the statutory income tax rate. Understanding this difference will enable the analyst to better estimate future earnings and cash flow.

When estimating future earnings and cash flows, the analyst should understand each element of the reconciliation, including its relative impacts, how each has changed with time, and how each is likely to change in the future. Often the analyst will need additional information from management to determine the future direction of each element.

In analyzing trends in tax rates, it is important to only include reconciliation items that are continuous in nature rather than those that are sporadic. There are no general rules for the kinds of items that are continuous or sporadic. The disclosures of each financial statement should be reviewed based on the footnotes and management discussion and analysis.

Nevertheless, items including different rates in different countries, tax-exempt income, and non-deductible expenses tend to be continuous. Others items are almost always sporadic, such as the occurrence of large dollar amounts of asset sales and tax holiday savings.

Example: Analyzing the tax rate reconciliation

Novelty Distribution Company (NDC) does business in the United States and abroad. The company's reconciliation between effective and statutory tax rates for three years is provided in Figure 11.

Figure 11: Statutory U.S. Federal Income Tax Rate Reconciliation

	2003	2004	2005
Statutory U.S. federal income tax rate	35.0%	35.0%	35.0%
State income taxes, net of related federal income tax benefit	2.1%	2.2%	2.3%
Benefits and taxes related to foreign operations	(6.5%)	(6.3%)	(2.7%)
Tax rate changes	0.0%	0.0%	(2.0%)
Capital gains on sale of assets	0.0%	(3.0%)	0.0%
Special items	(1.6%)	8.7%	2.5%
Other, net	0.8%	0.7%	(1.4%)
Effective income tax rates	29.8%	37.3%	33.7%

	2003	2004	2005
Taxable income	$2,330.00	$1,660.00	$2,350.00
Statutory U.S. federal income tax	815.50	581.00	822.50
State income taxes, net of related federal income tax benefit	48.93	36.52	54.05
Benefits and taxes related to foreign operations	(151.45)	(104.58)	(63.45)
Tax rate changes	–	–	(47.00)
Capital gains on sale of assets	–	(49.80)	–
Special items	(37.28)	144.42	58.75
Other, net	18.64	11.62	(32.90)
Effective income taxes	$694.34	$619.18	$791.95

Analyze the trend in effective tax rates over the three years shown.

Answer:

For some trend analysis, the analyst may want to convert the reconciliation from percentages to absolute numbers. However, for this example, the trends can be analyzed simply by using the percentages. Nevertheless, both percentages and the absolute numbers are provided.

The effective tax rate is upward trending over the 3-year period. Contributing to the upward trend is an increase in the state income tax rate and the loss of benefits related to taxes on foreign income. In 2003, a loss related to the sale of assets partially offset an increase in taxes created by special items. In 2003 and 2005, the special items and the other items also offset each other. The fact that the special items and other items are so volatile over the 3-year period suggests that it will be difficult for an analyst to forecast the effective tax rate for NDC for the foreseeable future without additional information. This volatility also reduces comparability with other firms.

Analyzing Disclosures About Deferred Tax Items

Companies are required to disclose details on the source of the temporary differences that cause the deferred tax assets and liabilities reported on the balance sheet. Changes in those balance sheet accounts are reflected in deferred income tax expense on the income statement. Here are some common examples of temporary differences you may encounter on the exam.

- A long-term deferred tax liability results from using the MACRS *depreciation* schedule for the tax returns and straight-line depreciation for the financial statements. The analyst should consider the firm's growth rate and capital spending levels when determining whether the difference will actually reverse.
- *Impairments* generally result in a deferred tax asset since the writedown of assets is recognized immediately for financial reporting, but not for tax purposes until the asset is sold.
- *Restructuring* generates a deferred tax asset because, for financial reporting purposes, the costs are recognized when restructuring is completed, but not expensed for tax purposes until actually paid. Note that restructuring usually results in significant cash outflows (net of the tax savings) in the years following when the restructuring costs are reported.
- In the U.S., firms that choose to use LIFO for financial statement purposes are required to use LIFO for tax purposes, so no temporary differences result. However, in countries for which this is not a requirement, temporary differences can result from the *choice of inventory accounting method.*
- *Post-employment benefits* and *deferred compensation* are both recognized when earned by the employee for book purposes but not expensed for tax purposes until actually paid. This will result in a current deferred tax asset or liability.
- A deferred tax adjustment is made to stockholder's equity to reflect gains or losses from carrying *available-for-sale marketable securities* at market value.

Example: Analyzing deferred tax item disclosures

WCCO Inc.'s income tax expense has consistently been larger than taxes payable over the last three years. WCCO disclosed in the footnotes to its 2005 financial statements the major items recorded as deferred tax assets and liabilities (in millions of dollars), as shown in Figure 12.

Figure 12: Deferred Tax Disclosures in Footnotes to WCCO Inc. Financial Statements

	2005	2004	2003
Employee benefits	$278	$310	$290
International tax loss carryforwards	101	93	115
Subtotal	379	403	405
Valuation allowance	(24)	(57)	(64)
Deferred tax asset	355	346	341
Property, plant and equipment	452	361	320
Unrealized gains on available-for-sale securities	67	44	23
Deferred tax liability	519	405	343
Deferred income taxes	$164	$59	$2

Use Figure 12 to explain why income tax expense has exceeded taxes payable over the last three years. Also explain the effect of the change in the valuation allowance on WCCO's earnings for 2005.

Answer:

The company's deferred tax asset balance results from international tax loss carryforwards and employee benefits (most likely pension and other post-retirement benefits) offset by a valuation allowance. The company's deferred tax liability balance results from property, plant, and equipment (most likely from using accelerated depreciation methods for tax purposes and straight-line on the financial statements) and unrealized gains on securities classified as available-for-sale (because the unrealized gain is not taxable until realized).

Income tax expense is equal to taxes payable plus deferred income tax expense. Because the deferred tax liabilities have been growing faster than the deferred tax assets, deferred income tax expense has been positive, resulting in income tax expense being higher than taxes payable.

Management decreased the valuation allowance by $33 million in 2005. This resulted in a reduction in deferred income tax expense and an increase in reported earnings for 2005.

Estimating Taxable Income from Deferred Tax Expense

Recall that deferred tax expense results from the difference between taxable income on the tax returns and pretax income on the financial statements. We can use the deferred tax expense and the statutory tax rate to estimate the difference between taxable income and pretax income attributable to specific temporary differences:

$$(\text{pretax income} - \text{taxable income}) = \frac{\text{deferred tax expense}}{\text{statutory tax rate}}$$

Example:

In 2005 WCCO reported depreciation expense on the statement of cash flows of $426 million. The deferred tax liability related to depreciation increased from $361 million in 2004 to $452 million in 2005. Assuming a statutory tax rate of 35%, compute the tax basis depreciation for 2005 and the cumulative financial reporting tax difference for net property, plant, and equipment as of fiscal year end 2005.

Answer:

The additional depreciation expense under tax reporting is equal to the change in the deferred tax liability divided by the statutory rate: ($452 − $361) / 0.35 = $260. Total tax basis depreciation for 2005 was $426 + $260 = $686.

The reporting difference in accumulated depreciation is approximately $1,291 ($452 / 0.35). The tax basis for property, plant, and equipment is $1,291 million less than the net amount reported on the balance sheet.

Effect of Disclosures on Financial Statements and Ratios

If the deferred tax liability or asset is expected to reverse, it is valued for accounting purposes at its undiscounted value. Because the payments may occur far into the future, an analyst should revalue the liability or asset at its present value. The difference between the stated value and the present value of deferred taxes should be treated as equity.

Example: Adjusting deferred taxes

Company A and Company B each have debt of $1,000,000, deferred tax liabilities of $200,000, and equity of $2,000,000. The deferred tax liabilities were created as a result of depreciation for tax purposes being greater than depreciation for financial reporting purposes. For Company A, there is no slowdown in capital expenditures expected, while for Company B, the growth in capital expenditures will stop. Therefore, it is reasonable to expect $75,000 of Company B's deferred tax liabilities to reverse. These deferred tax liabilities have a present value of $50,000.

Analyze the effect of the deferred liabilities on the financial statements and debt-to-equity ratio for both Company A and Company B.

Answer:

Analysis of Company A:

The unadjusted debt-to-equity ratio for Company A is:

$$\text{unadjusted debt-to-equity for Company A} = \frac{\$1,000,000 + \$200,000}{\$2,000,000} = 0.60$$

Since the deferred tax liabilities are not expected to reverse, they should be treated as equity. Therefore, the revised debt-to-equity ratio is:

$$\text{adjusted debt-to-equity for Company A} = \frac{\$1,000,000}{\$2,000,000 + \$200,000} = 0.45$$

This is a significant improvement over the unadjusted debt-to-equity ratio.

The right-hand side of the balance sheet (liabilities plus equity) stays constant. There is no additional wealth created or lost, and there has only been a reclassification between liabilities and equity.

Analysis of Company B:

The initial debt-to-equity ratio for Company B is also 0.60. Since some of the deferred tax liabilities are expected to reverse, the portion expected to reverse will be treated as a liability and the remaining amount treated as equity. Therefore, $50,000 of the deferred tax liability will remain as a liability, and $150,000 will be reclassified as equity. The revised debt-to-equity ratio is:

$$\text{adjusted debt-to-equity for Company B} = \frac{\$1,000,000 + \$50,000}{\$2,000,000 + \$125,000 + \$25,000} = 0.49$$

As with Company A, there is no change to the total value of the right-hand side of Company B's balance sheet because it still has to equal the total value of the assets. However, the reclassification of the deferred tax liabilities under present value assumptions means that the analyst has to increase the value of the equity by the amount of deferred tax liabilities that are not expected to reverse plus the difference between the absolute value and the present value of the deferred tax liabilities that are expected to reverse. Therefore, the value of equity is $2,000,000 + $125,000 + ($75,000 – $50,000) = $2,150,000.

Generally, if a company's deferred tax liabilities are not expected to reverse (and are therefore reclassified as equity), there will be a corresponding reduction in the firm's debt-to-equity ratio.

KEY CONCEPTS

1. Taxable income on the tax return is equivalent to pretax income on the income statement; taxes payable on the tax return is equivalent to tax expense on the income statement.

2. Deferred tax assets are balance sheet amounts that result from an excess of taxes payable over income tax expense that are expected to be recovered from future operations. Deferred tax liabilities are balance sheet amounts that result from an excess of income tax expense over taxes payable that are expected to result in future cash outflows.

3. Deferred tax assets and liabilities are calculated using the liability method, in which the assets and liabilities are calculated at any one time to reflect the current tax rate.

4. A valuation allowance reduces the value of a deferred tax asset when its eventual recoverability is in doubt.

5. Deferred tax liabilities that are expected never to reverse, typically because of expected growth in capital expenditures, should be treated for analytical purposes as equity. If deferred tax liabilities are expected to reverse, they should be treated for analytical purposes as liabilities, but calculated at their present value.

6. Permanent differences between taxable income and pretax income should not create a deferred asset or liability but should be used to adjust the effective tax rate.

7. If the tax rate increases, the increase in deferred tax liabilities increases the income tax expense, and the increase in deferred tax assets decreases the income tax expense. A tax rate decrease has the opposite effect.

8. Firms are required to disclose a reconciliation between a company's effective income tax rate and the applicable statutory rate in the country where the business is domiciled. Looking at the trend of the individual items of the reconciliation can aid in understanding past earnings trends and in predicting future tax rates. Where adequate data is provided, they can also be helpful in predicting future earnings, cash flows, and in adjusting financial ratios.

CONCEPT CHECKERS: ANALYSIS OF INCOME TAXES

1. Which of the following statements is **TRUE**? The difference between taxes payable for the period and the tax expense recognized on the financial statements results from differences:
    A. in management control.
    B. between basic and diluted earnings.
    C. between financial and tax accounting.
    D. between state and federal tax policies.

2. Which of the following tax definitions is **FALSE**?
    A. Taxable income is income based upon IRS rules.
    B. Taxes payable is the amount due to the government.
    C. Pretax income is income tax expense divided by one minus the statutory tax rate.
    D. Income tax expense is the amount listed on the firm's financial statements.

Use the following data to answer Questions 3 through 10.

*   A firm acquires an asset for $120,000 with a 4-year useful life and no salvage value.
*   The asset will generate $50,000 of cash flow for all four years.
*   The tax rate is 40% each year.
*   The firm will depreciate the asset over three years on a straight-line (SL) basis for tax purposes and over all four years on a SL basis for financial reporting purposes.

3. Taxable income in year 1 is:
    A. $6,000.
    B. $10,000.
    C. $20,000.
    D. $50,000.

4. Taxes payable in year 1 are:
    A. $4,000.
    B. $6,000.
    C. $8,000.
    D. $20,000.

5. Pretax income in year 4 is:
    A. $6,000.
    B. $10,000.
    C. $20,000.
    D. $50,000.

6. Income tax expense in year 4 is:
    A. $4,000.
    B. $6,000.
    C. $8,000.
    D. $20,000.

7. Taxes payable in year 4 are:
    A. $4,000.
    B. $6,000.
    C. $8,000.
    D. $20,000.

8. At the end of year 2, the firm's balance sheet will report a deferred tax:
    A. asset of $4,000.
    B. asset of $8,000.
    C. liability of $4,000.
    D. liability of $8,000.

9. Suppose tax rates rise during year 2 to 50%. At the end of year 2, the firm's balance sheet will show a deferred tax liability of:
    A. $5,000.
    B. $6,000.
    C. $8,000.
    D. $10,000.

10. Suppose tax rates rise during year 2 to 50%. What will be the income tax expense in year 2?
    A. $5,000.
    B. $8,000.
    C. $10,000.
    D. $11,000.

11. In its first year of operations, a firm produces taxable income of –$10,000. The prevailing tax rate is 40%. The firm's balance sheet will report a deferred tax:
    A. asset of $4,000.
    B. asset of $10,000.
    C. liability of $4,000.
    D. liability of $10,000.

12. An analyst is comparing a firm to its competitors. The firm has a deferred tax liability and is expected to continue to grow in the foreseeable future. How should the liability be treated for analysis purposes?
    A. It should be treated as equity at its full value.
    B. It should be treated as a liability at its full value.
    C. The present value should be treated as a liability with the remainder being treated as equity.
    D. It should be considered neither a liability nor equity.

13. An analyst is comparing a firm to its competitors. The firm has a deferred tax liability and is expected to have capital expenditures decline in the future. How should the liability be treated for analysis purposes?
    A. It should be treated as equity at its full value.
    B. It should be treated as a liability at its full value.
    C. The present value should be treated as a liability with the remainder being treated as equity.
    D. It should be considered neither a liability nor equity.

14. Which one of the following statements is **TRUE**? Under the liability method of accounting for deferred taxes, a decrease in the tax rate at the beginning of the accounting period will:
    A. increase taxable income in the current period.
    B. reduce income tax expense for the current period.
    C. reduce the deferred tax liability.
    D. increase the beginning-of-period deferred tax asset.

15.   An analyst gathered the following information about a company:
- Taxable income is $40,000.
- Pretax income is $50,000.
- Current tax rate is 50%.
- Tax rate when the reversal occurs will be 40%.

What is the company's deferred tax liability at the end of year 1?
A. $3,500.
B. $4,000.
C. $4,500.
D. $5,000.

16.   While reviewing a company, an analyst identifies a permanent difference between taxable income and pretax income. Which of the following statements identifies the **CORRECT** financial statement adjustment?
A. The amount of the tax implications of the difference should be added to the deferred tax liabilities.
B. The present value of the amount of the tax implications of the difference should be added to the deferred tax liabilities.
C. The effective tax rate for calculating tax expense should be adjusted.
D. Taxes payable should be reduced.

17.   An analyst is reviewing a company with a large deferred tax asset on its balance sheet. In reviewing the company's performance over the last few years, the analyst has determined that the firm has had cumulative losses for the last three years and has a large amount of inventory that can only be sold at sharply reduced prices. Which of the following adjustments should the analyst make to account for the deferred tax assets?
A. Record a deferred tax liability to offset the effect of the deferred tax asset on the firm's balance sheet.
B. Recognize a valuation allowance to reflect the fact that the deferred tax asset is unlikely to be realized.
C. Do nothing. The difference between taxable and pretax income that caused the deferred tax asset is likely to reverse in the future.
D. Decrease tax expense by the amount of the deferred tax asset unlikely to be realized.

ANSWERS – CONCEPT CHECKERS: ANALYSIS OF INCOME TAXES

1. **C**   The difference between taxes payable for the period and the tax expense recognized on the financial statements results from differences between financial and tax accounting.

2. **C**   Pretax income and income tax expense are not always linked because of temporary and permanent differences.

3. **B**   Annual depreciation expense for taxes is ($120,000 – 0) / 3 = $40,000. Taxable income is $50,000 – $40,000 = $10,000.

4. **A**   Taxes payable is taxable income × tax rate = $10,000 × 40% = $4,000. (The $10,000 was calculated in question #3).

5. **C**   Annual depreciation expense for financial income is ($120,000 – 0)/ 4 = $30,000. Pretax income is $50,000 – $30,000 = $20,000.

6. **C**   Because there has been no change in the tax rate, income tax expense is pretax income × tax rate = $20,000 × 40% = $8,000. (The $20.000 was calculated in question #5).

7. **D**   Note that the asset has been fully depreciated for tax purposes after year 3, so taxable income is $50,000. Taxes payable for year 4 = taxable income × tax rate = $50,000 × 40% = $20,000.

8. **D**   The difference between pretax income (calculated in question #5) and taxable income (calculated in question #3) each year is $20,000 – $10,000 = $10,000. The cumulative difference after two years is (2 × $10,000) = $20,000. The deferred tax liability is $20,000 × 40% = $8,000. It is a liability because pretax income exceeds taxable income.

9. **D**   The deferred tax liability is now $20,000 × 50% = $10,000. (Multiply the cumulative income difference by the new tax rate.)

10. **D**   Taxes payable in year 2 is now taxable income × 50% = $10,000 × 50% = $5000. The deferred tax liability at the end of year 1 was $4,000 (before restatement under the new tax rates). Tax expense = taxes payable + increase in deferred taxes = $5,000 + ($10,000 – $4,000) = $11,000.

11. **A**   Tax loss carryforwards are deferred tax assets and would be equal to the loss multiplied by the tax rate.

12. **A**   The firm has a deferred tax liability and is expected to continue to grow in the foreseeable future. The liability should be treated as equity at its full value.

13. **C**   The firm has a deferred tax liability and is expected to have capital expenditures decline in the future. The present value should be treated as a liability with the remainder being treated as equity.

14. **C**   If the tax rate falls, balance sheet DTL and DTA are both reduced. Taxable income is unaffected. Income tax expense could increase if the balance sheet DTA is greater than the DTL.

15. **B**   The tax rate that should be used is the expected tax rate when the liability reverses. The deferred tax liability will be $10,000 × 40% = $4,000.

16. **C**   If a permanent difference between taxable income and pretax income is identifiable, the effective tax rate for calculating tax expense should be adjusted.

17. **B**   A valuation allowance is used to offset deferred tax assets if it is unlikely that those assets will be realized. Because the company has a history of losses and inventory that is unlikely to generate future profits, it is unlikely the company will realize its deferred tax assets in full.

ANALYSIS OF FINANCING LIABILITIES

EXAM FOCUS

One crucial point in this topic review is that when a company issues a bond, the initial liability posted to the balance sheet is the amount received, not the par amount, and the effective interest rate is the market rate, not the coupon rate. The discount or premium is amortized over the bond's life so that the liability is equal to par at maturity. Candidates should understand the difference between cash interest costs and interest expense, how cash flow from operations is distorted by discount/premium bonds, and why market values of debt are more appropriate than book values for calculating leverage and for valuation purposes. Some advantages of various types of debt would be good to know, as would the balance sheet treatment of convertible bonds and bonds with attached warrants.

BOND TERMINOLOGY

The various forms of debt and financing activities are important aspects of the analysis of a firm's short-term liquidity and long-term solvency.

This review emphasizes balance sheet debt, including current liabilities, long-term liabilities from financing activities, the various debt instruments, and the effect of interest rate changes.

- The **face value** is also known as the bond's maturity value, or par value. This is the value of the bond if market interest rates equal the coupon rate on the date of bond issuance.
- The **coupon rate** is multiplied by the face value to calculate the periodic *coupon payments* to be made to investors.
- The **market rate of interest** is used to value debt obligations. Do not confuse the market rate of interest, which is the compensation required by financial markets for default risk, liquidity, the time value of money, etc., with the coupon rate, which is the rate of interest stated on the debt contract. For fixed-rate debt, the coupon rate does not change over the life of the contract. However, the market rate changes every day and will cause differences between the book value of the debt and the market value of the debt. This concept is explained in greater detail later in this topic review.

TYPES OF BALANCE SHEET DEBT

Current liabilities are defined as those liabilities due within one year or operating cycle.

Current liabilities are reported on the balance sheet according to their (1) order by maturity, (2) descending order by amount, or (3) order in the event of liquidation. Current liabilities are reported at their full maturity value. Current liabilities may result from operating activities (e.g., trade credit) or from financing activities (e.g., current portion of long-term debt):

- Operating and trade liabilities—these are the result of credit granted to the company by its suppliers.
- Advances from customers—these occur when customers pay in advance and when the firm must deliver the service or good in the future. These should be considered a prediction of future revenues rather than a prediction of future cash outflows.
- Short-term debt from the credit markets.

- Current portion of long-term debt payable within the year.

The first two categories (operating and trade liabilities, and advances) are consequences of operating decisions and arise in the normal course of business. The last two categories (short-term debt and current portion of long-term debt) are consequences of financing decisions and indicate a future need for cash or refinancing. It is necessary to monitor the relative levels of these two categories. A shift from operating to financing sources may indicate the beginning of a liquidity crisis, and the inability to repay short-term credit is a sign of financial distress.

Long-term debt contracts are obligations that are not payable within one year or one operating cycle, whichever is longer. Long-term debt may be obtained from many sources and may differ in the structure of interest and principal payments and the claims creditors have on the assets of the firm. Some creditors may have a claim on specific assets and other creditors may have only a general claim. Some creditors may have claims that rank below (are *subordinated* to) the claims of other creditors whose claims have priority (are *senior* to the other claims).

- Debt is equal to the present value of the future interest and principal payments. For *book values*, the discount rate is the interest rate in effect when the debt was incurred. For *market values*, the rate is the current market interest rate.
- Interest expense is the amount paid to the creditor in excess of the amount received. Although the total amount of interest to be paid is known, the allocation to specific time periods may be uncertain.

Bonds are a contract between the borrower and the lender that obligates the bond issuer to make payments to the bondholder over the life of the bond. Two types of payments are involved:

- Periodic payment of interest [affects cash flows from operations (CFO)].
- Repayment of principal at maturity [affects cash flow from financing (CFF)].

Interest expense each period = interest rate at issuance × balance sheet liability

The interest expense of bonds issued at a discount rises over time because of the increasing value of the liability. The interest expense of bonds issued at a premium will fall over time because of the decreasing value of the liability, and the interest expense of par bonds will remain constant.

The **balance sheet liability** is the present value of the remaining cash payments using the market rate when the bonds were issued. At maturity, the value of the liability will equal the par value of the bond.

The bond contract does not determine the amount the borrower receives or the allocation between interest and principal. That depends on the current market rate of interest. The market interest rate depends on the maturity and risk of the bond and may be equal to, less than, or greater than the coupon rate on the date of issue.

- When the market rate equals the coupon rate, the bond is called a *par* bond.
- When the market rate is greater than the coupon rate, the bond is called a *discount* bond.
- When the market rate is less than the coupon rate, the bond is called a *premium* bond.

LOS 45.a: Compute the effects of debt issuance and amortization of bond discounts and premiums on the financial statements and ratios, and discuss the effect on the financial statements from issuing zero-coupon debt.

Bonds Issued at Par

When a bond is issued at par, its effects on the financial statements are very straightforward.

- **Balance sheet impact.** Bonds are always initially listed as liabilities equal to the amount of the proceeds received at issuance. For a par bond the proceeds are equal to face value, so the bond liability remains at face value over the life of the bond.
- **Interest expense.** Interest expense is always equal to the book value of the bonds at the beginning of the period multiplied by the market rate of interest *at issuance*. In the case of par value bonds, this is the same as the coupon rate of the bond.
- **Cash flow.** CFO includes a deduction for interest expense. For bonds issued at par, the interest expense is equal to the coupon payment. CFF is increased by the amount received. Upon repayment of the bond at maturity, CFF is reduced by the bond's par value.

Bonds Issued at a Premium or Discount

When the market rate of interest is not equal to the coupon rate, the present value of the coupon payments plus the present value of the face value is not equal to par value, and a *premium* or *discount* occurs. The premium or discount is usually relatively small for coupon bonds.

If the market rate of interest is less than the coupon rate, the proceeds received will be greater than face value, and a premium results. Recall from our basic bond valuation that if the market rate of interest is less than the coupon rate, investors will *pay more* to obtain the higher coupon payment attached to the bond in question. Hence, the bond will sell at a premium.

If the market rate of interest is greater than the coupon rate, the proceeds received will be less than the face value, and a discount results. Here, the coupon rate is low relative to bonds that are being issued at par value. Hence, individuals will *pay less* than face value for bonds with low coupons relative to the current market rate. These are called discount bonds.

Balance sheet impact

- Bonds are always initially listed as liabilities based on the proceeds received from the bonds, which is the present value of all future payments. At any point in time, the book value of the bonds can be calculated as the present value of all future payments at the market rate of interest.

Professor's Note: The rate of interest used in all calculations for book values is the market rate at the time the bonds were issued. This is an extremely important point.

- Bonds that were originally sold at a premium will always be shown at a premium on the balance sheet. This premium will be amortized toward zero over the life of the bond.
- Bonds that were originally sold at a discount will always be recorded on the balance sheet at a discount. This discount will be amortized toward zero over the life of the bond. Hence, the book value of both premium and discount bonds will *converge* to the bonds' par or face values at maturity.

Interest expense

- Interest expense is always equal to the book value of the bonds at the beginning of the period multiplied by the market rate of interest. *Market rate of interest* refers to the rate in effect when the bonds are issued.
- In the case of premium bonds, the interest expense will be lower than the coupon. The amortization of the bond's premium will serve to *reduce* the interest expense that is shown on the income statement. In general, interest expense will equal the coupon payment less the premium amortization.
- In the case of discount bonds, the interest expense will be higher than the coupon. Here, the amortization of the bond's discount will serve to *increase* the interest expense that is reported on the

income statement. In general, interest expense will equal the coupon payment plus the discount amortization.

Professor's Note: In the case of a discount bond, the coupon is too low relative to the market's required rate of return. The purpose of amortizing the discount is to (1) increase the bond's book value over time and (2) increase interest expense so that the coupon + discount amortization is approximately equal to the interest expense that would have prevailed had the bond been issued at par with a higher coupon. This argument is easily reversed for premium bonds.

Cash flow

- The coupon represents the cash flow component of the bond and is the amount deducted in calculating CFO for accounting purposes. However, from an analytical perspective, the interest expense and the amortization of the premium or discount should be separated. Amortization should be included in CFF, not CFO.
- *For premium bonds*, the cash coupon is higher than interest expense; consequently, CFO is understated and CFF is overstated relative to a company that does not have premium bonds in its capital structure.
- *For discount bonds*, the cash coupon is lower than interest expense; consequently, CFO is overstated and CFF is understated relative to a company that does not have discount bonds.
- Analysts can make adjustments to CFO by correcting for the difference between the coupon payment and the interest expense—this adjustment will be positive for premium bonds and negative for discount bonds.
- Upon issuance, CFF is increased by the amount of the proceeds, and upon repayment at maturity, CFF is reduced by the par value or payoff amount.
- In our review of the statement of cash flows, it is argued that all debt-related cash flow should be excluded from CFO and included in CFF. This takes the adjustments just discussed one step further. From an economic perspective, this approach is desirable because it separates investment decisions from financing decisions and gives a more clear picture of the profitability of operations.

Example: Book values and cash flows

On December 31, 2002, a company issued a 3-year, 10% annual coupon bond with a face value of $100,000.

Part A: Calculate the book value of the bond at year-end 2002, 2003, and 2004, and the interest expense for 2003, 2004, and 2005, assuming the bond was issued at a market rate of interest of (1) 10%, (2) 9%, and (3) 11%.

Part B: The financial statements for 2003 show that cash flow from operations was $50,000. Assuming that the market rate of interest was 9% when the bond was issued, how should this cash flow be analyzed when comparing it to other companies?

Answer: Part A

Bond issued at par. If the market rate of interest at issuance is 10%, the book value of the bonds will always be $100,000, and the interest expense will always be $10,000, which is equal to the coupon payment of 0.10 × $100,000. There is no discount or premium to amortize.

Premium bonds. If the market rate of interest is 9%, the present value of the cash payments (a 3-year annuity of $10,000 and a payment in three years of $100,000) is $102,531.

N = 3; PMT = 10,000; FV = 100,000; I/Y = 9; CPT → PV = $102,531

Professor's Note: The present value computed in this manner will have a minus sign.

Figure 1 shows the interest expense (IE) and book value (BV) at the end of each year.

Figure 1: Interest Expenses and Book Value for a Premium Bond

Year	(1) Beginning Book Value	(2) Interest Expense (1) × 9%	(3) Coupon	(4) Ending Book Value (1) + (2) – (3)
2003	$102,531	$9,228	$10,000	$101,759
2004	101,759	9,158	10,000	100,917
2005	100,917	9,083	10,000	100,000

The premium amortization for 2003 is 10,000 – 9,228 = $772. For 2004, the amortization is 10,000 – 9,158 = $842. Finally, for 2005, premium amortization is $917. Note that the premium has been fully amortized upon maturity such that the book value of the bond equals par value.

Discount bonds. If the market rate of interest is 11%, the present value of the cash payments (a 3-year annuity of $10,000 and a payment in three years of $100,000) is $97,556.

N = 3; PMT = 10,000; FV = 100,000; I/Y = 11; CPT → PV = $97,556

Figure 2 shows the interest expense and book value at the end of each year.

Figure 2: Interest Expense and Book Value for a Discount Bond

Year	(1) Beginning Book Value	(2) Interest Expense (1) × 11%	(3) Coupon	(4) Ending Book Value (1) + (2) – (3)
2003	$97,556	$10,731	$10,000	$98,287
2004	98,287	10,812	10,000	99,099
2005	99,099	10,901	10,000	100,000

Again, the pattern of discount amortization is such that the discount is fully amortized upon maturity, when the book value of the bond equals par value.

Answer: Part B

For the premium bond (9% market rate at issuance), the cash component of interest expense was overstated. CFO was understated in 2003 because CFO is reduced by the coupon of $10,000 instead of by the true interest expense of $9,228. For analysis, cash flow from operations should be adjusted by adding $772 ($10,000 – $9,228). Note that since CFO is understated, CFF will be overstated over the life of a premium bond. While the proceeds of issuance are a positive CFF (+$102,531), the negative CFF at maturity is only the face value ($100,000). Over the life of the bond, net CFF (+2,531) is positive, by the same amount that CFO is understated.

Summary of Financial Statement Effects of Issuing a Bond

Statement of Cash Flows

Figure 3: Cash Flow Impact of Issuing a Bond

	Cash Flow from Financing	*Cash Flow from Operations*
Issuance of debt	Increased by cash received (Present value of the bond at the market interest rate)	No effect
Periodic interest payments	No effect	Decreased by interest paid [(coupon rate) × (face or par value)]
Payment at maturity	Decreased by face (par) value	No effect

Figure 4: Economic or Analytic Perspective of Interest Payments

	Cash Flow from Financing	*Cash Flow from Operations*
Premium bonds	Overstated	Understated
Discount bonds	Understated	Overstated

Income Statement

$$\text{Interest expense} = \binom{\text{the market rate}}{\text{at issue}} \times \left(\begin{array}{c} \text{the balance sheet value} \\ \text{of the liability at} \\ \text{the beginning of the period} \end{array} \right)$$

Figure 5: Income Statement Impact of Issuing a Bond

Issued at Par	*Issued at a Premium*	*Issued at a Discount*
Market rate = coupon rate Interest expense = coupon rate × face value = cash paid	Market rate < coupon rate Interest expense = cash paid – amortization of premium	Market rate > coupon rate Interest expense = cash paid + amortization of discount
Interest expense is constant	Interest decreases over time	Interest increases over time

Balance Sheet

Long-term debt is carried at the present value of the remaining cash payments discounted at the market rate existing when the debt was issued.

Figure 6: Balance Sheet Impact of Issuing a Bond

Issued at Par	*Issued at a Premium*	*Issued at a Discount*
Carried at face value	Carried at face value plus premium The liability decreases as the premium is amortized to interest expense	Carried at face value less discount The liability increases as the discount is amortized to interest expense

The Effect on Reported Cash Flows of Issuing Zero-Coupon Debt

Zero-coupon debt is debt issued with no periodic payments of interest and principal is paid back with one lump sum payment upon maturity. Zero-coupon bonds are also known as *pure discount* instruments because they are issued at a discount from par value, and their annual interest expense is *implied*. Actual interest is all paid at maturity when the bonds are paid off (at their par value). The effects of zero-coupon debt on financial statements are qualitatively the same as those of discount debt—only the impact is larger because the discount is larger.

For discount bonds, the coupon understates the cash component of interest expense and CFO is overstated. With zero-coupon bonds, there is no coupon, so for operating cash flow purposes there is no interest expense deducted. This *severely overstates CFO*. The difference shows up at maturity when the zero-coupon bond is paid off. The cash flow when the bond is paid off is charged to CFF, and for discount debt this negative cash flow is greater than the positive CFF at issuance. Thus CFF is understated over the life of the bond.

Example: Effect of zero-coupon debt on CFO

Two companies have an identical value for cash sales less cash inputs and cash operating expenses of $50,000. The only difference between the two companies is their financing. At the beginning of this year, Company A sold $1,000,000 of face value zero-coupon bonds maturing in three years. Company B sold $750,000 of 10% coupon bonds maturing in three years. Assume the market rate of interest on these bonds is 10%.

- How much did Company A receive for its bonds?
- What would interest expense be for Company A over the three years of the bond's life?
- Compute the cash flow from operations for Company A and Company B for year 1 (ignore taxes).

Assume that both bonds are *annual pay* and are valued using annual pay assumptions.

Professor's Note: For the exam, know that most zero-coupon bonds in the U.S. are valued using a semiannual pay convention.

Answer:

The present value of $1,000,000 in three years is $1,000,000 / $(1.1)^3$ = 751,315.

N = 3; I/Y = 10; FV = 1,000,000; PMT = 0; CPT→ PV = $751,315

Interest expense in year 1 is $751,315 × 10% = $75,131.

Book value in year 1 is $751,315 + $75,131 = $826,446.

Interest expense in year 2 is $826,446 × 10% = $82,645.

Book value in year 2 is $826,446 + $82,645 = $909,091.

Interest expense in year 3 is $909,091 × 10% = $90,909.

Book value at the end of year 3 = $909,091 + $90,909 = $1,000,000.

Note that the "interest expense" for Company A is entirely composed of *discount amortization*. There is no cash interest component to Company A's interest expense.

CFO for Company A = $50,000 because there is no cash interest expense.

CFO for Company B = $50,000 – $75,000 = –$25,000. Company B's cash coupon payment reduces CFO significantly.

Without any adjustments, Company A's CFO appears significantly higher than Company B's CFO. An analyst should either adjust B's cash flow upward or A's downward when comparing the companies. Note that at issuance CFF is approximately +$750,000 for both A and B (A was issued for $751,315), but at maturity CFF is –$750,000 for Company B and –$1,000,000 for Company A.

LOS 45.b: Determine the appropriate classification for debt with equity feaures and calculate the effect of issuance of such instruments on the debt to total capital ratio.

Convertible Bonds

When convertible bonds are issued, under U.S. Generally Accepted Accounting Principals (U.S. GAAP), they are recorded on the balance sheet as if there were no conversion feature, and interest expense is recorded exactly as it is for option-free bonds. A change in this treatment is currently under consideration.

From an analytic perspective, however, the equity feature of convertible bonds can be an important distinction. In general, when the stock price is significantly above the conversion price, it should be treated like equity for the purposes of calculating the debt ratios. Such treatment will decrease debt to equity and debt to total capital. At the other extreme, when the stock price is significantly lower than the conversion price, convertible debt should be treated like debt in calculating ratios.

When the stock price is close to the conversion price, the classification is not as clear and the effect on the debt to total capital ratio is uncertain. The analyst should compute debt ratios treating the convertible bonds alternatively as debt and as equity to gauge the impact of the assumption used. Choosing one treatment over the other should depend on the purpose of the analysis and the analyst's estimate of the probability of conversion over the relevant time horizon.

Bonds With Warrants

When bonds are issued with warrants attached, the proceeds are allocated between the two components. The bond portion is recognized (at a discount) as a liability at fair market value and the discount is amortized over the life of the issue. The warrants are recognized as equity at fair market value, and the cash received when the warrants are exercised is added to equity capital. Overall, debt ratios will be increased less by the issuance of bonds with warrants attached than by the issuance of convertible bonds.

Non-convertible preferred shares are treated by the analyst as equity unless they are redeemable by the holder, in which case they should be treated as debt and the dividends treated as interest. This treatment is required by International Accounting Standards (IAS) and under consideration by the Financial Accounting Standards Board (FASB).

The liability recorded for conventional bonds and convertible bonds is greater than for an equivalent amount of bonds with warrants attached. Because a portion of the proceeds of a bond with attached warrants is classified as equity, both debt-to-equity and debt-to-total capital will be *lower* than if conventional or convertible debt were issued.

LOS 45.c: Describe the disclosures relating to financing liabilities, and discuss the advantages/ disadvantages to the company of selecting a given instrument and the effect of the selection on a company's financial statements and ratios.

There are various disclosures related to financing liabilities that will aid an analyst.

- On the balance sheet, we will find the present value of the promised future liability payments, discounted at the rate in effect at issuance.
- On the income statement, or in a footnote, we will find interest expense for the period.

- On the cash flow statement, we will find cash interest expense and we can compare this to interest expense to see the effect of the issuance of zero-coupon or discount debt.
- For a publicly-traded firm, filings with the SEC will detail all outstanding securities and their relevant terms.
- For off-balance-sheet liabilities, such as leases, take-or-pay contracts, and other material financial obligations of the firm, we will find details of each liability in the footnotes to the financial statements.

When raising funds, the firm must decide which instrument it will use among a wide variety of security types. Each instrument has advantages and disadvantages. Which is most advantageous for the firm will depend on the specific circumstances of the firm. Some key points will help you to understand which instrument would be the best choice, given the firm's circumstances.

As noted previously, *zero-coupon debt* reduces the firm's cash interest costs and may be advantageous when near-term cash flow is low or quite uncertain. If the firm faces restrictions on its cash interest coverage ratio or has financing costs tied to this ratio, zero coupon debt could offer the most advantages.

Variable-rate debt (also called floating-rate debt) carries an interest rate that is periodically reset to market rates. This typically has the effect of keeping the market value of the debt close to its par value. If a firm has operating cash flows that tend to go up (down) when short-term interest rates increase (decrease), then issuing variable-rate debt can reduce stress on net cash flows. On the other hand, when this is not the case, issuing variable-rate debt can increase the variability of net cash flows as interest rates rise and fall.

When management believes that interest rates will fall in the future, the issuance of variable-rate debt may be based on speculation. If management is right, the variable-rate debt can be replaced with fixed-rate debt in the future after rates have fallen. Thus we can draw a distinction between managements that issue variable-rate debt for valid business purposes and those that issue for speculative reasons.

One final advantage can arise when short-term interest rates are significantly lower than longer term rates. If this situation persists, the firm can reduce total interest costs over the planning horizon by issuing variable-rate debt, since the variable rate is typically a short-term rate. Be aware, however, that the firm will be accepting cash interest variability along with a potential reduction in total interest costs and that often, higher long-term rates may be an indication that short-term rates will be significantly higher in the future.

Firms can issue **debt denominated in a foreign currency**. This type of liability can be advantageous if the firm has future cash flows in that currency. By matching the currency of this cash flow to future liabilities, the firm may hedge (reduce) some currency risk that they would otherwise have. If a firm, for some reason, has a lower borrowing cost in foreign markets, this could make the issuance of debt denominated in a foreign currency attractive.

Each of the types of debt securities with equity features discussed previously has its own potential advantages. Issuing **convertible debt** will decrease borrowing costs, reducing both interest expense and cash interest expense. The trade-off here is simply the value of the option to convert into common stock that is included in the security. There are no specific balance sheet differences between issuing convertible debt and issuing an equivalent amount of non-convertible debt.

Issuing **bonds with warrants attached** can also reduce interest costs relative to conventional corporate bonds but, given the balance sheet treatment of the liability, interest expense will be greater than for equivalent convertible bonds. When warrants are attached, the value attributed to the warrants is treated as a bond discount at issuance and is amortized over the term of the bond. The balance sheet liability is less than both a conventional and convertible bond for this same reason. This will, of course, affect related debt ratios. Assuming the stated coupon rate is the same for a convertible bond and an equivalent bond with warrants attached, the cash interest will be the same for both, and less than the cash interest costs for a conventional bond.

Debt convertible into the shares of a company other than the issuing company is referred to as **exchangeable debt**. There are several potential advantages to issuing exchangeable debt. As with convertible debt, the exchange option will decrease the required yield, and therefore interest expense, of the borrowing. At the same time, the exchange price will typically be some premium over the current market value of the shares. A holding of the shares of the other company may, at the same time, offer some strategic business advantage. If there is a significant capital gain in the shares, the firm may be avoiding significant tax consequences of selling the position and at the same time realizing its value. If the block of exchangeable shares is relatively large, the firm can reduce the market impact of a sale of the entire block by calling the exchangeable debt periodically, releasing shares to the market in a piecemeal manner.

Commodity-linked bonds may reduce (hedge) cash flow risk for producers of the commodity. Consider an oil company that issues bonds with a coupon rate tied to the price of oil. Presumably, when oil prices are high, operating cash flows are relatively high and more cash is available to pay interest costs. More importantly, cash interest expense would fall when oil prices are low. In this case, the times interest earned and cash interest coverage ratios will tend to be more stable over an economic cycle than if conventional debt were issued.

The issuance of **perpetual debt** or conventional bonds with very long maturities (e.g. 100 years) issued at par will not have balance sheet, income statement, or cash flow effects appreciably different from those of conventional fixed-rate bonds with more typical maturities. The analyst, however, may choose to treat these securities more like equity, given their similarity to a preferred stock. The idea here is that perpetual debt is more similar to permanent capital than to conventional debt. Just as issuing variable-rate debt has a potential advantage over fixed rate debt if rates subsequently decrease, issuing perpetual debt has a potential advantage if it is timed to coincide with low market interest rates.

Conventional **preferred shares** have no set maturity and pay a dividend than can be omitted without forcing bankruptcy, so they are treated as equity. However, the distinction between debt and equity securities is often not clear in the case of preferred stock. Just as perpetual debt has characteristics similar to equity, some preferred shares have characteristics more similar to debt than to equity. When preferred shares are redeemable by the shareholder or required to be redeemed by a sinking fund provision, their value should be treated like debt. Also, preferred shares that pay an adjustable short-term interest rate (so called adjustable-rate or market-rate preferred) have the characteristics of short-term debt and should be treated as such by the analyst.

LOS 45.d: Determine the effects of changing interest rates on the market value of debt and on financial statements and ratios.

Under U.S. GAAP, balance sheet values for outstanding debt must be based on the market rate on the date of issuance.

Changes in market interest rates lead to changes in the market values of debt. *Increases (decreases) in the market rate of interest decrease (increase) the market value of debt.* These gains (from the decrease in market value of debt) or losses (from the increase in market value of debt) are not reflected in the financial statements. Hence, the book value of debt will not equal the market value.

With variable-rate debt, neither balance sheet values nor market values of the debt change with market rates, but interest expense does. Rising market rates increase interest expense on variable-rate debt and decrease net income.

For purposes of analysis, market values may be more appropriate than book values. For example, firms that issue debt when interest rates are low are relatively better off when interest rates increase. This increase should be reflected in a higher value of equity and a lower value of debt. Adjusting the firm's debt down to market value will reduce it to the amount the firm would currently have to pay to retire the debt, and will decrease the debt-to-equity ratio. If interest rates decrease, adjusting the debt to market value will have the opposite effects.

SFAS 107 requires disclosures about the fair value of outstanding debt based on year-end or quarter-end prices. These disclosures are made in the notes to the financial statements.

Note: Market value disclosures are not required for non-U.S. firms.

Estimating market values for publicly traded debt is easy. For debt that is not publicly traded, we can find the present value of the future cash flows. Typically, these cash flows are disclosed by the company. The relevant market rate for finding the present values can be found by considering the maturity and other terms of the debt and then using:

- Other similar issues of the company which are publicly traded.
- Rates on publicly traded debt of similar companies.
- A risk premium added to the U.S. bond rate for that maturity.

LOS 45.e: Explain the role of debt covenants in protecting creditors by limiting a company's freedom to invest, pay dividends, or make other operating and strategic decisions.

Debt covenants are restrictions imposed by the bondholders on the issuer in order to protect the bondholders' position. The bondholder can demand repayment of the bonds after a violation of one of the covenants (this is called a technical default). An analysis of the bond covenants is a necessary component of the credit analysis of a bond. Bond covenants are typically disclosed in the footnotes.

Examples of covenants include restrictions on:

- Dividend payments and share repurchases.
- Mergers and acquisitions, and sale, leaseback, and disposal of certain assets.
- Issuance of new debt.
- Repayment patterns (e.g., sinking fund agreements and priority of claims).

Other covenants require the firm to maintain ratios or financial statement items, such as equity, net working capital, current ratio, or debt-to-equity ratio at certain levels. Covenants will specify whether GAAP is to be used when calculating the ratios or whether some adjustment is required. Covenants protect bondholders from actions the firm may take that would negatively affect the value of the bondholders' claims to firm assets and earnings (i.e. decrease credit quality). To the extent that covenants restrict, for example, the firm's ability to invest, take on additional debt, or pay dividends, an analysis of covenants can be important in valuing the firm's equity (especially involving its growth prospects) as well as in analyzing and valuing its debt securities.

KEY CONCEPTS

1. Issuance of discount bonds will lead to an understatement of CFF and an overstatement of CFO, and issuance of premium bonds will have the opposite effect because coupon interest (cash) payments are not equal to interest expense.
2. The amortization of bond premiums and discounts will provide the correct interest expense for the period since the coupon payment does so only for bonds issued at par.
3. The issuance of zero-coupon (pure discount) bonds causes the most severe overstatement of CFO and eventual understatement of CFF.
4. Debt with equity features should be treated for analytical purposes as having both a debt and equity component.

5. The following table summarizes the key issues related to financing liabilities in this topic review.

Financing Liability	Advantages (from the perspective of the issuer)	Analyst Treatment
Discount/zero-coupon debt	• CFO overstated • Cash interest reduced	• Increase interest expense and decrease CFO by amount of discount amortization
Convertible debt	Versus conventional debt: • Lower interest expense • Higher operating cash flow • Same balance sheet liability	• Treat as equity if stock price > conversion price • Treat as debt if stock price < conversion price
Exchangeable debt	• Lower interest expense • Generate cash without selling investment • Reduce market impact of selling investment • Delay tax impact of gain and control timing of gain	• Similar to convertible
Bonds with warrants	Versus conventional debt: • Lower interest expense • Higher operating cash flow • Lower balance sheet liability	• Classify bond value as debt, warrant value as equity
Commodity bonds	• Converts interest expense from fixed to variable cost • Can reduce interest coverage variability	• May reduce risk compared to conventional debt
Perpetual debt	• Lock in long-term rates when rates are low	• Treat as equity
Preferred stock	• Create a debt/equity hybrid security	• Classify redeemable preferred shares as debt and dividends as interest • Classify variable-rate shares as short-term liabilities

6. Market values of fixed-rate debt change as interest rates change, but reported book values do not. Use market values for analysis and valuation purposes, with the offsetting adjustment to equity.

7. Evaluation of a firm's credit risk and growth prospects should include an analysis of bond covenants.

CONCEPT CHECKERS: ANALYSIS OF FINANCING LIABILITIES

1. The book value of debt equals the present value of interest:
   A. payments at the current discount rate.
   B. payments using the discount rate at the time of issue.
   C. and principal payments using the current discount rate.
   D. and principal payments using the discount rate at the time of issue.

2. Annual interest expense is the:
   A. sum of the annual coupon payments.
   B. amount paid to creditors in excess of par.
   C. book value of the debt times the current interest rate.
   D. book value of the debt times the market interest rate when it was issued.

Use the following data to answer Questions 3 through 10.

A firm issues a $10 million bond with a 6% coupon rate, 4-year maturity, and annual interest payments when market interest rates are 7%.

3. The bond can be classified as a:
   A. discount bond.
   B. zero-coupon bond.
   C. par bond.
   D. premium bond.

4. The annual coupon payments will each be:
   A. $600,000.
   B. $676,290.
   C. $700,000.
   D. $723,710.

5. Total cash payment due the bondholders is:
   A. $12,400,000.
   B. $12,738,721.
   C. $12,800,000.
   D. $13,107,960.

6. The initial book value of the bonds is:
   A. $9,400,000.
   B. $9,661,279.
   C. $10,000,000.
   D. $10,338,721.

7. For the first period the interest expense is:
   A. $600,000.
   B. $676,290.
   C. $700,000.
   D. $723,710.

8. If the market rate changes to 8%, the book value of the bonds at the end of the first period will be:
    A. $9,484,581.
    B. $9,661,279.
    C. $9,737,568.
    D. $9,745,959.

9. The total interest expense reported by the issuer over the life of the bond will be:
    A. $2,400,000.
    B. $2,738,721.
    C. $2,800,000.
    D. $3,107,960.

10. How much will cash flow from operations (CFO) in year 1 be understated or overstated by these bonds?
    A. Overstated by $76,290.
    B. Overstated by $100,000.
    C. Understated by $76,290.
    D. Understated by $100,000.

11. Interest expense reported on the income statement is based on the:
    A. market rate at issuance.
    B. coupon payment.
    C. current market rate.
    D. unamortized discount.

12. The actual coupon payment on a bond is:
    A. reported as an operating cash outflow.
    B. reported as a financing cash outflow.
    C. reported as a financing cash inflow and operating cash outflow.
    D. not reported since only the interest expense is reported.

13. A 2-year bond is carried on the books at a premium because it was issued at a coupon rate of 0.25% higher than the market rate. After one year, market rates have gone down by 0.5%. The bond will now be listed on the books as having:
    A. the same premium it had when originally issued.
    B. a lower premium than when it was originally issued.
    C. par value.
    D. a discount.

14. Wolfe Inc. had a capital structure consisting of $10 million of liabilities and $15 million of equity. Wolfe then issued $0.7 million of preferred shares and $1.0 million of bonds with warrants attached (debt component comprises 80% of the value) for total cash proceeds of $1.7 million. Which of the following amounts is the *revised* debt to total capital ratio upon the issuance of the two new financial instruments?
    A. 0.404.
    B. 0.431.
    C. 0.679.
    D. 0.757.

15. A company has convertible bonds on its books with a conversion price of $20 per share. The stock price is currently $40 per share. For analytical purposes, the bonds should be treated as:
    A. debt.
    B. preferred stock.
    C. equity.
    D. a hybrid of debt and common stock.

16.   The relative effects on interest expense and operating cash flow from issuing convertible bonds versus conventional bonds are:

	Interest Expense	Operating Cash Flow
A.	Lower	Lower
B.	Lower	Higher
C.	Higher	Higher
D.	Higher	Lower

17.   Which of the following is *least likely* a motivation for issuing exchangeable debt?
A. The issuing firm reports an immediate gain when the debt is issued.
B. Interest expense is lower than issuing conventional debt.
C. The market impact of selling the underlying shares all at once is mitigated.
D. The issuing firm generates cash while retaining control of the underlying shares.

ANSWERS – CONCEPT CHECKERS: ANALYSIS OF FINANCING LIABILITIES

1. **D** The book value of debt is equal to the present value of interest and principal payments. Book value is based on the market interest rate in effect at the time the debt was issued.

2. **D** Annual interest expense is the book value of the debt times the interest rate at the time of issuance.

3. **A** This bond is issued at a discount since the coupon rate < market rate.

4. **A** Coupon payment = (coupon rate × face value of bond) = 6% × $10,000,000 = $600,000

5. **A** Four coupon payments and the face value = $600,000 × 4 + $10,000,000 = $12,400,000

6. **B** The present value of a 4-year annuity of $600,000 plus a 4-year lump sum of $10 million, all valued at a discount rate of 7%, equals $9,661,279. C and D can be eliminated because the bond is selling at a discount.

7. **B** Market interest rate × book value = 7% × $9,661,279 = $676,290

8. **C** The change in interest rates is ignored. The new book value = beginning book value + interest expense – coupon payment = $9,661,279 + $676,290 – $600,000 = $9,737,569. The interest expense was calculated in Question 7. Alternatively, changing N from 4 to 3 and calculating the PV will yield the same result.

9. **B** Coupon payments + amortized interest = coupon payments + (face value – issue value) = $2,400,000 + ($10,000,000 – $9,661,279) = $2,738,721

10. **A** The true interest expense is $676,290, while the coupon being deducted to calculate CFO is only $600,000. This means CFO is overstated by the difference of $76,290.

11. **A** Interest expense reported on the income statement is based on the market rate at issuance and reflects the coupon rate plus or minus the amortization of the discount or premium.

12. **A** The actual coupon payment on a bond is reported as operating cash outflow.

13. **B** The premium will be lower because of the amortization of the premium over time. The change in interest rates has no impact.

14. **A** The $0.7 million of preferred shares are treated as equity. For the warrants, $0.8 million would be treated as debt and $0.2 million as equity.

    Liabilities = $10 million + $0.8 million = $10.8 million

    Equity = $15 million + $0.7 million + $0.2 million = $15.9 million

    Debt to total capital ratio = liabilities / (liabilities + equity) = $10.8 million / ($10.8 million + $15.9 million) = 0.404.

15. **C** The bonds should be treated as equity for analytical purposes because the stock price is significantly above the conversion price.

16. **B** Issuing convertible bonds instead of conventional bonds reduces interest expense (because convertibles carry lower yields, all else equal) and increases operating cash flow.

17. **A** One of the advantages of issuing exchangeable debt is to *delay the income tax impact of a potential gain* from selling the shares until the investors exchange the shares. The other three choices are motivations for issuing exchangeable debt.

LEASES AND OFF-BALANCE-SHEET DEBT

EXAM FOCUS

The key to this topic review is differentiating between an operating lease and a capital lease. With an operating lease, there is no recognition of an asset or liability on the balance sheet. The lease payment is charged to the income statement as rent expense and reduces cash flow from operations. With a capital lease, a depreciable asset and a liability are reported on the balance sheet, much as if the asset were purchased and financed with debt. Each lease payment is composed of interest expense and amortization of the lease liability. For the Level 1 exam, be prepared for questions asking for the differences in financial statements and ratios depending on whether an operating lease or a capital lease is used. You should also be able to make lease accounting calculations. Finally, expect questions about how off-balance-sheet financing activities, such as take-or-pay contracts, throughput arrangements, and sales of receivables, affect the financial statements.

LOS 46.a: Discuss the motivations for leasing assets instead of purchasing them and the incentives for reporting the leases as operating leases rather than capital leases.

Leases are classified as either capital leases or operating leases. A lessee must classify a lease as a **capital lease** if *any one* of the following criteria is met:

- The title to the leased asset is transferred to the lessee at the end of the lease period.
- A bargain purchase option exists. A bargain purchase option is a provision that permits the lessee to purchase the leased asset for a price that is significantly lower than the fair market value of the asset on the date that the purchase option becomes exercisable.
- The lease period is at least 75% of the asset's economic life.
- The present value of the lease payments is equal to or greater than 90% of the fair value of the leased asset. The interest rate used to discount the lease payments is the *lower of* the lessee's incremental borrowing rate or the interest rate implicit in the lease.

Professor's Note: The implicit interest rate in the lease is the discount rate that the lessor used to determine the lease payments. It is the lease's internal rate of return because it is the interest rate that equates the present value of lease payments to the fair value of the leased asset. Using the lower of the two discount rates increases the present value of the lease payments and increases the likelihood that the lease will satisfy the 90% criterion and therefore be classified as a capital lease.

A lease not meeting any of these criteria is classified as an **operating lease**.

To have the use of assets in production a firm can buy the asset, rent it for a short term, or lease it for a longer term. There are two different accounting treatments for leases, one for operating leases and one for capital leases. We will address these different treatments shortly, but first let's look at some reasons for leasing rather than purchasing an asset that are not related to the differences in accounting treatment. The **lessee** is the firm that is leasing the asset for use. The **lessor** is the firm from which they are leasing the asset.

Reasons for leasing rather than purchasing an asset include:

- The period of use is short relative to the asset's useful life. For example, a construction company may lease some equipment for the duration of a 1- or 2-year construction project.

- The lessor may be better able to resell the asset. For example, a lessor of copy machines may be well equipped to refurbish and sell a used machine.
- The lessee may not want the risk of resale (the uncertainty about the value of the asset at the end of the period of use, when it will be sold). For example, with high technology equipment, whether it will still be the best technology at the end of the lease period can have a large effect on its resale value.
- If the lessor has market power, the lessor may maximize profits through leasing the asset and maintaining more control of its use. For example, the sole manufacturer of specialized machinery may want to set lease terms based on the intensity of use of the machine, which it could not control or charge for under an outright sale.
- Assets less specialized to the firm are more likely to be leased. For example, office space is often leased.
- There may be risk reduction benefits, especially to privately held firms, from leasing when firm assets have highly correlated values over time. Some of the risk of changes in asset value are effectively borne by the lessor who, in effect, retains ownership of the asset.

Capital Versus Operating Leases

As we will discuss in more detail shortly, an operating lease is accounted for like a rental—no asset or liability is shown on the firm's balance sheet and the periodic lease payments are simply an expense in the current period. In contrast, a capital lease is treated like a purchase of the asset, with the present value of future minimum lease payments treated as a balance sheet liability and the (equal) value of the asset for the lease period shown as an asset on the balance sheet.

Professor's Note: Most of the "incentives" below favor the operating lease. There are very few (if any) incentives for the lessee to classify a lease as a capital lease.

The incentives for structuring a lease as an **operating lease** are:

- If the lessor is in a higher marginal tax bracket than the lessee, the lease should be structured as an operating lease so that the lessor can take advantage of the depreciation of the leased equipment to reduce its taxable income and, thereby, the taxes it pays.
- An operating lease avoids recognition of an asset and a liability on the lessee's balance sheet. Relative to a company that uses capital leases, the operating lease company will have higher profitability ratios (e.g., return on assets) and lower leverage ratios. The lessee may have bond covenants governing its financial policies (e.g., a maximum debt-to-equity ratio).
- Management compensation can be linked to returns on invested capital and operating leases will result in lower invested capital than capital leases.

Capital leases involve the effective transfer of all the risk and benefits of the property to the lessee. Capital leases are economically equivalent to sales (i.e., to a purchase with a transfer of title) and for accounting purposes are treated as sales. Advantages of a capital lease (to the lessee) include the following:

- In the early years of the lease, total expense is greater, potentially leading to tax savings.
- Operating cash flow is higher under a capital lease relative to an operating lease.

LOS 46.b: Determine the effects of capital and operating leases on the financial statements and ratios of the lessees and lessors.

Reporting by Lessee

Operating lease: At the inception of the lease, no entry is made. During the term of the lease, *rent expense*, the lease payment, is charged to income and to *cash flow from operations*. Footnote disclosure of the lease payments for each of the next five fiscal years is required.

Capital lease: At the inception of the lease, the *present value* of minimum lease payments is recognized as an asset and as a liability on the lessee's balance sheet. During the term of the lease, the leased asset is *depreciated* on the income statement. (The depreciation period is the lease period if there is no title transfer or bargain purchase option; if there *is* a title transfer or bargain purchase option, the leased asset is depreciated over its estimated economic life).

- The lease payment is separated into *interest expense* (the discount rate times the lease liability at the beginning of the period) and *principal payment* on the lease liability (the lease payment less the interest expense).
- *Cash flow from operations* is reduced by the interest expense and *cash flow from financing* is reduced by the principal payment on the lease liability.

Example: Effects of a capital lease

Affordable Leasing Company leases a machine for its own use for four years with annual payments of $10,000. At the end of the lease, the lessor regains possession of the asset, which will be sold for scrap value. The lessor's implicit rate on the lease is 6%, and Affordable Leasing's incremental borrowing rate is 7%. Calculate the impact of the lease on Affordable Leasing's balance sheet and income statement for each of the four years, including the immediate impact. Affordable Leasing depreciates all assets on a straight-line (SL) basis. Assume the lease payments are made at the end of the year.

Answer:

The lease is classified as a capital lease because the asset is being leased for at least 75% of its useful life (we know this because at the end of the lease term, the asset will be sold for scrap). The discount rate that should be used to value the lease is 6%, which is the lower of the lessor's implicit rate on the lease and Affordable Leasing's incremental borrowing rate. The present value of the lease payments at 6% is $34,651.

N = 4; I/Y = 6; PMT = 10,000; FV = 0; CPT → PV = $34,651

This amount is immediately recorded as both an asset and a liability.

Over the next four years, depreciation will be $34,651 / 4 = $8,663 per year.

The asset value will decline each year by the depreciation amount and will be: $25,988; $17,326; $8,663; and $0 at the end of each of the next four years, respectively.

The interest expense and liability values are shown in Figure 1. Note that the *principal repayment* equals the lease payment minus interest expense.

Figure 1: Affordable Leasing Example: Capitalized Lease Calculations

Year	(1) Beginning Leasehold Value	(2) Interest Expense (1) × 6%	(3) Lease Payment	(4) Ending Leasehold Value (1) + (2) − (3)	(5) Book Value of the Asset
0				$34,651	$34,651
1	$34,651	$2,079	10,000	26,730	25,988
2	26,730	1,604	10,000	18,334	17,326
3	18,334	1,100	10,000	9,434	8,663
4	9,434	566	10,000	0	0

Column 5 contains the annual book value of the asset. Notice that because the asset is being depreciated at a rate that is different from the rate of amortization for the liability, the two values are equal only at the inception and termination of the lease.

Financial Statement and Ratio Effects of Operating and Capital Leases

Balance sheet. Capital leases create an asset and a liability. Consequently, turnover ratios that use total or fixed assets in their denominator will appear lower for capital leases relative to operating leases. Return on assets will also be lower for capital leases. Most importantly, leverage ratios such as the debt-to-assets ratio and the debt-to-equity ratio will be higher with capital leases because of the recorded liability. The next lease payment is recognized as a current liability on the lessee's balance sheet. This reduces the lessee's current ratio and its working capital (current assets minus current liabilities).

Since operating leases do not affect the lessee's liabilities, they are sometimes referred to as *off-balance-sheet financing.*

Income statement. *All else held constant, operating income* will be higher for companies that use capital leases relative to companies that use operating leases. This is because the depreciation expense for a capital lease is lower than the lease payment. Interest expense is not included in the calculation of operating income.

Let's assume Affordable Leasing can treat the lease as either an operating or a capital lease. The table in Figure 2 compares the income statement (IS) effects for operating and capital leases.

Figure 2: Affordable Leasing: Leasing Decision Impact on Cash Flow

	Operating Lease	Capital Lease		
	Operating Expense = Total Expense	Operating Expense	Nonoperating Expense	
Year	Rent	Depreciation	Interest	Total Expense
1	$10,000	$8,663	$2,079	$10,742
2	10,000	8,663	1,604	10,267
3	10,000	8,663	1,100	9,763
4	10,000	8,663	566	9,229
Total	40,000			40,000

Total expense over the life of the lease will be the same for operating and capital leases because the sum of the depreciation plus the interest expense will equal the total of the lease payments. However, although the lease payments and depreciation are constant, the interest expense is higher in the first few years (this behavior of interest expense is typical of an amortizing loan). Consequently, net income in the first few years of the lease will be lower for capital leases because the sum of depreciation and interest expense exceeds the lease payment early in the lease's life.

Cash flow. Total cash flow is unaffected by the accounting treatment of a lease as either a capital or operating lease. In our example, total cash outflow is $10,000 per year. However, if the lease is an *operating lease* (rent expense = $10,000), then the *total cash payment* reduces cash flow from *operations*. If the lease is a *capital lease*, then *only* the portion of the lease payment that is considered *interest expense* reduces cash flow from operations. The part of the lease payment considered *payment on principal* reduces cash flow from *financing* activities. The data in Figure 3 illustrate that if a lease is a capital lease, there is greater cash flow from operations (CFO) and less cash flow from financing (CFF).

Figure 3: Affordable Leasing: Leasing Decision Impact on Cash Flow

Year	Capital Lease		Operating Lease
	CF Operations	CF Financing	CF Operations
1	–$2,079	–$7,921	–$10,000
2	–1,604	–8,396	–10,000
3	–1,100	–8,900	–10,000
4	–566	–9,434	–10,000

For example, assume that Affordable Leasing reports CFO of $15,000. If it reports the lease as a capital lease, CFO equals $12,921 (15,000 – 2,079). If it reports the lease as an operating lease, CFO equals $5,000 (15,000 – 10,000). Hence, companies with capital leases will show higher levels of CFO relative to firms that use operating leases (all else the same).

The tables in Figure 4 and Figure 5 summarize the differences between the effects of capital leases and operating leases on the financial statements of the lessee.

Figure 4: Financial Statement Impact of Lease Accounting

Financial Statement Totals	Capital Lease	Operating Lease
Assets	Higher	Lower
Liabilities (current and long term)	Higher	Lower
Net income (in the early years)	Lower	Higher
Net income (later years)	Higher	Lower
Total net income	Same	Same
EBIT (operating income)	Higher	Lower
Cash flow from operations	Higher	Lower
Cash flow from financing	Lower	Higher
Total cash flow	Same	Same

Figure 5: Ratio Impact of Lease Accounting

Ratios	Capital Lease	Operating Lease
Current ratio (CA/CL)	Lower	Higher
Working capital (CA – CL)	Lower	Higher
Asset turnover (Sales/TA)	Lower	Higher
Return on assets* (EAT/TA)	Lower	Higher
Return on equity* (EAT/E)	Lower	Higher
Debt/assets	Higher	Lower
Debt/equity	Higher	Lower

* in the early years of the lease

In sum, all the ratios in Figure 5 are worse when the lease is capitalized. The only improvements in financial statement items and ratios from capitalization are an improvement in EBIT (because interest is not subtracted), an increase in CFO (because principal reduction is CFF), and higher net income in the later years of a lease (because interest plus depreciation is less than the lease payment in the later years).

Professor's Note: For the lessor, a lease can be classified as an operating lease or a capital lease. If it is a capital lease it can be classified as a sales-type lease or as a direct financing lease. The effects on the financial statements of the lessor of these various classifications are covered in the final LOS of this review.

LOS 46.c: Describe the types and economic consequences of off-balance-sheet financing and determine how take-or-pay contracts, throughput arrangements, and the sale of receivables affect selected financial ratios.

Professor's Note: Operating leases are the most prevalent type of off-balance-sheet financing.

Operating leases are just one example of contractual obligations that are not recognized as liabilities on the balance sheet. All financial statements should be adjusted to reflect the economic reality of the following off-balance-sheet financing activities.

Under a **take-or-pay contract** or **throughput arrangement**, the purchasing firm commits to buy a minimum quantity of an input (usually a raw material) over a specified period of time. Prices may be fixed or related to market prices. Neither the asset nor any borrowings used to secure the commitment are recognized on the balance sheet. However, the purchaser must disclose the nature and minimum required payments in the footnotes to the financial statements.

For analysis purposes, the present value of the assets and debt commitments should be added to the balance sheet assets and debt to compute leverage ratios.

Under a **sale of receivables with recourse**, a firm may sell its accounts receivable to unrelated parties, but the firm continues to service the original receivables and transfers any collections to the new owner of those receivables. Although such transactions are recorded as a sale, thereby decreasing accounts receivable and increasing operating cash flow, the buyer usually has limited exposure (the risk of not collecting a receivable is borne by the seller). Therefore, the transaction is nothing more than a collateralized borrowing.

For analysis purposes, accounts receivable and current liabilities should be increased by the amount of receivables that were sold before computing ratios (e.g., the current ratio, receivables turnover, and leverage ratios). Also, cash flow from operations should be adjusted by classifying the sale of the receivables as cash from financing instead of cash from operations.

Although all majority-owned subsidiaries must be consolidated (their assets and liabilities added to the parent's balance sheet), **financial subsidiaries** for which the parent owns less than 50% are not consolidated. For example, if a firm owns 49% of a financial company, the investment in that company on the parent's balance sheet represents 49% of the subsidiary's assets and liabilities. But those liabilities (and an equal amount of assets) are not recognized on the parent's balance sheet.

For analysis purposes, the proportionate share of receivables and liabilities in the subsidiary should be added back to the parent's accounts when computing consolidated debt-to-equity, receivables turnover, and interest coverage ratios. You'll learn more about proportionate consolidations at Level 2.

Firms may obtain operating capacity through **investments in affiliated firms** (suppliers and end users). **Joint ventures** may provide economies of scale and disperse risks. Financing is frequently acquired through take-or-pay or throughput contracts. Direct or indirect debt guarantees may also be present in joint ventures. These guarantees will be disclosed in footnotes to the financial statements.

For analysis, the debt guarantees should be added to the debt of the company. If there are no guarantees, the proportionate share of the debt of the joint venture or affiliate should be added to the debt of the company.

Off-Balance-Sheet Financing and Financial Ratios

Because the debt on take-or-pay contracts and throughput arrangements is off-balance-sheet, it has the effect of lowering leverage ratios such as the debt ratio and the debt-to-equity ratio. That is why, for analytical purposes, the present value of the minimum purchase obligation should be added to both long-term liabilities and long-term assets before calculating leverage ratios.

The sale of receivables artificially reduces the receivables balance and short-term borrowings. Consequently, leverage ratios are too low, receivables turnover is too high, and the current ratio (assuming it is greater than 1.0) is too low. That is why, for analytical purposes, the receivables and short-term debt should be added back to the book value balances and the ratios should be calculated with these restated values.

Let's work through an example of the sale of receivables. Assume that a firm reports selling $170,000 of receivables, and footnote disclosures reveal the sale has not transferred the risk (i.e., the receivables were sold with recourse). In addition, the reported debt is $1,300,000, the reported equity is $580,000, and the interest rate associated with the receivables sale is 9%.

For purposes of analysis we should *treat the sale as a borrowing, reinstate the receivables, and treat the proceeds of the sale as debt.* We can adjust the end-of-period balance sheet as shown in Figure 6.

Figure 6: Balance Sheet Adjustments

	As Reported	Adjusted
Debt	$1,300,000	$1,470,000
Equity	$580,000	$580,000
Debt-to-equity ratio	2.24	2.53

We also need to make an adjustment to the income statement to show the change in interest. We add interest on the receivables to both income and expense. (Assuming a 9% interest rate, interest expense would be $15,300.) Hence, net income will not be affected, but the coverage ratios will be lower than reported. EBIT increases because the discount (implicit interest) on the sale of the receivables is taken as an operating loss.

Figure 7: Income Statement Adjustments

	As Reported	Adjusted
EBIT	$265,000	$280,300
Interest expense	$102,000	$117,300
Coverage ratio	2.60	2.39

The cash flow statements also need to be adjusted by reducing the cash flow from operations and increasing the cash flow from financing by the amount of the receivables sold. CFI and total cash flows are not affected.

LOS 46.d: Distinguish between a sales-type lease and a direct financing lease and determine the effects on the financial statements and ratios of the lessors.

A lessor must classify a lease as a capital lease if any of the four criteria used for a lessee hold and the following two criteria hold:

• The collectiblity of lease payments is predictable.

©2007 Schweser

- There are no significant uncertainties about the amount of unreimbursable costs yet to be incurred by the lessor.

The incentive for structuring a lease as a capital lease is that the *lessor* will have earlier recognition of revenue and income by reporting a completed sale even though the substance of the transaction is similar to an installment sale or financing. The lessor will have higher profitability and turnover ratios.

Sales-Type and Direct-Financing Leases

If the lease is a capital lease and the lessor is a dealer or seller of the leased equipment, then the lease is a **sales-type lease** on the books of the lessor. This means that the implicit interest rate is such that the present value of the minimum lease payments is the *selling price* of the leased asset. Thus, *at the time of the lease's inception, the lessor recognizes a gross profit* equal to the present value of the minimum lease payments (MLPs) less the cost of the leased asset. Interest revenue is equal to the implicit interest rate times the net lease receivable at the beginning of the period.

If the lease is a capital lease and the lessor is not a dealer in the leased asset (e.g., a finance company), then the lease is a **direct financing lease**. *No gross profit is recognized at lease inception*, and all profit is interest revenue. The implicit rate is such that the present value of the minimum lease payments equals the *cost* of the leased asset. Interest revenue equals the implicit interest rate times the net lease receivable at the beginning of the period.

Professor's Note: The lessor always uses the implicit rate on the lease to calculate the interest revenue and determine the net investment in the lease. The lessee uses the lower of the lessor's implicit rate and the lessee's incremental borrowing rate.

Accounting for Sales-Type Leases

Accounting at sale. When the sale is made, two transactions are set up.

- First, the sale is recorded as the present value of the lease payments, with the cost of goods sold being equal to the net difference between the cost of the asset being leased and the present value of the estimated future salvage value of the asset (its terminal value). The profit shows up on the income statement. That same amount is reported as an operating cash inflow and an investment cash outflow, so net cash flow is zero.
- The second transaction sets up an asset account called the *net investment in the lease*, which is the present value of all future lease payments and the estimated salvage value.

Periodic transactions. Interest income is calculated each year by multiplying the year's beginning value of the net investment in the lease by the discount rate on the lease. The interest income affects both the income statement and cash flow from operations. The net investment in the lease at the end of each year is calculated by subtracting the difference between the lease payment and interest income from the beginning net investment balance. The reduction in net investment on the lease is an investing cash flow, not an operating cash flow.

Ending balance. After the lease is completed, the salvage value remains as an asset. If the asset is sold, this cash inflow is an investing cash flow.

Sales-Type vs. Operating Lease

Balance sheet effect. As shown in Figure 8 (assuming a 4-year lease), leased assets are larger at lease inception (by the amount of the gross profit on sale), under a sales-type lease compared to an operating lease, but at the end of the lease both methods report the asset at its salvage value.

Figure 8: Balance Sheet Effect of Sales-Type Versus Operating Lease

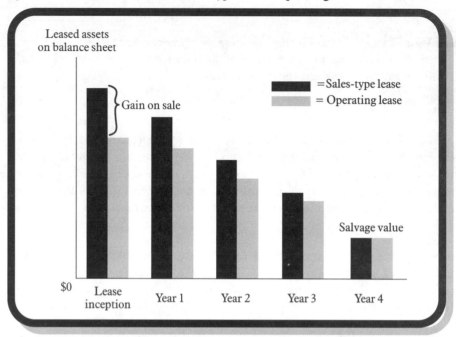

Income statement effect. As shown in Figure 9 (assuming a 4-year lease), total income over the life of the lease will be the same under both methods, but income will be "front-loaded" under the sales-type lease because the gain on sale will be reported at the inception of the lease. After the inception, only interest expense is reported under the sales-type lease. Under the operating lease, income each year is rental revenue less depreciation.

Figure 9: Income Statement Effects of Sales-Type Versus Operating Lease

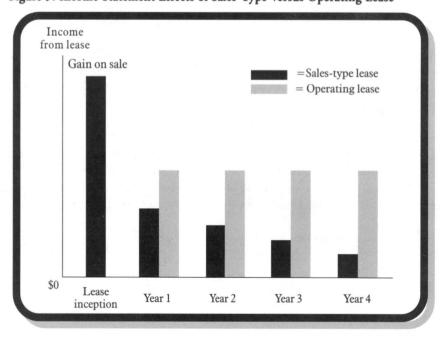

Cash flow statement effect. As shown in Figure 10 (assuming a 4-year lease), total cash flow over the life of the lease will be the same under both methods, but cash flow from operations (CFO) will be "front-loaded" under the sales-type lease because the gain on sale is reported at the inception of the lease but offset by an outflow classified as cash flow from investing (CFI).

Figure 10: Cash Flow Statement Effects of Sales-Type Versus Operating Lease

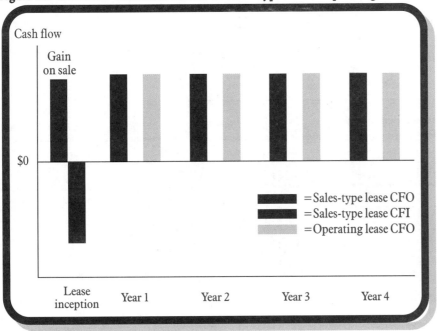

In the detailed example that follows, we will demonstrate these effects, but keep the big-picture perspective and don't get lost in the details of the calculations.

Example: Analyzing the financial statement effects on lessor

Silvio Leasing Company leases a machine to an oil company. The lease is for the oil company's own use for four years with annual payments of $10,000. It cost Silvio $30,000 to produce the machine. Silvio estimates it will be able to sell the machine in four years for $6,000. At the end of the lease, Silvio regains possession of the asset, which will be sold for scrap value. The collectiblity of the lease payments is predictable, and there are no significant uncertainties about Silvio's unreimbursable costs. The implicit discount rate on the lease is 6%. Assume the lease payments are made at the end of the year.

- Determine whether the lease should be classified by Silvio as a sales-type capital lease or an operating lease.
- Analyze the effects on Silvio's financial statements of classifying the lease as a sales-type capital lease versus an operating lease.

Answer:

The lease should be classified by Silvio as a sales-type capital lease because the asset is being leased for at least 75% of its useful life (we know this because at the end of the lease term the asset will be sold for scrap) and because it meets the other two criteria for a sales-type capital lease.

The present value of the lease payments at 6% is $34,651.

N = 4; I/Y = 6; PMT = 10,000; FV = 0; CPT → PV = $34,651

The present value of the salvage value is $4,753.

N = 4; I/Y = 6; PMT = 0; FV = 6,000; CPT → PV = $4,753

The cost of goods sold is then $30,000 – $4,753 = $25,247.

The profit on the sale is $34,651 – $25,247 = $9,404.

The net investment in the lease is $34,651 + $4,753 = $39,404.

The lease amortization schedule is shown in Figure 11 (remember that Silvio is the *lessor*).

Figure 11: Silvio Lease Amortization Schedule

Year	Payment	Interest income	Reduction in net investment	Net investment in lease
0				$39,404
1	$10,000	$2,364	$7,636	$31,768
2	$10,000	$1,906	$8,094	$23,674
3	$10,000	$1,420	$8,580	$15,094
4	$10,000	$906	$9,094	$6,000
Total	$40,000	$6,596	$33,404	

The effects on Silvio's balance sheet, income statement, and cash flow statement are shown in Figures 12, 13, and 14.

Figure 12: Effect on Silvio's Balance Sheet

	Sales-Type Capital Lease			Operating Lease		
	Net Investment In Lease:			Assets under lease	Accumulated depreciation	Net assets under lease
Year	Current	Long-term	Total			
0	$7,636	$31,768	$39,404	$30,000	$0	$30,000
1	$8,094	$23,674	$31,768	$30,000	$6,000	$24,000
2	$8,580	$15,094	$23,674	$30,000	$12,000	$18,000
3	$9,094	$6,000	$15,094	$30,000	$18,000	$12,000
4	$6,000	$0	$6,000	$30,000	$24,000	$6,000

Let's assume that the company owned the asset prior to the lease and reported it on the balance sheet at a cost of $30,000. In that case, if the lease is categorized as a sales-type capital lease, it is reported on the balance sheet at $39,404, and total assets increase by $9,404. If it's recorded as an operating lease, the asset remains at $30,000 and total assets don't change. Prior to the termination of the lease, assets are higher with the sales-type capital lease versus the operating lease.

Figure 13: Effect on Silvio's Income Statement

Year	Sales-Type Capital Lease	Income	Operating Lease Revenue	Operating Lease Depreciation	Operating Lease Income
0	Gain on sale	$9,404			
1	Interest	$2,364	$10,000	$6,000	$4,000
2	Interest	$1,906	$10,000	$6,000	$4,000
3	Interest	$1,420	$10,000	$6,000	$4,000
4	Interest	$906	$10,000	$6,000	$4,000
Total		$16,000	$40,000	$24,000	$16,000

Total income over the life of the lease ($16,000) will be the same for operating and capital leases. However, recognition of much of the income for a capital lease will be reported immediately at the initiation of the lease as a gain on sale ($9,404). Income will be recognized earlier for the sales-type capital lease than for the operating lease, but in this example net income is higher under the operating lease in years 1 through 4.

Figure 14: Effect on Silvio's Cash Flow Statement

Year	Sales-Type Capital Lease CFO	Sales-Type Capital Lease Cash from investing	Sales-Type Capital Lease Total	Operating Lease CFO
0	$9,404	($9,404)	$0	$0
1	$2,364	$7,636	$10,000	$10,000
2	$1,906	$8,094	$10,000	$10,000
3	$1,420	$8,580	$10,000	$10,000
4	$906	$9,094	$10,000	$10,000
Total	$16,000	$24,000	$40,000	$40,000

For a capital lease, only the gain on sale and interest income are reported as cash flow from operations, whereas all of the lease payments for an operating lease are considered operating cash flows. Total cash flow from operations over the life of the lease will be higher for an operating lease ($40,000) than a capital lease ($16,000), but total cash flows (including cash flows from investing of $24,000) will be the same under both methods ($40,000).

Accounting for Direct Financing-Type Leases

There is no sales or manufacturing profit in a direct financing-type lease, so the only profit element is interest income. Compared to a sales-type lease, a direct financing lease will result in lower net income, lower retained earnings, and lower equity by the amount of the profit on sale that is recorded for a sales-type lease.

Example: Direct financing type leases

Assume Johnson Company purchases an asset for $69,302 to lease to Carver, Inc. for four years with an annual lease payment of $20,000 at the end of each year. At the end of the lease, Carver will own the asset for no additional payment. The implied discount rate on the lease is therefore 6% (N = 4, PV = –69,302, PMT = 20,000, FV = 0, CPT → I/Y = 6). Determine how Johnson should account for the lease payments from Carver.

Answer:

Because ownership of the asset transfers for no additional payment at the end of the lease, Johnson (the lessor) treats this as a direct financing-type capital lease. Johnson would record an asset—net investment in the lease—in the amount of $69,302. The lease payments would be recorded as follows:

Figure 15: Accounting for Lease Payments to Lessor

Year	(1) Beginning Investment in Lease	(2) Interest Income (1) × 6%	(3) Lease Payment	(4) Ending Investment in Lease (1) + (2) – (3)
0				$69,302
1	$69,302	$4,158	$20,000	53,460
2	53,460	3,208	20,000	36,668
3	36,668	2,200	20,000	18,868
4	18,868	1,132	20,000	0

Interest income received each year would increase income and cash flow from operations as lease payments are received. The principal reduction amount (column 3 – column 2) reduces the asset net investment in lease and is treated as an inflow to CFI.

KEY CONCEPTS

1. A lease is classified as a capital lease by a lessee if any one of the following holds:
   - If the title is transferred to the lessee at the end of lease period.
   - A bargain purchase option exists.
   - The lease period is at least 75% of the asset's life.
   - The present value of the lease payments is at least 90% of the fair value of the asset.

   Otherwise, it is classified as an operating lease.

2. Capital leases are recorded on the lessee's financial statements as assets and liabilities—the assets are depreciated, and the lease payments are split into principal repayments and interest expense. The recorded liability is amortized over the life of the lease.

3. Relative to operating leases, capital leases provide a lessee with higher assets, higher liabilities, deferred net income, and higher operating cash flow.

4. Relative to operating leases, capital leases provide a lessor with earlier recognition of profit, larger assets, and lower cash flow from operations.

5. Various off-balance-sheet financing methods include take-or-pay and throughput arrangements, sales of receivables, finance subsidiaries, and joint ventures.

6. Off-balance-sheet financing methods make debt balances look artificially low, and receivables sales and finance subsidiaries make receivables look artificially low. For analytical purposes, the debt and receivables should be restated before calculating ratios.

7. Capital leases are sales-type leases if the lessor is a manufacturer or dealer of the asset being leased and allow the lessor to record the sale at the beginning of the lease, while operating leases force the lessor to wait until the lease payments are received to recognize revenue from the lease.

CONCEPT CHECKERS: LEASES AND OFF-BALANCE-SHEET DEBT

1. Compared to a capital lease, a firm with an equivalent operating lease will show *higher*:
    A. return on assets if a lessee and higher profitability ratios if a lessor.
    B. initial leverage ratios if a lessee and avoid recognition of debt on the balance sheet.
    C. profitability ratios if a lessee and avoid recognition of debt on the balance sheet, and higher cash flow from operations if a lessor.
    D. return on assets if a lessor, higher profitability ratios and initial leverage ratios if a lessee, and avoid recognition of debt on a lessee's balance sheet.

2. Which of the following statements about leases is **FALSE**?
    A. A lease is considered a capital lease if the lease period is at least 75% of the asset's economic life.
    B. In a capital lease, substantially all benefits and risks of ownership are transferred to the lessee.
    C. The lessee should book capital leases to the leased asset and lease obligation accounts, and then amortize the lease obligation and depreciate the leased assets.
    D. To record leased assets, the lessee determines the present value of the lease payments using the greater of the implicit rate in the lease or the lessee's incremental borrowing rate.

3. A firm leases a machine for ten years.
    *   Lease payments are $3,500 per year at the end of each year.
    *   The firm has an option to buy the machine for $15,000 at the end of the lease term.
    *   The fair market value of the machine is $30,000.
    *   The machine's economic life is 15 years.
    *   There will be zero salvage value in 15 years.
    *   The implicit rate in the lease is 8.25%.

    The firm should:
    A. treat the lease as an operating lease.
    B. capitalize the lease because it involves a bargain purchase.
    C. capitalize the lease because the lease term is less than 75% of the economic life of the asset.
    D. capitalize the lease because the present value of future lease payments exceeds 90% of fair market value.

4. For a lessee:

Operating leases are accounted for like:	Operating lease payments are reported as:
A. contracts	lease expense
B. asset purchases	lease expense
C. contracts	interest expense
D. asset purchases	interest expense

5. For a lessee, a capital lease results in:
    A. an asset.
    B. a short-term liability.
    C. a long-term liability.
    D. all of the above.

6. For a company that has sold receivables but retained the credit risk, which of the following do **NOT** have to be adjusted?
    A. Accounts receivable.
    B. Inventory turnover.
    C. Current ratio.
    D. Debt-to-equity.

7. Which of the following is **NOT** an off-balance-sheet financing method?
    A. Sale of receivables.
    B. Finance subsidiaries.
    C. Throughput arrangements.
    D. Convertible bonds.

8. Which of the following statements about capital and operating leases is **FALSE** for a lessee?
    A. Total cash flows are not affected by the accounting treatment of the lease.
    B. When a capital lease is initiated, the present value of the leased asset is treated as a financing cash flow.
    C. As compared to an operating lease, a capital lease will report higher operating cash flows and lower financing cash flows.
    D. Over the life of a capital lease the total expenses will equal those of a similar operating lease; but the operating lease will have lower expenses in the earlier years, while the capital lease will have lower expenses in the later years.

9. A capital lease results in the following net income to a lessee compared to a comparable operating lease:

	Early Years	Later Years
A.	Lower	Lower
B.	Lower	Higher
C.	Higher	Lower
D.	Higher	Higher

10. For a lessee, capital lease interest expense is equal to the:
    A. interest rate multiplied by the beginning leasehold liability.
    B. interest rate multiplied by the lease payment.
    C. lease payment.
    D. depreciation expense.

11. Compared to an operating lease, the lessee's debt-to-equity ratio for a capital lease is:
    A. higher.
    B. lower.
    C. not affected.
    D. higher in the early years and lower in the later years.

12. For a lessee, an operating lease compared to a capital lease will *most likely* result in a:
    A. lower debt-to-equity ratio.
    B. higher financing cash flow.
    C. lower cash flow from operations.
    D. lower net income in the earlier years of the lease.

13.   Which of the following statements concerning a lessee is **FALSE**?
       A. All else equal, when a lease is capitalized, income will rise over time.
       B. Lease capitalization increases a firm's operating cash flows and decreases the firm's financing cash flows relative to cash flows for an operating lease.
       C. In the first years of a capital lease, the firm's debt-to-equity ratio will be greater than if the firm had used an operating lease.
       D. In the first years of a capital lease, the firm's current ratio will be greater than it would have been had the firm used an operating lease.

Use the following data to answer Questions 14 through 18.

•   A firm has just signed a 5-year lease on a new machine.
•   Lease payments are $20,000 per year, payable at the end of the year.
•   The machine has no salvage value at the end of the lease term.
•   The machine has a 5-year useful life.
•   The firm's incremental borrowing cost is 11%.
•   The lessor's implicit rate on the lease is 10%.
•   The lease is classified as a capital lease.

14.   What will be the leasehold asset at the inception of the lease?
       A. $0.
       B. $20,000.
       C. $73,918.
       D. $75,816.

15.   What will the firm report as interest expense in the first year?
       A. $7,582.
       B. $8,131.
       C. $12,418.
       D. $20,000.

16.   What will be straight-line (SL) depreciation expense in the first year?
       A. $10,000.
       B. $12,418.
       C. $15,163.
       D. $20,000.

17.   How much of the first-year lease payment will be deducted from cash flow from operations?
       A. $0.
       B. $7,582.
       C. $12,418.
       D. $20,000.

18.   How much of the first-year lease payment will be deducted from cash flow from financing?
       A. $0.
       B. $7,582.
       C. $12,418.
       D. $20,000.

COMPREHENSIVE PROBLEMS: LEASES AND OFF-BALANCE-SHEET DEBT

1. Consider the effects on the following financial statement items and ratios of capitalizing a lease rather than treating it as an operating lease. Indicate the effect of capitalizing the lease on the following during the first year of the lease (circle one).

CFF	higher	lower	no change
CFO	higher	lower	no change
CFI	higher	lower	no change
total cash flow	higher	lower	no change
EBIT	higher	lower	no change
net income	higher	lower	no change
D/A	higher	lower	no change
D/E	higher	lower	no change
ROA	higher	lower	no change
ROE	higher	lower	no change
total asset turnover	higher	lower	no change

2. Babson Corp. sold $550,000 of receivables during the most recent period. Meg Jones, CFA, is adjusting balance sheet items and some ratios for this sale of receivables because significant credit risk on these remains with Babson. Indicate increase, decrease, or unchanged to reflect the effect of adjustment on the indicated items and ratios.

Debt	Cash	Current ratio (= 1)
Debt-to-equity	Receivables	Working capital
Receivables turnover	Cash conversion cycle	Interest coverage
CFO	CFF	CFI

3. Ed's Supply Corp. is examining the effects on the financial statements of classifying the lease of equipment to Excavations Inc. If Ed's (the lessor) classifies this 4-year lease as a sales-type capital lease rather than as an operating lease, the effects on the following in the first year and the third year of the lease are (indicate +, −, or = for no change):

	1st year of lease	3rd year of lease
Revenues		
Interest income		
Net income		
Retained earnings		
CFO		
CFI		
Assets		

ANSWERS – CONCEPT CHECKERS: LEASES AND OFF-BALANCE-SHEET DEBT

1. **C** Structuring a lease as an operating lease results in higher profitability ratios for the lessee and avoidance of recognition of debt on the lessee's balance sheet, and higher cash flow from operations for the lessor. The other statements each have an incorrect component. As compared to a capital lease, an operating lease results in lower profitability ratios for a lessor, lower initial leverage ratios for the lessee, and a lower return on assets for the lessor.

2. **D** Lease payments are valued using the *lower* of the implicit lease rate or lessee's incremental borrowing rate.

3. **A** The purchase option is not a bargain because it is one-half the original price when only one-third of the asset life remains; title is not transferred at the end of the lease term; lease period is only 2/3 of the asset's life; 90% of fair value is $27,000, while the present value of lease payments at the implicit rate is $23,222. Because none of the capital lease criteria hold, the lease is treated as an operating lease.

4. **A** Operating leases are accounted for like contracts (capital leases are like purchases), and operating lease payments are reported as lease expense.

5. **D** For a lessee recording a capital lease, both a long-term asset and long-term liability will be recognized, as well as a short-term liability being recognized for next year's lease payment.

6. **B** The inventory turnover ratio does not need to be adjusted.

7. **D** Convertible bonds are not an off-balance-sheet financing method.

8. **B** The accounting treatment of a lease affects the classification of cash flows but not the total cash flows. Also, a capital lease will report higher operating cash flows and lower financing cash flows than an operating lease. For a lessee there is typically no cash flow at initiation. The principal portion of each lease payment is treated as a cash flow from financing.

9. **B** In the early years, a capital lease results in lower net income because interest plus depreciation expense is greater than rent expense under an operating lease. This effect reverses in the later years of the lease.

10. **A** Interest expense is calculated each year by multiplying the year's beginning value of the leasehold liability by the discount rate on the lease. This *interest expense* is charged to income and operating cash flow.

11. **A** A capital lease will cause the debt-to-equity ratio to increase due to the ratio's denominator effect when adding assets and liabilities to the balance sheet. No debt is booked related to the operating lease.

12. **D** A capital lease results in lower net income in the early years of the lease due to the capital lease recognizing interest expense and depreciation expense. A capital lease will also have a *higher* operating cash flow due to payments being split between operating and financing cash flows.

13. **D** A firm's current ratio will be less when using a capital lease due to the next year's lease payment being classified as a current liability.

14. **D** The appropriate discount rate is the 10% rate implicit in the lease (it's less than the lessee's incremental borrowing rate of 11%). The present value of the lease payments at a 10% discount rate is $75,816. Using a financial calculator:

    I/Y = 10; PMT = 20,000; N = 5; CPT → PV = $75,816

15. **A** Interest expense is the leasehold value multiplied by 10%, which is $7,582.

16. **C** Depreciation is the leasehold value divided by 5, or 75,816 / 5 = $15,163.

17. **B** Only the interest expense is deducted from CFO.

18. C   The financing cash flow is the principal component of the lease, which is the lease payment of $20,000 less the interest component of $7,582.

ANSWERS – COMPREHENSIVE PROBLEMS: LEASES AND OFF-BALANCE-SHEET DEBT

1.   With a capital lease:
    • CFF is lower.
    • CFO is higher.
    • CFI is unchanged.
    • Total cash flow is unchanged.
    • EBIT is higher.
    • Net income is lower in the early years.
    • D/A is higher.
    • D/E is higher.
    • ROA is lower.
    • ROE is lower.
    • Asset turnover is lower.

2.   To adjust these items, we treat the sale of receivables as if it were a short-term borrowing and add back the amount of receivables sold. This will increase debt and the D/E ratio. Receivables increase and current liabilities increase by the same amounts so that working capital, the current ratio (because it's equal to 1), and cash position are unchanged by the adjustment. The receivables turnover is decreased by adding back AR so the cash conversion cycle is longer. The cash generated by the sale is CFF after adjustment rather than CFO, so CFF increases and CFO decreases. The increase in interest from adjusting debt upward will decrease the interest coverage ratio, assuming EBIT > interest expense. CFI is unaffected.

3.

	1st year of lease	3rd year of lease
revenues	+	−
interest income	+	+
net income	+	−
retained earnings	+	+
CFO	+	−
CFI	−	+
Assets	+	+

In the first year of the lease, capitalization of a sales-type lease increases revenues because it is reported as a sale. The profit on the sale increases net income and retained earnings. The recognition of the sale also increases CFO in the first year and decreases CFI by the investment in the lease. Assets are higher for the capitalized lease until the end of the lease term because of the recognition of the profit on the sale at lease inception. Interest income is recognized for the capital lease but not for the operating lease (payments are all rental income), so interest income is always higher for the capital lease.

Revenues are lower for the sales-type lease after the first year because only interest income is recognized and this is lower than the lease payment. Net income is lower in later years for the lessor with a sales-type lease. The income on the sales-type lease is CFI and CFO. For the operating lease, the entire rental payment is CFO. The interest portion of the sales-type lease is CFO, so it goes down each year and the difference between sales-type lease CFO and operating lease CFO is greater each year.

Retained earnings are higher for a sales-type lease in the initial year because of the profit recognition, and will remain higher until the end of the lease term, when total net income over the lease is equal for both treatments.

FORMULAS

free cash flow = operating cash flow − net capital expenditures

$$\text{common-size income statement ratios} = \frac{\text{income statement account}}{\text{sales}}$$

$$\text{common-size balance-sheet ratios} = \frac{\text{balance sheet account}}{\text{total assets}}$$

$$\text{current ratio} = \frac{\text{current assets}}{\text{current liabilities}}$$

$$\text{quick ratio} = \frac{\text{cash + marketable securities + receivables}}{\text{current liabilities}}$$

$$\text{cash ratio} = \frac{\text{cash + marketable securities}}{\text{current liabilities}}$$

$$\text{receivables turnover} = \frac{\text{net annual sales}}{\text{average receivables}}$$

$$\text{average receivables collection period} = \frac{365}{\text{receivables turnover}}$$

$$\text{inventory turnover} = \frac{\text{cost of goods sold}}{\text{average inventory}}$$

$$\text{average inventory processing period} = \frac{365}{\text{inventory turnover}}$$

$$\text{payables turnover ratio} = \frac{\text{cost of goods sold}}{\text{average trade payables}}$$

$$\text{payables payment period} = \frac{365}{\text{payables turnover ratio}}$$

$$\text{cash conversion cycle} = \left(\begin{array}{c}\text{average receivables}\\\text{collection period}\end{array}\right) + \left(\begin{array}{c}\text{average inventory}\\\text{processing period}\end{array}\right) - \left(\begin{array}{c}\text{payables payment}\\\text{period}\end{array}\right)$$

$$\text{total asset turnover} = \frac{\text{net sales}}{\text{average total net assets}}$$

$$\text{fixed asset turnover} = \frac{\text{net sales}}{\text{average net fixed assets}}$$

$$\text{equity turnover} = \frac{\text{net sales}}{\text{average equity}}$$

$$\text{gross profit margin} = \frac{\text{gross profit}}{\text{net sales}}$$

$$\text{operating profit margin} = \frac{\text{operating profit}}{\text{net sales}} = \frac{\text{EBIT}}{\text{net sales}}$$

$$\text{net profit margin} = \frac{\text{net income}}{\text{net sales}}$$

$$\text{return on total capital} = \frac{\text{net income} + \text{interest expense}}{\text{average total capital}}$$

$$\text{return on total equity} = \frac{\text{net income}}{\text{average total equity}}$$

$$\text{return on common equity} = \frac{\text{net income} - \text{preferred dividends}}{\text{average common equity}} = \frac{\text{net income available to common}}{\text{average common equity}}$$

$$\text{business risk} = \frac{\sigma \text{ of operating income}}{\text{mean operating income}} = \frac{\text{std. deviation of EBIT}}{\text{mean EBIT}}$$

$$\text{debt-to-equity ratio} = \frac{\text{total long-term debt}}{\text{total equity}} = \frac{\text{long-term liabilities} + \text{deferred taxes} + \left(\begin{array}{c}\text{present value of}\\\text{lease obligations}\end{array}\right)}{\text{common} + \text{preferred equity}}$$

$$\text{long-term debt-to-total long-term capital} = \frac{\text{total long-term debt}}{\text{total long-term capital}}$$

$$\text{total debt ratio} = \frac{\text{current liabilities} + \text{total long-term debt}}{\text{total debt} + \text{total equity}}$$

$$\text{interest coverage} = \frac{\text{earnings before interest and taxes}}{\text{interest expense}}$$

$$\text{fixed financial cost ratio} = \frac{\text{EBIT} + \text{ELIE}}{\text{gross interest expense} + \text{ELIE}}$$

$$\text{cash flow coverage of fixed financial costs} = \frac{\text{CFO} + \text{interest expense} + \text{ELIE}}{\text{interest expense} + \text{ELIE}}$$

$$\text{cash flow to long-term debt} = \frac{\text{CFO}}{\text{BV of long-term debt} + \text{PV of operating leases}}$$

$$\left(\begin{array}{c}\text{cash flow to}\\ \text{total interest-bearing debt}\end{array}\right) = \frac{\text{CFO}}{\text{total long-term debt} + \text{current interest-bearing liabilites}}$$

$$\text{original DuPont equation: ROE} = \left(\begin{array}{c}\text{net profit}\\ \text{margin}\end{array}\right)\left(\begin{array}{c}\text{asset}\\ \text{turnover}\end{array}\right)\left(\begin{array}{c}\text{equity}\\ \text{multiplier}\end{array}\right)$$

$$\text{extended DuPont equation: ROE} = \left[\left(\frac{\text{EBIT}}{\text{sales}}\right)\left(\frac{\text{sales}}{\text{assets}}\right) - \left(\frac{\text{interest expense}}{\text{assets}}\right)\right]\left(\frac{\text{assets}}{\text{equity}}\right)(1-t)$$

$$\text{basic EPS} = \frac{\text{net income} - \text{preferred dividends}}{\text{weighted average number of common shares outstanding}}$$

$$\begin{array}{c}\text{diluted}\\ \text{EPS}\end{array} = \frac{\left[\text{net income} - \begin{array}{c}\text{preferred}\\ \text{dividends}\end{array}\right] + \left[\begin{array}{c}\text{convertible}\\ \text{preferred}\\ \text{dividends}\end{array}\right] + \left(\begin{array}{c}\text{convertible}\\ \text{debt}\\ \text{interest}\end{array}\right)(1-t)}{\left(\begin{array}{c}\text{weighted}\\ \text{average}\\ \text{shares}\end{array}\right) + \left(\begin{array}{c}\text{shares from}\\ \text{conversion of}\\ \text{conv. pfd. shares}\end{array}\right) + \left(\begin{array}{c}\text{shares from}\\ \text{conversion of}\\ \text{conv. debt}\end{array}\right) + \left(\begin{array}{c}\text{shares}\\ \text{issuable from}\\ \text{stock options}\end{array}\right)}$$

ending inventory = beginning inventory + purchases − COGS

current cost of inventory (FIFO) = LIFO inventory + LIFO reserve

$\text{COGS}_{\text{FIFO}} = \text{COGS}_{\text{LIFO}} - (\text{ending LIFO reserve} - \text{beginning LIFO reserve})$

$$\text{straight-line depreciation} = \frac{\text{cost} - \text{salvage value}}{\text{useful life}}$$

$$\text{DDB depreciation} = \left(\frac{2}{\text{useful life}}\right)(\text{cost} - \text{accumulated depreciation})$$

$$\text{sum of the years' digits: depreciation in year x} = \frac{(\text{original cost} - \text{salvage value}) \times (n - x + 1)}{\text{SYD}}$$

$$\text{where SYD} = \frac{n(n+1)}{2}$$

$$\text{average age in years} = \frac{\text{accumulated depreciation}}{\text{depreciation expense}}$$

$$\text{average age as a percentage} = \frac{\text{accumulated depreciation}}{\text{ending gross investment}}$$

$$\text{average depreciable life} = \frac{\text{ending gross investment}}{\text{depreciation expense}}$$

$$\text{income tax expense} = \text{taxes payable} + \Delta DTL - \Delta DTA$$

$$\text{interest expense} = \left(\begin{array}{c}\text{the market rate}\\\text{at issue}\end{array}\right) \times \left(\begin{array}{c}\text{the balance sheet value}\\\text{of the liability at}\\\text{the beginning of the period}\end{array}\right)$$

INDEX

A

accelerated depreciation 147
accelerated depreciation methods 168
accounting changes 25
accrual accounting 17
amortization 209
analyzing effective tax rates 195
antidilutive securities 109
ARO. See asset retirement obligation
asset retirement obligation 177
audit opinion 13
auditor 13
average age 174
average cost method 124
average depreciable life 174
average inventory processing period 81
average receivables collection period 81

B

balance sheet 11
basic EPS 107
bonds 206
bonds with warrants 213
book value 145, 167
business risk 84

C

capital leases 222
capitalized interest 158
capitalizing interest costs 159
carrying values 145
cash conversion cycle 82
cash flow coverage 87
cash flow from financing 44, 51
cash flow from investing 43, 51
cash flow from operations 43, 51
cash flow to long-term debt 87
cash ratio 80
CFF. See cash flow from financing
CFI. See cash flow from investing
CFO. See cash flow from operations
common-size statements 77
completed contract method 21

complex capital structure 106
components of net income 18
convertible bonds 213
cost recovery method 21
current cost method 132
current ratio 80

D

debt-to-equity ratio 85
declining balance method 147
deferred tax asset 187
deferred tax assets 191
deferred tax liabilities 186, 188, 191
depletion 149
depreciable lives 172
depreciation 146
diluted EPS equation 110
dilutive securities 109
direct financing lease 229
direct method 53
direct-financing lease 228
discarded assets 148
discontinued operations 25
double-declining balance 168
DuPont analysis, extended 91
DuPont analysis, original 89

E

earnings per share 106
economic depreciation 167
EPS. See earnings per share
equity turnover 83
exchangeable debt 215
exchanging assets 149
extraordinary items 25

F

FCF. See free cash flow
FIFO 124
FIFO to LIFO conversion 129
financial reporting terminology 185
financial risk 85
financial subsidiaries 227

fixed asset turnover 82
fixed financial cost 87
free cash flow 60

G

GAAP. See Generally Accepted Accounting Principles
Generally Accepted Accounting Principles 9
goodwill 149
gross profit margin 83
growth analysis 87

H

harmonization 73
hierarchical model 73
historical cost 167

I

IAS GAAP 60
impact of depreciation methods 172
impact of impairment 176
impaired assets 175
income smoothing 27
income statement 18
income statement approach (tax reporting) 191
income tax expense 191
income taxes payable 191
indirect method 44, 53, 58
installment sales method 21
intangible assets 145, 149, 160
interest coverage 86
inventory accounting 124, 130
inventory turnover 81
investments in affiliated firms 227

J

joint ventures 227

L

LCM. See lower of cost or market
lessee 222
lessor 222
liability method 187
LIFO 124
LIFO liquidation 135
LIFO reserve 128
LIFO to FIFO conversion 128
liquidity ratios 80

long-term asset 145
long-term debt-to-total capital 86
lower of cost or market 127, 135

N

natural resources 145, 149
net profit margin 84
net realizable value 135
noncash investing and financing 44
noncash transactions 53

O

operating leases 222
operating leverage 85
operating profit margin 83
operating profitability ratios 82, 83

P

payables payment period 81
payables turnover ratio 81
percentage-of-completion method 21
permanent differences 190
prior-period adjustments 26
property, plant, and equipment 146

Q

quick ratio 80

R

receivables turnover 81
recoverability test 176
relative age 174
return on common equity 84
return on total capital 84
return on total equity 84
revaluation 161
revenue recognition 19, 20
risk analysis 84
ROTC. See return on total capital

S

sale of receivables with recourse 227
sales basis method 20
sales variability 85
sales-type lease 228, 229
salvage values 172

service hours 170
SFAS 107 (debt disclosures) 216
SFAS 109 (tax disclosures) 194
SFAS 143 (asset retirement) 177
simple capital structure 106
sinking fund depreciation 171
statement of cash flows 42, 53
statement of stockholders' equity 29
straight-line depreciation 147, 167
sum-of-year's digits 168
sustainable growth rate 88

T

take-or-pay contract 227
tangible assets 145
tax return terminology 185
temporary differences 189, 190
throughput arrangement 227
total asset turnover 82
total debt ratio 86
treasury stock method 110

U

units-of-production 170
units-of-production method 147
unusual or infrequent items 24

V

valuation allowance 188
variable-rate debt 214

W

weighted average number of common shares 107, 109

Notes

Notes

Notes

Notes

Notes

Notes